A GUIDE TO THE STUDY OF terrestrial ecology

contours: studies of the environment

Series Editor
William A. Andrews
Associate Professor of Science Education
The Faculty of Education
University of Toronto

A Guide to the Study of ENVIRONMENTAL POLLUTION
A Guide to the Study of FRESHWATER ECOLOGY
A Guide to the Study of SOIL ECOLOGY
A Guide to the Study of TERRESTRIAL ECOLOGY

A GUIDE TO THE STUDY OF

terrestrial ecology

Contributing Authors:
William A. Andrews
Daniel G. Stoker
Donna K. Moore
Larry N. Doble
Elaine C. McKnight

Editor:
William A. Andrews

Prentice-Hall, Inc., Englewood Cliffs, New Jersey

Library of Congress Cataloging in Publication Data

ANDREWS, WILLIAM A.   1930-
A guide to the study of terrestrial ecology.

(Contours: Studies of the environment)
SUMMARY: Deals with land-based ecological systems such as forests, meadows, parks,
and sand dunes, and describes field and laboratory procedures for investigating these areas.
1. Ecology. (1. Ecology) I. Title.
QH541.A53   574.5'264   73-11163
ISBN 0-13-370940-X
ISBN 0-13-370932-9 (pbk.)

A Guide to the Study of
TERRESTRIAL ECOLOGY
© 1974 by W. A. Andrews
Published by Prentice-Hall, Inc.
Englewood Cliffs, New Jersey.
Printed in the United States of America.
10 9 8 7 6 5 4 3 2 1

Prentice-Hall International, Inc., *London*
Prentice-Hall of Australia, Pty., Ltd., *Sydney*
Prentice-Hall of Canada, Ltd., *Toronto*
Prentice-Hall of India Private Ltd., *New Delhi*
Prentice-Hall of Japan, Inc., *Tokyo*

Design by Jerrold J. Stefl, cover illustration by Tom Daly,
text illustrations by James Loates.

Title page photo DPI: Lizabeth Corlett

PREFACE

Ecology is the study of the relationships between living things and their environments. This book is about terrestrial ecology. Therefore it deals with the interrelationships found in forests, woodlots, meadows, parks, bogs, sand dunes, and other land-based ecological systems. It provides you with the background knowledge and the procedures required to investigate, in the laboratory and in the field, the many relationships that exist in such areas.

What kind of soil do earthworms prefer? Why? What factors determine the insect population of a field? How is rich soil formed in an area that was once covered with sand? How do various animals respond to changes in relative humidity, temperature, light intensity, and other factors? These questions are typical of the type that you will investigate in this book. The pursuit of the answers to such questions should provide you with many exciting and rewarding weeks of field and laboratory work.

After you have completed the material in this book, you should understand the basic principles of ecology well enough that you can and will apply them in your everyday lives. You should be able to debate rationally the commonly used practice of clear-cutting as a method of obtaining lumber. You should know how to react to a government proposal to open up a sand dune area to commercial enterprises. You should understand and appreciate the important roles of many organisms in nature. You should understand how man's continued presence on this planet is linked to the continued success of other species of living things. In short, you should become the type of citizen that is desperately needed to help restore and maintain an environment that is needed by man and all living things.

ACKNOWLEDGMENTS

This program was developed at the Faculty of Education, University of Toronto. The resources of the Faculty and the knowledge and skills of many student-teachers in the Environmental Studies option contributed greatly to the quality of the material contained in this book and its companion volumes.

The authors wish to acknowledge the competent professional help received from the Publisher. In particular, we extend our thanks to Sue Barnes, Norma Soden, and Jane Standen for their skillful editorial work. We also thank John Perigoe and Kelvin Kean for their assistance in the planning and development of this program in Environmental Studies.

The authors are particularly appreciative of the attractive, imaginative, and accurate art work of Jim Loates. Jim has been a valued member of our team since its inception. We are equally appreciative of the work of Lois Andrews who prepared the manuscript with great care and dedication.

W.A.A.
D.G.S.
D.K.M.
L.N.D.
E.C.M.

CONTENTS

FIELD AND LABORATORY STUDIES: ABIOTIC FACTORS 90

3

FIELD AND LABORATORY STUDIES: BIOTIC FACTORS 140

4

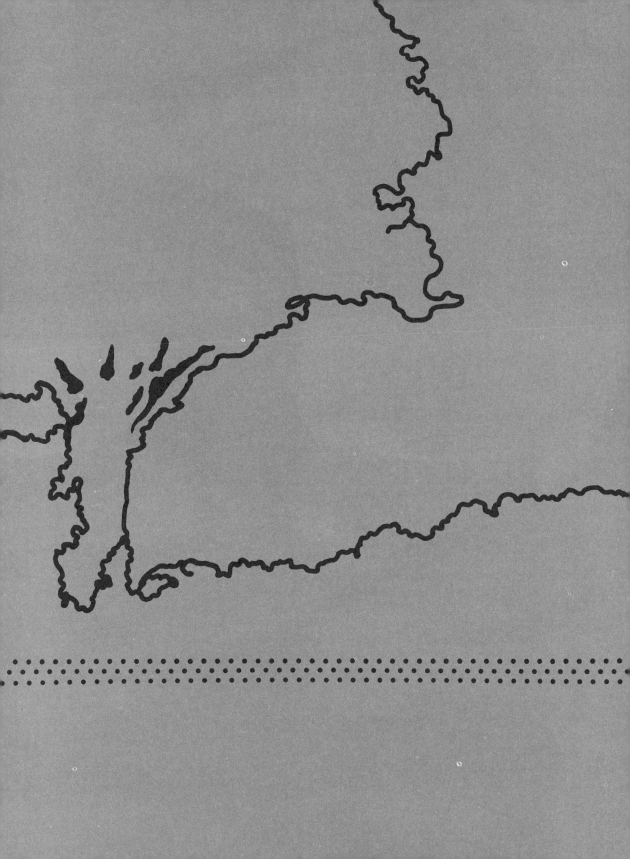

Introduction to Basic Principles

1

At first glance an oak forest and a grassy meadow appear very different. What a contrast there is between the imposing oaks of the forest and the small herbs and grasses of the meadow! Even a closer look at the forest and meadow reveals very few species common to both. *Shade-tolerant* trilliums cover the forest floor. Squirrels are numerous. Birds abound in the trees. Characteristic of the meadow are *sun-tolerant* herbs and grasses, noisy crickets, and active grasshoppers. Many birds also live in the meadow, but the species are generally quite different from those in the forest. Yet, in spite of these differences, there are many close similarities between the oak forest and the grassy meadow. Through photosynthesis, the oaks and other green plants of the forest provide food for organisms such as insects and chipmunks that are unable to manufacture their own. The grasses and herbs of the meadow similarly provide food for crickets, grasshoppers, and other non-photosynthetic organisms. Shelter for thousands of organisms is another necessity provided by the oaks of the forest and the grasses and herbs of the meadow. Don't think, however, that the plants of the forest or meadow are independent of the animals they feed and shelter. The plants are almost as dependent on the animals as the animals are on the plants.

The study of the relationships among organisms and between organisms and their environments is called *ecology*.

It is characteristic of any science to have a few key concepts which are the product of many observations. Even though ecology is a young science, its key concepts have been clearly defined. You must know some of these basic concepts or principles before you start your field studies. Can you define *community, ecosystem, niche,* and *succession*? If not, read on.

1.1 AN INTRODUCTION TO THE ECOSYSTEM CONCEPT

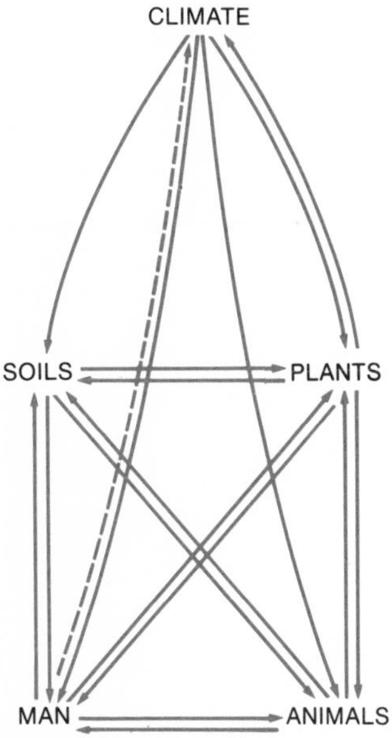

This section provides an overview of one of the most important concepts of science, the ecosystem concept. Read it carefully, since it is the base upon which you will build your understanding of the complex but exciting interactions that occur in terrestrial ecosystems.

A naturally occurring group of organisms (plants, animals, and protists) living in a particular habitat, depending on and sustaining each other, is termed a *biotic* (living) *community*. Such a community cannot exist in a vacuum. It is influenced by and dependent upon *abiotic* (non-living) *factors* such as sunlight, soil, topography, wind, temperature, moisture, and minerals. The interaction of biotic and abiotic factors creates what is called an *ecosystem*. A forest is an ecosystem as is a pond, a meadow, or a classroom terrarium. So intricately knit is the web of interacting factors within an ecosystem that should one vital strand be broken, the ecosystem may be destroyed. A simplified diagram of the interacting biotic and abiotic factors is illustrated in Figure 1-1.

Consider how complex an ecosystem must be that has hundreds of different plant and animal species! Suppose, for example, that a lumber company completely strips a forested area of its large trees. What effects will this have on the forest ecosystem? The trees will no longer add humus to the soil since they will no longer be dropping leaves onto the ground. Snails, slugs, earthworms, and other animals that thrive in the leaf litter will decrease in numbers and, perhaps, vanish completely. Animals that prey on these organisms will be affected. Soil erosion may occur since the leaf canopy is no longer present to absorb the energy of a heavy rainfall. If the soil erodes, many plant species will disappear. The animals that eat these plants will move away or die of starvation. Plants like mushrooms and ferns that require abundant shade and moisture will likely die. Broad-leafed plants like Jack-in-the-pulpit, trillium, and Mayapple cannot live in direct sunlight. Thus they too will be affected.

Fig. 1-1
An ecosystem is a complex network of abiotic and biotic factors in which each factor is affected by the others.

On the positive side, many species of plants that require intense sunlight will now be able to grow in the area. Grasses, goldenrod, and other sun-tolerant plants will gradually become established. Shrubs and tree species that could not grow in the shade of the forest will appear. New insect populations will be established, and new bird and mammal species will make their homes there. But the original ecosystem is gone, perhaps forever.

The chain of events that occurs when one factor in an ecosystem is altered is long and involved. But it is certain to occur. Try now to imagine further changes that would occur in the forest that has been lumbered. Do you think that neighboring ecosystems will be affected? Would a nearby stream, pond, or meadow experience any changes as a result of lumbering in the forest?

You may feel that lumbering is a poor example for showing how ecosystems change. After all, most of us live a long way from a forest. But think again! How much of Canada and the United States was once forest? Most of you can assume that deer and bear once walked through forests where your school is now located. In fact, the very spot where you are sitting may once have been a secluded forest nook where a deer fawn found refuge beneath the boughs of a tree. How things have changed! And, every day, still more natural terrestrial habitats are bulldozed to make room for new homes, shopping plazas, schools, and roads. Where will it all end? Can anyone predict the long-term effects of these changes?

The answer to the last question is "Yes." Ecologists have sufficient knowledge of the structure and functioning of ecosystems to predict disasters like soil erosion, depletion of soil minerals on farmland, and flooding due to poor land management. Yet these things still happen. Why? Perhaps it is because the rest of us know so little about the structure and functioning of ecosystems that we fail to understand their advice. Instead, in our relentless pursuit of the dollar, we press on with our "development" of the countryside. Perhaps it is time that we stopped. But that is a judgment which you can make after you have studied the structure and functioning of ecosystems. These topics are surveyed briefly in this section and then dealt with in greater depth in later sections of this Unit.

The structure of ecosystems. Let us first consider the basic similarities in the biotic structure of ecosystems. In any ecosystem there is a continual demand for energy—the plants, animals, and protists require energy to sustain life processes. The sun supplies this energy as light. The *producers* (green plants) of the ecosystem use the light energy to form high-energy organic compounds such as glucose from the basic inorganic compounds, water and carbon dioxide. The process by which they do this is called *photosynthesis* (*photo* means "light" and *synthesis* means "putting together"). The high-energy compounds formed by the producers are used by them for their growth and metabolism. As a result, producers are called *autotrophic* (self-feeding) organisms.

Ecosystems also have *heterotrophic* (other-feeding) organisms. These are known as *consumers* since they are animals which eat plants or other animals to obtain their nourishment. Those animals which eat plants are called *herbivores* (plant-eaters). They are also called *first-order consumers* since they obtain their energy requirements by feeding directly on the producers. Deer and rabbits are herbivores. Animals which eat other animals are called *carnivores* (flesh-eaters). Those carnivores which feed on herbivores are called *first-order carnivores* or *second-order consumers*. The wolf and fox are first-order carnivores. Note that, indirectly, they too obtain their energy from producers. *Third-order consumers* (*second-order carnivores*) are also present in many ecosystems. What are some third-order consumers? Ecosystems also have what is called a top carnivore. What do you think is meant by that term?

Clover is food for the rabbit. The rabbit, in turn, is food for the fox. This statement can be summarized in the following way:

$$Clover \rightarrow Rabbit \rightarrow Fox$$

This is called a *food chain*. However, most animals have several sources of food. Food chains, then, are not really distinct but interconnect to form a *food web*. Each species—clover, rabbit, and fox—has a function or *niche* in the food chain. In this case, the niches are, respectively, producer, herbivore, and carnivore. It is rather obvious that some species do not have one particular niche in the food web but may have many. The fox may be a carnivore when it feeds on a rabbit, but is a herbivore when it eats berries. Such a complex pattern as the food web is only one of the highly integrated relationships that occur among the organisms of an ecosystem.

Another group of organisms common to all ecosystems are the *decomposers*. They are specialized consumers which feed on dead organic matter, returning basic substances such as minerals and water to the soil. Most decomposers are microscopic organisms like bacteria and yeast. But snails and many fungi are also decomposers.

Producers, consumers, and decomposers are the necessary biological parts of any ecosystem (Fig. 1-2). However, in each ecosystem these roles may be carried out by quite different organisms. See if you can name producers, consumers, and decomposers for each of these ecosystems: a forest, a meadow, a pond, a swamp. Other differences in the biotic structure of ecosystems include population numbers, population distribution, and population growth.

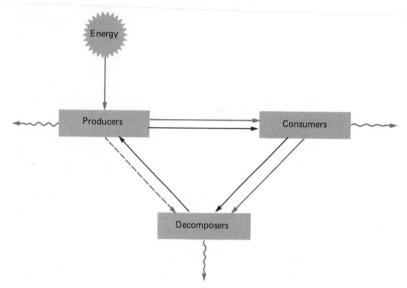

Fig. 1-2
The four basic parts of an ecosystem are a source of energy, the producers, the consumers, and the decomposers. The green arrows indicate energy flow; the wavy lines represent energy lost at each level. The black lines indicate the flow of nutrients. What is the meaning of the broken green arrow?

Now, let us consider briefly the abiotic structure of ecosystems. Basically all ecosystems require the same nutrients—the elements carbon, nitrogen, oxygen, and hydrogen. Also, all ecosystems are regulated by physical factors such as temperature, moisture, light, wind, and nature of the soil. However, all ecosystems have different limits for each of these factors. How these factors vary and how the organisms of each ecosystem are adapted to them is another aspect to be studied in the structure of an ecosystem.

The functioning of ecosystems. No ecosystem is static. Energy and nutrients are flowing continuously through the ecosystem. The functioning of the ecosystem is measured by the rates of energy flow and nutrient cycling. However, it is not easy to measure such rates. In fact, the study of the functioning of ecosystems has lagged behind the study of their structure because of this problem. Therefore your study of the functioning of ecosystems will generally be descriptive, rather than quantitative. For example, you will not measure the rate of energy flow, but you will study the direction of energy flow.

Since energy is gradually lost along a food chain through respiration of the plants and animals, the flow of energy is one-way. Little, if any, energy is recycled. That is, the organisms at the end of a food chain do not return appreciable quantities of energy to the producers. (Can you explain why this is so?) As a result of this one-way flow, energy must enter all ecosystems to replace that lost along food chains. In all natural ecosystems this energy comes from the sun.

Nutrients, on the other hand, are continuously recycled. The decomposers in the soil break down organic matter from plants and animals, releasing mineral nutrients. These are then absorbed by the roots of plants. If it weren't for the decomposers, the flow of nutrients would also be one-way.

Man's effect on ecosystems. If an ecosystem is a highly integrated complex of interacting factors, what results from changing one part of it? The immediate consequences of the removal of photosynthetic plants from an ecosystem are obvious. Solar energy cannot be transformed to biochemical energy, and the ecosystem ceases to function. You have already seen how lumbering can radically change a forest ecosystem.

Not as dramatic, but just as deadly to the ecosystem, is man's excessive use of pesticides. Not only may he do away with a particular rodent or insect, but he may kill, directly or indirectly, those organisms dependent on that rodent or insect. The dependent organism may be killed directly by consuming its poisoned prey or indirectly by starvation if it cannot alter its diet.

Often man is unaware of the broad ecological consequences when he manipulates and alters ecosystems to his own advantage. However, he is also a dependent organism and part of an ecosystem. It is therefore important for his own survival that he develop an ecological awareness of his actions.

For Thought and Research

1 a) Distinguish between a habitat and a niche.
   b) Distinguish between a community and an ecosystem.
2 Read the sections on food chains and food webs in at least two books of *Recommended Readings* 1 to 6.
3 Complete the following food chains:
   a) In a meadow: grass → crickets → . . .
   b) In a mixed forest: saplings → deer → . . .

c) In an oak forest: acorns → squirrels → . . .
d) In a garden: seedlings → earthworms → . . .

Compare your results with those of others. What do you find?

4 What niche(s) does man occupy in his food web? Are these niches the same as they were 50,000 years ago? Explain.

5 Try developing food chains, each composed of at least five different organisms, for the following regions:

a) the Arctic tundra;
b) the African savanna;
c) the Florida Everglades;
d) the Amazon jungle;
e) Central Park, New York, today and as it was 600 years ago.

6 Find out all you can about the processes of photosynthesis and respiration by consulting one or more of *Recommended Readings* 3 to 6. Write the summation equation for each process and account for each term in the equation. What relationship exists between the two equations? What roles do these processes play in the functioning of ecosystems? If you wish to perform laboratory studies of these processes, consult Unit 6 of *Recommended Reading* 8.

Recommended Readings

For interesting descriptions of food chains and food webs, consult any one of the first six books in this list. All of these books are written at the beginner's level.

1 *Basic Ecology* by Ralph and Mildred Buchsbaum, Boxwood Press, 1957.

2 *Ecology,* ed. by Peter Farb, Life Nature Library, Time, Inc., 1963.

3 *Biological Science: An Ecological Approach*, B.S.C.S. Green Version, Rand McNally, 1973.

4 *Biological Science: An Inquiry into Life*, B.S.C.S. Yellow Version, Harcourt Brace Jovanovich, 1973.

5 *Biological Science: Molecules to Man,* B.S.C.S. Blue Version, Houghton Mifflin, 1973.

6 *Modern Biology* by J. H. Otto and A. Towle, Holt, Rinehart & Winston, 1973.

7 *Readings in Conservation Ecology* by G. W. Cox, Meredith, 1969. This book contains an interesting article by E. P. Odum on the structure and functioning of ecosystems.

8 *A Guide to the Study of Environmental Pollution* by W. A. Andrews et al., Prentice-Hall, 1972.

1.2 STRUCTURE OF AN ECOSYSTEM— BIOTIC FACTORS

Section 1.1 pointed out that ecosystems have common structural characteristics. You may remember that producers, consumers, and decomposers are common to all ecosystems. But each ecosystem has features which differentiate it from any other.

If you were asked how an oak forest differs from a grassy meadow, your first answer would probably be that they have different species. Yet *species composition* is just one criterion of the biotic structure of an ecosystem. The number of species present also varies from one ecosystem to another. An ecosystem with a great many species is said to be highly diversified. *Species diversity,* then, is another distinguishing feature of an ecosystem. In an oak forest most of the birds nest in the trees. But there are few trees in the meadow for birds to nest in so they must nest on the ground. Thus the *distribution* of species also characterizes an ecosystem. A further factor that characterizes an ecosystem is the *abundance* of living things. The study of species abundance comes under a special field of ecology called *population ecology.*

COMMUNITY COMPOSITION AND SPECIES DIVERSITY

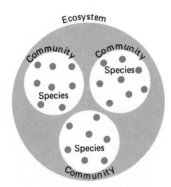

Fig. 1-3
Relationships of the biotic components of an ecosystem.

A natural community is defined by the various species composing the community (Fig. 1-3). But before we can discuss the composition of a community, we should define what we mean by *species.* Is it enough that two organisms look alike? The horse and the donkey look much alike, but they are different species. Appearances can be deceiving. If organisms interbreed, can we consider them to be of the same species? The brown bear and the polar bear interbreed in zoos and produce fertile offspring, yet no such offspring have ever been found in nature. The barrier is that these bears occupy different habitats. The brown bear lives in the northern forest and the polar bear lives on ice floes and snowfields in the Arctic. How, then, can we define species? A species can perhaps be best defined as a group of individuals that are more or less similar in appearance and that are able to interbreed to produce fertile offspring in their natural environments.

Once the species of a community have been identified, the reasons for their presence must be established. In other words, what determines the composition of a particular community? The prevailing climate—temperature, moisture, wind—determines, to a large extent, what species will be present. An element of chance is also involved. Can you think of some ways in which chance can play a role in the composition of a community?

Natural communities have a tremendous number of plant and animal species. When you attempt species identification on a field trip, you will soon realize that a feature of most communities is that there are very few species which are abundant and a great many species which are rare. The few abundant species in a community are called *dominants*. Ecologists first concentrate on the dominant organisms of a community in order to fathom some of the mysteries of the particular ecosystem. The dominant organisms, usually plants, influence the physical conditions for the other organisms and may, therefore, determine their distribution. Why do you think this is so? Often a community is named after the dominant plant. Thus ecologists speak of a spruce bog, a cedar wetlands, and a maple-beech forest.

Variations in the physical environment cause much of the diversity of species in a community. In general, the greater the variety in the physical environment, the greater the diversity. Even in an artificially created situation such as in a cornfield, it is almost impossible to limit the community to one species. Many small plants and numerous animals will find a place to live. Why?

There is a gradation of diversity of species with respect to the size of the organism. For example, there are many species of insects and few of mammals. To date, over 1,000,000 animal species have been identified, three-quarters of them insects. How do you account for such great variation in insects and relatively little in mammals?

DISTRIBUTION OF PLANT AND ANIMAL SPECIES

The distribution of plant species in a terrestrial community can be described both vertically and horizontally. Ecologists have subdivided communities vertically into several layers which reflect the type of plants present in the community. The layer or *stratum* closest to the ground is called the *ground stratum*. It includes mosses, lichens, and herbs. The next layer above the ground stratum is called the *shrub stratum*. Shrubs and saplings are included in this layer. The uppermost layer is the *tree stratum*. These three layers are the main ones (Fig. 1-4). In some cases more layers are required to describe a community. The tropical rain forest, for example, has more than one tree layer because some of the trees are considerably taller than others. Table 1 indicates the average vertical height of the three major strata in a deciduous forest in Ontario.

The *stratification* of the vegetation determines the stratification of the wildlife. Each stratum has its own characteristic animals, although considerable interchange does take place between the layers. As a result, a community that has the most layers generally has the broadest variety of wildlife. Not all communities are equally stratified. A natural forest community is more highly stratified than a grassland commu-

Fig. 1-4
Stratification in a deciduous forest. How many layers can you see?

TABLE 1

Layer	Average vertical height
Ground layer	0.3 meters
Shrub layer	1.8 meters
Tree layer	15 meters

nity. Most forests, therefore, have a great diversity of wildlife associated with them. Can you see why some artificially created forests have been called "biological wastelands"?

The individuals of a plant species are distributed in a horizontal plane as well as in a vertical one. Horizontal distribution may be *regular*, with individuals spaced at specific distances from one another. This occurs when a barren area is reforested with pines. Distribution may also be *clumped*, as often happens when seeds germinate under the parent plant. The most common type of distribution is, of course, *random*. Here the species shows no special pattern. Whether the distribution is regular, clumped, or random, the ecologist who wishes to determine population numbers must know which it is. Generally it is too time-consuming to count all of the individual members of a species. (Imagine yourself counting the number of grass plants in a meadow!) Instead, the estimate of a population's size within a large area is made from a count of the numbers within a smaller representative area. If the species has a clumped distribution or if the sample area is too small, the estimate of the population number could be quite inaccurate. For instance, three clumps of thistles may exist in a cornfield. If you sampled only one small area of the cornfield, you would likely conclude that no thistles existed, which is untrue. How could you increase your chances of locating some thistles but still sample only a small portion of the total cornfield area?

The distribution of a species may be discontinuous or continuous from one community to another. Where the distribution of species is discontinuous, definite boundaries can be identified. A wheat field next to a fenced woodlot is an example of such a distribution. Wheat plants are on one side of the fence and trees are on the other. No gradual merging of the two species can be seen. However, most natural communities do not have distinct boundaries. They have a continuity of species between them. Some species are not as tolerant of the conditions in the neighboring community as they are of the conditions in their own. Other species may be more successful under the conditions in the neighboring community. As a result, the less tolerant species will be less plentiful or nonexistent in the neighboring community and the more tolerant ones will be more plentiful. This causes a gradual blending of the two communities.

The transition zone where two communities blend is called the *ecotone*. Generally, the variety and density of organisms is greater there than in either of the two communities (Fig. 1-5). For example, there are normally more bird species in the ecotone between a forest and a meadow than there are in either the forest or the meadow. Members of each community share the ecotone. Because the ecotone has such diversity of species, it is an excellent region in which to conduct field studies. Bear this in mind when you are selecting study sites. And don't forget to compare the ecotone with the communities on either side of it.

Fig. 1-5
An ecotone between a deciduous forest and a grassy field. Why would you expect more species of plants and animals here than in either the forest or field?

For Thought and Research

1   a)   Distinguish between species composition and species diversity.

    b)   Which community do you think would have the greater species diversity: A desert or a tropical forest? A grassland or a deciduous forest? Account for your answers.

2   Explain how the dominant species in each of the following communities influences the physical conditions for the other organisms of the community:

    a)   the hickory and oak trees of a forest community in North Carolina;

    b)   the black spruce trees of a spruce bog community in northern Canada;

    c)   the grasses of a grassland community in the midwest;

    d)   the lichens of a tundra community in the Arctic;

    e)   the clumps of sand grass growing in a desert community in Arizona.

3   a)   Examine a greenbelt area near your home or school. How many strata are shown by the vegetation growing there? Estimate the average height of each stratum. Identify, if possible, the dominant plants of each stratum. Make a note of any animals (including birds and insects) that seem to prefer a particular stratum. Try to determine why they prefer it.

    b)   Describe an ecotone that exists in the greenbelt area. What particular factors appear to make the ecotone more attractive to many animals than either of its bordering communities?

4   a)   Name a species of plant that you have seen which generally exhibits a clumped distribution. Why does it have such a distribution?

    b)   Why must the sample area be large if the species being counted during a population study has a clumped distribution?

    c)   What factors do you think should determine the size of the sample area when estimates of population numbers are being made? How would you know that the sample area was large enough?

Recommended Readings

1 *Population Dynamics* by J. Cairns, Jr., B.S.C.S. Patterns of Life Series, Educational Programs Improvement Corporation, 1966. This small book is written at the beginner's level.
2 *Elements of Ecology* by G. L. Clarke, John Wiley & Sons, 1966. This book has thorough and interesting sections on the community concept, ecotones, and community composition.
3 *Concepts of Ecology* by E. J. Kormondy, Prentice-Hall, 1969. Consult this book for further information on ecological communities and population ecology.
4 *Ecology and Field Biology* by R. L. Smith, Harper & Row, 1966. This book has advanced but interesting descriptions of types of communities and population ecology.
5 *Recommended Readings* 1-5 of Section 1.1 also have portions dealing with the topics introduced in this section.

1.3 STRUCTURE OF AN ECOSYSTEM — ABIOTIC FACTORS

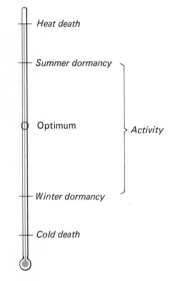

Organisms are affected by many abiotic factors, the common ones being temperature, moisture, light, wind, and soil characteristics. Each organism has a range of tolerance for each of these factors. This range depends on the abiotic factor and on the organism. When the range is exceeded, in either direction, the organism suffers. Within each range of tolerance there is an *optimum* at which the organism lives best. Obviously optimal conditions cannot exist in an environment for all organisms all of the time. Organisms are different and abiotic factors fluctuate. Even if the environment were stable, optimal conditions for one stage in the life cycle of an organism might not be optimal for another stage. Most organisms, therefore, spend much of their lifetimes in suboptimal conditions. Those with the broadest tolerance to all factors generally survive best and have the widest distribution.

Fig. 1-6
Scale of tolerance to temperature. All organisms live within a particular temperature range and live best at an optimal temperature. Some organisms live in a state of suspended animation at high temperatures, others at low temperatures. Beyond these extreme limits, death will occur.

TEMPERATURE

The ability to tolerate variation in temperature is different for every organism. Nematode eggs can withstand temperatures well below −200°C. Some pollen grains, fern spores, seeds, and bacteria spores can survive temperatures as low as −100°C. Many fungus spores can withstand temperatures as high as 150°C. However, for each species there are temperatures below and above which it cannot live. Between these limits, each species prefers a particular temperature range, and lives best at an *optimal temperature* in this range (Fig. 1-6).

The environmental temperature regulates the temperature within a plant and thereby regulates its metabolic processes. For example, the rate of photosynthesis increases with increasing temperature and decreases when the temperature is lowered (Fig. 1-7). Germination of many types of seeds is triggered by lower than average temperatures in temperate climates. The seeds of some pines will not germinate until they have been frozen. Chilling is also an important factor for flower development in some species. Best growth, flowering, and fruiting in tomato plants occur when warm day temperatures (26°C) are followed by cool night temperatures (10°C). Temperatures also vary seasonally and plants must be able to adapt to the changing temperatures. In order to survive freezing winter temperatures, many species of plants become dormant.

The environmental temperature also affects animals. Some animals have body temperatures which vary with the external temperature. These are called *poikilotherms* (*poikilo* means "various" and *therm* means "heat"). Among the poikilotherms are fish, reptiles, amphibians, arthropods, and all of the animals that are structurally simpler than these. Mammals and birds, however, have a temperature-regulating mechanism which maintains a constant body temperature despite varying environmental temperatures. Thus they are called *homoiotherms* (*homoio* means "alike") (Fig. 1-8).

Since the metabolic processes of poikilotherms are affected by the external temperature, the metabolism of poikilotherms may become deranged in extreme temperatures. Within limits, however, the metabolic processes of homoiotherms are governed only by the internal body temperature. Environmental temperature therefore affects the growth and development of poikilotherms more than it does homoiotherms.

Adaptations to daily and seasonal temperature fluctuations are important to both poikilotherms and homoiotherms. The body temperature of poikilotherms changes to adjust to these fluctuations. To avoid extreme temperatures, some poikilotherms burrow or become dormant. In contrast, homoiotherms maintain a constant body temperature when the environmental temperature varies. For example, when the environmental temperature becomes very low, a homoiothermic animal produces more heat to maintain a constant body temperature. It must, of course, either eat more food or engage in less activity to be able to supply this heat without wasting away. Some mammals prefer the latter and, consequently, hibernate. Can you name some?

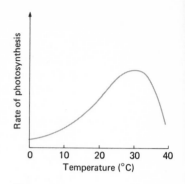

Fig. 1-7
The rate of photosynthesis increases with increasing temperature up to a maximum, beyond which it decreases again. Can you explain this?

Fig. 1-8
One animal that must maintain a constant body temperature is the red fox. How does it do so on very cold days? (U.S.D.A. Photo by Tom Beemers.)

Adaptation, then, is the key to survival for poikilotherms, homoiotherms, and plants. And the study of adaptation to variation is the key to studying any abiotic factor. Studying temperature changes and distributions within an ecosystem can be a rewarding exercise only if you try to determine how temperature affects the organisms of the ecosystem and how the organisms adapt to meet the particular temperature changes.

MOISTURE

No environmental factor is more important to living organisms than water. This is because all living cells require water as a component of their protoplasm. In addition, they require it as a reactant in many life processes. Green plants, for example, require water as a reactant in the process of photosynthesis.

As with temperature, organisms have optimal moisture conditions. They can, of course, live within a range of moisture conditions. Depending on their ability to adapt to adverse moisture conditions, the range may be narrow or wide. In any case, an overall water balance must be maintained between organisms and their environments. Too little water can cause the death of terrestrial plants and animals through dehydration. Too much water may drown many species of animals. It may even drown a plant by preventing sufficient oxygen from reaching the roots. Birds often die as a result of chilling from excessive exposure to moisture.

Precipitation. Terrestrial plants and animals depend largely on precipitation for their moisture requirements. As a result, the distribution of precipitation over the surface of the earth plays an important role in determining the distribution of plants and animals. However, precipitation does not act alone in determining the distribution of plants and animals. Equally important is the temperature. Precipitation and temperature, together, are largely responsible for the *climate* of a region. The prevailing climate determines the distribution of plants and animals. It determines whether an area is a tropical rain forest, a desert, a boreal forest, or another type of community.

The total amount of precipitation is not nearly as important to a biotic community as is its distribution over the year. If you live in an area that experiences snowfall, you know that rain during the growing season is of greater value to plants than is snow during the winter. We generally think of tropical regions as being continuously wet. Yet most tropical regions have unequal distribution of rainfall over a year. Two tropical regions were compared that have approximately the same annual precipitation. In one region it is distributed more or less evenly over the year. The vegetation in this region is chiefly evergreen. The other region has seasonal changes in precipitation. That is, it has wet and dry seasons. In this region the vegetation is largely deciduous—the leaves drop during the dry season.

Precipitation is affected by many factors. Three of the most important ones are the direction of the prevailing winds, the topography of the land, and the temperature. If the prevailing winds blow over large expanses of water, precipitation will usually be high on nearby land masses. The presence of a high mountain range generally results in heavy precipitation on the windward side of the mountains. Warm winds can pick up and hold more moisture than can cool winds. Figure 1-9 shows how these three factors can act together to cause unusually heavy precipitation on the windward side of a mountain range. Can you name regions in North America where this phenomenon occurs?

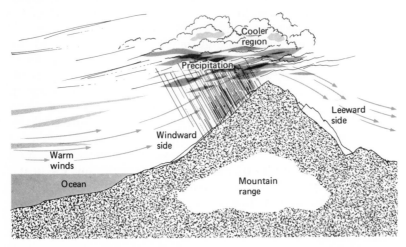

Fig. 1-9
Winds that strike a mountain range are forced up into the cooler regions of the atmosphere. If the winds are moisture-laden, this moisture condenses into precipitation and falls on the windward side.

Atmospheric humidity. Water vapor in the air also has a significant effect on living organisms. This water vapor is called atmospheric humidity. It is most commonly determined by measuring the relative humidity. *Relative humidity* is defined as the ratio of the mass of water present in a given volume of air to the mass of water required to saturate that same volume of air at a constant temperature. It is commonly expressed as a percentage. Thus a relative humidity of 80% means that the air contains 80% of the water that it is capable of holding at that particular temperature.

Plants give off water vapor through pores in their leaves by a process called *transpiration*. This process is essential to plants. It helps moderate the temperature of plant leaves on hot days in much the same manner that perspiration helps to cool your body. More important, though, is its role in transporting essential minerals from the roots to the leaves of plants. Without transpiration, sufficient water would not pass through a plant to carry necessary quantities of trace minerals to the leaves.

You know that on a hot humid day, sweat accumulates on your skin. This happens because sweat cannot evaporate as quickly when the relative humidity is high. In general, plants are affected in a similar way. When the relative humidity is high, the transpiration rate is low; when the relative humidity is low, the transpiration rate is high. Fortunately most plants have adaptations that tend to prevent excessive transpiration that might otherwise cause death through dehydration. Evergreens like pines and spruces have their pores (stomata) located in a groove on the underside of their leaves (needles). Cacti have very few pores. What does the average house or garden plant do when it is subjected to very dry conditions? How does this adaptation reduce water loss?

Moisture content of soil. You have probably noticed adjacent biotic communities where the precipitation is obviously the same but where the plant species are quite different. Such a situation is commonly found on the slope of a hill in a forested region. Mosses, ferns, and other moisture-loving plants abound at the base of the hill. Yet these plants are not common at the top of the hill. Relative humidity undoubtedly has something to do with this unequal distribution of plants. It is usually higher at the base of the hill since that area is protected from the drying effects of wind and sun. In fact, you may have noticed the damp feeling that encompasses you as you walk from the top of a forest hill down to its base. However, the main reason for the difference in plant species at the top and bottom of a hill is the water content of the soil. With time, organic matter in the form of decaying leaves is added to the soil on the forest floor. Much of this is washed or blown down to the base of the hill. Organic matter increases the ability of the soil to retain moisture. Thus the moisture content of the soil at the base of a forested hill is usually high. Moisture draining from the hill helps to keep it high. Also assisting is the fact that the base of the hill is closer to the water table.

In some areas water retention by the soil is so high that the soil is permanently wet. Only plants that have adapted to this extreme moisture condition can survive in these areas. Such plants are called *hydrophytes*. Hydrophytic communities are found in and around ponds and lakes. They also occur along the banks of streams and rivers. In addition, most marsh plants are hydrophytes. The dominant plants of most hydrophytic communities grow with their roots anchored in the mud below water level and their leaves either floating on the surface or extending into the air above. Pond lilies, bulrushes, cattails, pickerel weed, and arrowhead are in this category (Fig. 1-10). Other hydrophytes grow totally submerged in water. *Elodea* and *Cabomba,* two common aquarium plants, are examples of this type. Still others (some species of algae) float freely in the water. Duckweed, which commonly covers ponds with a thick blanket of green, is an example of a hydrophyte that floats on the surface. Examine illustrations of some of these hydrophytes and see if you can figure out how they have adapted to their environments. (See *Recommended Reading* 1.)

Where a combination of low precipitation, low relative humidity, and low water retention by soil creates an excessively dry environment, a completely different type of plant community occurs. The plants of this community are called *xerophytes*. The desert is an extreme example of a xerophytic community (Fig. 1-11). Deserts are formed in regions that have scant rainfall throughout the year and in regions that experience long periods of drought. Less extreme xerophytic conditions occur on sand dunes and rocky slopes. Common xerophytic plants are cacti of deserts, sage-brush of dry

Fig. 1-10
The plants of this pond community have special adaptations that permit them to survive in a hydrophytic environment. What are some of these adaptations?

Fig. 1-11
The xerophytic plants of a desert have developed structural features that make it possible for them to live there. What do you suppose some of these adaptations are? (S.C.S. U.S.D.A. Photo by Bluford W. Muir.)

Fig. 1-12
A forest in a mesophytic area usually exhibits luxuriant growth. (U.S.D.A. Photo.)

prairies, lichens that grow on rocks, and sand grass that colonizes sand dunes. The evergreen trees of the northern forest are usually considered xerophytes. Water may be plentiful in a northern forest, but during the winter this water is frozen. In such a state, it cannot be absorbed by plants. All xerophytes show adaptations to lessen the loss of water by transpiration from the leaves. The leaves and stems of many xerophytes are thick and fleshy to permit the storage of water. The leaves of xerophytes are usually small; the spines on cacti are all that remain of leaves on these plants. The leaves have very few breathing pores (stomata) and almost all of them are located on the underside of the leaves. Why would this be so? Some xerophytes have long tap roots that extend deep into the ground to reach moisture. Other xerophytes, like sand grass, have profusely branched fibrous roots that efficiently absorb the small amount of moisture present.

Plants that prefer intermediate moisture conditions are called *mesophytes*. Most of the herbs, shrubs, and trees of a forest are mesophytes (Fig. 1-12). The common plants of meadows—buttercups, orchard grass, and sow thistles—are also mesophytes. Mesophytes thrive when moderate amounts of moisture are available throughout most of their growing seasons. Since moisture conditions are not extreme, it is difficult to spot any unusual adaptations among the plants of a mesophytic community.

Each plant community has associated with it an animal community whose members also show adaptations. What animals live among the bulrushes, cattails, and sedges on the margin of a pond? What adaptations to hydrophytic conditions do they show? What animals live in a desert? On sand dunes? What adaptations do they possess that permit them to live in a xerophytic area?

Adaptation to variations in environmental conditions is the key to survival of a species. Thus, although a particular species may prefer certain moisture conditions, it will not last long unless it can tolerate extremes from time to time. For example, most mesophytic areas experience periods in which xerophytic conditions dominate. The plants and animals of such areas have adaptations that permit them to survive through dry periods. The evergreens of a mesophytic forest have a waxy coating on their needles to slow down moisture loss during the xerophytic conditions of winter. Deciduous trees drop their leaves in winter to reduce water loss. Alfalfa and sweet clover develop long tap roots to obtain water in midsummer. Annuals (plants that live only one year) survive long periods of drought as seeds. The seeds germinate only when favorable moisture conditions return. Desert animals conserve moisture by burrowing during the day. They are active only at night when the temperature is lower and the relative humidity higher. Some desert animals like the kangaroo rat live on water produced by the breakdown of the cellulose in green plants. Many animals enter a period of dormancy during dry periods.

Adaptations to variations in moisture conditions are numerous among plants and animals. Watch for them during your field studies.

WIND

Wind has both desirable and undesirable effects on ecosystems. Foremost among the desirable effects is bringing precipitation to an area. Winds blowing over large bodies of water become laden with water vapor. As these winds move inland, the vapor precipitates out, thereby adding moisture to the land.

Hay fever sufferers are well aware that the pollen grains of many plants are transported by wind. In fact, without wind, many species of plants would not be pollinated at all. Thus seeds would not be produced and the species would vanish. Grasses depend largely on wind for pollination. Conifers like the pine tree have pollen grains that bear winglike attachments. This adaptation permits pine pollen to be carried many miles by wind.

Wind also plays an important role in increasing the distribution of plant species over a land mass. It carries spores from mushrooms and other fungi many miles. These spores land, germinate, and start new colonies. The wind also carries the seeds of many plants to new locations. How do the seeds of maple trees, ash trees, and dandelion plants ensure distribution by wind? Sometimes the wind moves an entire plant to help it disperse its seeds. For example, as the familiar tumbleweed is blown along, its seeds are gradually dislodged. One original plant may seed a strip several miles long.

Everyone is familiar with the eroding effects that strong winds have on soil. Clouds of dust often fill the air in farming regions where vast tracts of land are under intense cultivation. Much valuable farmland is lost due to the thoughtless agricultural practices that make dust storms possible. But the effects of wind on soil are not all bad. A great deal of rich farmland was created by wind action. During the glacial period, dust from the flood plains of glacial rivers was swept into the air by strong winds. It then settled uniformly over the surrounding countryside. Soil formed in this manner

Fig. 1-13
A blowout can destroy in hours a forest that took hundreds of years to develop. Blowouts are brought on by anything that breaks the continuous mat of vegetation—thoughtless lumbering practices, dune buggy operation, torrential rains.

Fig. 1-14
These pines indicate, like a weather vane, the direction of the prevailing wind.

is called *loess*. Loess soil covers thousands of square miles of land in Nebraska, Kansas, and Iowa. In some places this soil is over 15 meters deep. Being finely divided and rich in nutrients, it is an excellent medium for plant growth. In fact, the soil in these three states is considered some of the prime farmland of the world. Unfortunately, its fine texture makes loess an easy target for erosion by wind and water. It has been estimated that about 300 million tons of topsoil go down the Mississippi River every year. Further studies show that about one-third of the topsoil of the United States has vanished because of erosion by wind and water. Yet, even though the causes of erosion are understood and preventive measures have been developed, three-quarters of the farmland in North America is still being mismanaged.

Figure 1-13 shows another example of the harmful effects of winds on ecosystems. If a forest has developed on unstable soil as in a sand dune area, it can be destroyed overnight by a powerful wind.

Wind also affects the growth of plants. Strong winds blow away water vapor from the vicinity of plant leaves. The drier air outside the leaves encourages excessive transpiration by the leaves. Unless the plants have special adaptations to counteract this drying action, they will either die or be stunted in growth. Thus trees like spruces that are normally tall and slim become short and spreading when they grow in areas exposed to regular strong winds. The delicate growing tips do not develop properly because of the drying action of the wind. Only those branches close to the ground, out of the full force of the wind, develop.

Strong winds alter the physical appearance of trees in many other interesting ways (Fig. 1-14). The branches on the windward side of trees in exposed areas are often bent around until they permanently point in the direction of the prevailing wind. Also, cold dry winds often kill the twig-forming buds on the windward side of trees. This means that no limbs will grow on that side.

As well as deforming trees, strong winds can uproot them or break limbs from them. Such damage is most common in forests where man has removed the larger trees, thereby exposing the smaller trees to the full force of the wind. Since the smaller trees often have not developed extensive rooting systems, they are easily uprooted. Rooting systems are generally shallow and not very extensive in wet soils since the trees do not require large and deep roots to obtain moisture. Thus uprooting is particularly common in an area like a cedar wetland where the larger trees have been logged.

LIGHT

The sun gives off electromagnetic waves having a wide range of wave lengths. At one extreme are the very short gamma rays and X rays. Fortunately for life on the earth, little of this radiation passes through the atmosphere. At the other extreme are the long radio waves. Most of these pass through the atmosphere with ease. (What evidence do you have of this?) Between the two extremes are the ultraviolet, visible, and infrared bands of radiation (Fig. 1-15).

Radiation visible to the human eye has wave lengths between 400 and 750 millimicrons (mμ). Ultraviolet radiation has wave lengths less than 400 mμ and infrared radiation has wave lengths greater than 750 mμ. Some ultraviolet reaches the surface of the earth where it has both beneficial and harmful effects on organisms. You are probably familiar with its effects, good and bad, on humans. Some infrared also gets through the atmosphere. When it strikes the surface of the earth, it warms the soil, water, and atmosphere. Provided atmospheric conditions are normal, the visible band of radiation passes through the atmosphere with ease. Its effects on living organisms are many and varied.

Most living organisms depend on sunlight for survival. Green plants (producers) obtain their energy requirements by converting light energy to chemical energy through photosynthesis. Consumers also obtain their energy from the sun, although by a more indirect means. Light is, therefore, of unquestionable value in the functioning of an ecosystem. Yet, ironically, too much light kills most organisms. For example, the chlorophyll that is vital to green plants is destroyed by excessive light. Thus light is both an essential factor and a limiting factor—it must be present, but too much or too little can be harmful. This creates a real problem for plants and animals. They somehow have to seek out or create an environment that offers the right amount of light. Many of the structural features and behavior patterns of organisms are related to the solution of this problem. Can you think of some examples?

Fig. 1-15
The electromagnetic spectrum.

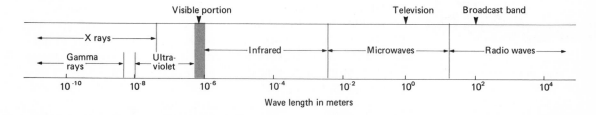

Within a particular ecosystem like a forest, the light conditions are not uniform throughout. The light may vary in intensity, duration, and quality from place to place and from time to time. For example, the light is not as bright (intense) at the forest floor as it is at the top of the leaf canopy. The sun does not shine on the forest for as many hours per day in March as it does in June. The light does not have the same color (quality) in the depths of the forest as it does in more open areas. It is convenient, therefore, to study the effects of light on organisms under the three headings—intensity, duration, and quality.

Intensity. Many factors affect light intensity. Among these are latitude, altitude, topography, time of year, time of day, and cloud cover. Over any particular community, provided it is not too large, these factors are reasonably uniform. Within a particular community, the stratum in which the organism is found can greatly affect the intensity of the light that reaches it. An organism in the upper or tree stratum in a forest will probably receive much brighter light than an organism in the lower or ground stratum. A combination of a thick canopy of leaves and prolonged cloudy periods can often reduce the light intensity to the *compensation intensity* for some plants. This is the intensity at which the light is just bright enough to make it possible for photosynthesis to replace the sugars as fast as respiration uses them. If the intensity is below this level for too long, some plant species will die. Most green plants have a compensation intensity of over 100 foot-candles.

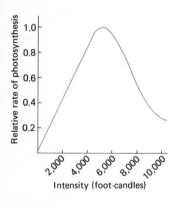

Light intensity has a controlling influence on any ecosystem because it determines, to a large extent, the degree of *primary production* in the ecosystem. (Primary production is the rate at which energy is stored by producers through the process of photosynthesis.) Up to a certain point, the rate of photosynthesis increases as the light intensity increases. But a *saturation intensity* exists, beyond which the rate of photosynthesis decreases (Fig. 1-16). For *shade-tolerant* plants, the maximum rate of photosynthesis occurs at very low intensities. This adaptation helps make it possible for many plants —ferns, mosses, trilliums, maple seedlings—to live in the dense shade of the forest floor.

Light intensity also plays a role in determining the *orientation* of plants and animals. That is, it helps to determine the direction of growth and movement of plants and the direction of movement of animals. Plants exhibit *tropisms* (from the Greek *trope* which means "turn"). Plants exhibit *geotropism,* or response to gravity. You can plant a seed any way

Fig. 1-16
The relationship between light intensity and rate of photosynthesis for a forest community.

you like, but the root will always turn down and the stem up. Plants also exhibit *phototropism,* or response to light. The growing tips of green plants head up toward the light. This is positive phototropism. Foresters make use of this and of crowding to ensure tall erect growth of trees that are to be used as lumber (Fig. 1-17). Sun-tolerant plants like geraniums turn their leaves toward the sun to obtain maximum exposure. Sunflowers follow the movement of the sun across the sky each day so they can present the broad sides of their leaves continuously to the sun. In areas where the light intensity is excessive most of the time, many plants exhibit negative phototropism. They turn their leaves so that the edges face the sun. Why do they do this?

Many animal species also orient themselves using light intensity. With animals, this orientation is not called a tropism but, instead, a *taxis*. You exhibit *geotaxis*. That is, you use gravity to keep yourself vertical as you walk around. Many animals exhibit *phototaxis*. The honey-bee determines its path from its hive to a nectar source by the angle between the path and the sun. What does it do when the sun is covered with clouds? All the bee needs is a small patch of blue sky. It then orients itself by using the angle of polarization of the light in this patch of sky. (See *For Thought and Research,* question 12.)

The migration of birds over long distances is just as amazing as the ability of bees to find their food supply. Birds may use prominent landmarks, prevailing wind direction, and other environmental factors to help orient themselves during migration. However, evidence exists which shows that many species of birds use the direction of the sunlight for this purpose. Further, they are apparently able to compensate for changes in the position of the sun during the day.

Duration. You are undoubtedly aware of the fact that seasonal changes occur in the behavior of plants and animals. At a certain time of year a particular plant flowers; at a certain time of year a particular bird migrates. What causes these seasonal changes in behavior? You may think that they are associated with the changes in light intensity that occur over the course of a year. Scientists believe, however, that these changes have more to do with changes in length of exposure, or duration, than with changes in intensity.

This response of organisms to the length of day is called *photoperiodism.* It is most clearly demonstrated by plants. Plants can be classified as *long-day, short-day,* or *day-neutral.* The flowering of day-neutral plants is not affected by the length of day. On the other hand, long-day plants will only

Fig. 1-17
These pine trees grow straight and tall with very little lateral growth as they compete for light and space. (Courtesy of Ontario Ministry of Natural Resources.)

flower when the length of day exceeds a certain critical value. This value is different for each species of plant. It usually exceeds 12 hours and is commonly about 14 hours. Such periods of long days and short nights occur in middle and upper latitudes in the late spring and summer. You probably know some of these long-day plants—red clover, spinach, timothy grass, oats, and radish. Attempts to grow these plants when the daily period of light is less than the critical value result in suppressed flowering and, frequently, stunted growth.

Short-day plants flower naturally only under conditions of short days and long nights. The critical length of day for these plants is less than 12 hours and commonly about 10 hours. In the middle and upper latitudes, days of this length occur in the early spring and in the late summer or early autumn. Trilliums, Jack-in-the-pulpits, and other spring flowers are short-day plants. Most of these plants are perennials. Their roots and buds were formed the previous year. You may have noticed that, in a deciduous woods, these plants flower before the leaves of the trees have fully developed. Why is this so?

Other short-day plants require a long period of growth before they are mature enough to flower. These plants develop during the bright sunny days of the summer. Then flowering is triggered by the shortened days of late summer or early autumn. Chrysanthemum, tobacco, goldenrod, cosmos, dahlia, ragweed, and aster are common plants in this category.

Since the duration of light controls flowering, it determines the season in which a particular plant flowers. Further, it influences the geographical distribution of a plant species. Consider, for example, a long-day plant that has a photoperiod of 14 hours. This plant could flower early in July in parts of the United States having the same latitude as Virginia. In Northern Ontario and places of similar latitude the length of day is 14 hours in May and again in August. Thus the plant could theoretically flower at either of those two times. In practice, however, it can flower only in August since the temperature is too low in May to permit flowering. Yet August flowering may mean that development of seeds could not be completed before frost kills the plant. In this way, therefore, plants are restricted to certain geographical areas. Plants that live in the Arctic must be able to tolerate long days since the duration of daylight is very long in the Arctic during the growing season. On the other hand, tropical plants are adapted to short days since the photoperiod there is about 12 hours.

The duration of light also controls the life cycles of many animals. The long days of late spring induce some mammals like ferrets to breed; the shorter days of autumn are required before the same process is initiated in deer. Photoperiodism also plays a role in the migration of birds. If you live in Canada or the northern United States, you know that birds arrive in the spring at about the same time every year. They may even leave their winter homes during a cold spell and arrive during a blizzard. Thus temperature appears not to be a major factor in determining migration times. The effect of photoperiodism is only secondary, however. The length of day controls the reproductive cycle. This, in turn, determines the times of migration. Birds need long periods of daylight for nest building and collecting food for their ever-hungry young. Therefore, under periods of long daylight, the process of raising young can be completed more quickly and, as a result, more successfully. Birds migrate north to breed because the length of day is longer there during the summer when food supply and temperature also favor reproduction. Southward migration in the fall occurs to escape the killing cold and limited food supply of northern areas in winter. Remember that although photoperiodism plays a role in migration, it does not explain how birds find their way during migration nor why this behavior evolved in the first place.

Quality. This term is used when referring to the color or wave length of light. As an ecological factor it is of less significance than intensity and duration. Of greatest significance ecologically is the role that light quality plays in photosynthesis. Not all wave lengths of the visible spectrum are used in photosynthesis. Only the violet and red ends of the spectrum are absorbed. The green portion is reflected. (See Fig. 1-18.) This is why chlorophyll-bearing plants appear green when exposed to daylight or its equivalent.

In general, quality is affected by the same factors that affect intensity—altitude, latitude, time of year, time of day, and atmospheric conditions. For example, smog cuts down light intensity. It also disperses blue light which means that less blue light reaches the earth. Since these factors are relatively constant over large areas, they are not as important ecologically as local variations such as the stratum in which the organism is located. For example, the ground stratum in a forest receives less red and blue light than the tree stratum. This is because the chlorophyll in the leaves of the tree stratum has absorbed much of this light. However, many species of plants have adapted to light of this quality. In fact, the

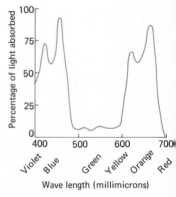

Fig. 1-18
The absorption curve of chlorophyll.

reduction in intensity appears to be more of a limiting factor in the ground stratum than does the change in quality.

The quality of light affects mainly those animals that have color vision. It is interesting to note that certain species of arthropods, fish, birds, and mammals have well-developed color vision while other species in the same groups do not. For example, primates are the only mammals that have well-developed color vision. What advantages do you think color vision gives to an animal?

SOIL

Soil is the most complex environmental factor affecting life in terrestrial ecosystems. No one factor alone describes soil. Texture, acidity, nutrients, organic content, and moisture content are just a few characteristics which must be considered. Also, life exists in the soil. Insects, other invertebrates, fungi, and bacteria interact with and affect the abiotic characteristics of the soil. In fact, the soil is an ecosystem in itself.

Soil formation begins with the weathering of rocks and rock fragments. As the weathered material accumulates, primitive plants take root. They contribute further to the breakdown of the rock and add organic debris to the soil surface. Bacteria and fungi decompose the organic matter from plant and animal remains to humus. This decomposition to humus is one of the first stages in the conversion of organic matter to soil material. Humus, in turn, is gradually decomposed by bacteria and fungi to simple compounds such as water, carbon dioxide, and minerals.

At any one time the soil has a certain mineral and organic content. But it does not have a uniform mixture of minerals and organic matter. Instead it has layers or *horizons*, each with its own characteristics. Together these horizons make up what is known as a *soil profile*. A soil profile is formed largely by the action of percolating water. The water leaches materials from the surface layers and deposits them in deeper layers of the soil. In this way layers (horizons) having different properties, like color, are formed. You have probably seen a profile similar to the one shown in Figure 1-19.

Another characteristic of the soil is the texture or size of the soil particles (Fig. 1-20). Soils consisting of sand-size particles are termed coarse-textured soils. Clay soils are fine-textured soils. Of course there is a range of textures between these two extremes. Particle size is important because it affects the water-holding capacity of the soil. Rain water percolates down into the soil. Some of this water is held be-

Fig. 1-19
A cut into the soil generally reveals a soil profile consisting of two or more horizons, each having a particular set of properties. (U.S.D.A. Photo.)

Fig. 1-20
A set of soil sieves can be used to study the texture of soil.

tween the particles. The rest percolates, under the influence of gravity, toward the water table. The amount of water remaining in the soil after the gravitational water has drained away is called the *field capacity* of the soil. Clay soils have a greater field capacity than sandy soils because more water is trapped between the fine particles than between the coarse particles. However, much of the water trapped by the fine particles is held there by very strong bonds. As a result this water is unavailable to plants. Coarse soils cannot bind as much water in this way. Therefore, although coarse-textured soils have a lower field capacity, they generally have more water that is available for plants.

The *p*H of the soil is another important factor. *p*H is a measure of acidity. It can vary from 0 to 14. The lower the *p*H number the higher the acidity. A soil with a *p*H between 0 and 7 is an acid soil. A soil of *p*H 7 is neutral and a soil of *p*H greater than 7 is alkaline or basic. The soil acidity usually varies from one horizon to the next. Generally more acid is present in the humus layer. This is because carbon dioxide is one of the products of organic breakdown and it dissolves in the water of the soil to produce carbonic acid.

There are many other soil factors which should be considered when you are planning your terrestrial studies. Among these are soil temperature, mineral content, percolation rate, capillarity, moisture content, organic content, pore space, and the types of organisms present in the soil. More information on these and other aspects of soil studies can be obtained from *Recommended Reading* 2.

You should keep in mind that although we have discussed temperature, moisture, light, wind, and soil under separate headings, they do not operate independently. You must not single out any one factor and study it independently of the others unless you are studying a controlled system in which you know that only one factor is changing. Such a system would normally be encountered only in a carefully designed laboratory situation.

MICROENVIRONMENTS

Abiotic factors like temperature, moisture, wind, light, and soil conditions act together to create the general environment over a broad region of land. This, in turn, determines the overall biotic nature of the region. Yet, within any given region, abiotic factors vary considerably from place to place. *Microenvironments* exist within the larger environment. For example, the soil may be richer in a hollow than on the hills around it.

The relative humidity is higher among tall grass than it is a meter above the grass; on a hot summer day, the temperature is many degrees higher next to the ground than it is a meter above the ground; conditions in a cave or rock crevice differ greatly from those in the immediate surroundings; the light intensity is lower and the moisture content higher under a fallen log than in the surrounding forest. Such microenvironments generally affect organisms more directly than does the overall environment.

Microenvironmental studies are often performed in caves, around fallen logs, in rock crevices, and in sheltered nooks. They are most commonly performed in that portion of the atmosphere which is within 1.5 meters of the soil.

The temperature and moisture conditions within a microenvironment act together to create a *microclimate* that usually differs greatly from the overall climate of the area. Among a dense stand of ferns in a northern forest on a hot summer day, the microclimate can be similar to the climate of a tropical rain forest.

When you are working in the field, it is important that you continually bear in mind that microenvironments exist. For example, if you wish to measure the overall temperature and relative humidity of a region, keep your instruments at least 1.5 meters from the ground. There are, of course, many occasions on which you will want to make measurements of the microenvironment. If you are trying to determine the conditions most suitable for the growth of maple seedlings in a forest, you would make all environmental measurements near the ground. The overall environment is not nearly as important to these seedlings as is the microenvironment.

For Thought and Research

1 a) Why do variations in the environmental temperature have a greater effect on the metabolism of poikilotherms than on the metabolism of homoiotherms?

b) Make a list of five homoiotherms and five poikilotherms. Explain how each of these animals protects itself from very high and very low temperatures.

2 a) What do you think would be the average relative humidity of a desert? Of a tropical rain forest?

b) Suppose that the relative humidity in a field was 80% at 5 p.m. The temperature was 25°C and the wind calm. By 9 p.m. the temperature was 10°C and the wind was still calm. What will happen to the relative humidity? Why? What evidence have you seen that supports your answer?

3 a) Which wind will dry out a terrestrial ecosystem more quickly, one with a relative humidity of 10% or one with a relative humidity of 70%? Assume that wind velocity, direction, and temperature are the same in both cases.

b)   The stomata (breathing pores) of pine and spruce trees are located in a groove on the underside of each needle. Examine one of these needles with a hand lens and draw what you see. If possible, examine the same needle with higher magnifications, using a dissecting microscope or a compound microscope. Mount a light source so that the top of the needle is illuminated. Add any further details that you see to your initial diagram. How does this adaptation help pine and spruce trees to withstand the drying effects of winds and high temperatures?

4   a)   How have cacti adapted to xerophytic conditions?

b)   Name three or four desert animals and explain how each animal has adapted to the xerophytic conditions of the desert.

c)   A spruce tree in the northern coniferous forest may be standing in 6 feet of snow, yet ecologists say that it is experiencing xerophytic conditions. Why?

5   a)   Why do deciduous trees enter a period of dormancy during the winter?

b)   Do you think that any life processes operate during this period? Give evidence to support your answer.

c)   The leaves of some species of maple and oak trees commonly become brightly colored in the fall. Find out what role, if any, is played by environmental factors in this color change.

6   Why do homeowners often add peat moss to the soil of their gardens and lawns?

7   a)   Hydrophytic plants that grow totally submerged in streams and rivers have grass-like or finely divided leaves. Why?

b)   The leaves of submerged hydrophytes have very thin cell walls and usually lack a cuticle (wax-like surface layer). Why?

c)   What do you think is the main function of the root of a submerged hydrophyte? Why?

8   a)   Why do wind-pollinated plants like pines and grasses lack colorful flowers?

b)   Which do you think produces more pollen grains, a flower on a wind-pollinated plant or a flower of similar size on an insect-pollinated plant? Why?

c)   Visit a local greenbelt area and sketch or photograph evidence of the impact of wind on that particular ecosystem.

9   a)   Collect pollen grains from a number of wind-pollinated plants. Examine the grains with a microscope and sketch their shapes. Repeat this procedure for several insect-pollinated plants. Describe and account for the differences.

b)   Coat a microscope slide with a thin film of a clear petroleum jelly. Place the slide in a location where it will not receive dust blown up from the ground, but where particles in the air can settle out on it. Leave the slide undisturbed for two or three weeks. Then examine it with a microscope, looking in particular for pollen grains. Use *Recommended Reading* 3 to determine the identity of the grains. Can you detect the "parent" plants nearby? From your observations would you conclude that wind-pollination is efficient or inefficient? Why?

10   a)   Why is soil erosion more pronounced now than it was 200 years ago?

b)   Deposits of loess reach their greatest extent in north-central China. Consult a map of the world and see if you can figure out why this is so.

11   a)   Grow a *Mimosa* plant from seed or buy a small plant from a florist. Use this plant to study thigmotropism (response to touch). Do environmental factors like light intensity and moisture content of the soil affect the degree of response to touch or the rate of recovery? What is the mechanism behind thigmotropism in the *Mimosa* plant? What other plants do you know that show thigmotropism?

b)   In addition to phototropism, geotropism, and thigmotropism, what other tropisms do plants exhibit? Describe and explain each one.

12 a)   In addition to geotaxis and phototaxis, what other taxes do animals exhibit? Describe and explain each one.

b)   Ask your teacher for a polarized piece of glass. Go outside and examine blue sky through the filter. Look in various directions but always keep the same side of the filter upward. Describe your results. If a bee saw what you saw, how could he use this to orient himself in flight? Find out all you can about polarization of sunlight.

c)   Obtain a photographer's light meter that reads in foot-candles. Design and carry out an experiment to determine the compensation intensities of a few species of house plants. Geraniums, African violets, and fibrous begonias are suggested.

13 a)   The chrysanthemum is a short-day plant that blooms naturally in the fall. Yet florists sell these plants in full bloom during the long days of June. How do you suppose florists encourage these plants to bloom at that time?

b)   Visit a greenhouse or flower shop and discuss your answer for part a) with the owner. Ask him for other examples of the use of photoperiodism in horticulture.

14 a)   What color would a "green" plant be if it is illuminated with green light only? With red light only? Explain your answers. Design an experiment to verify your answers.

b)   What are the chief wave lengths emitted by the special fluorescent lights that are used to promote plant growth?

c)   You can study the absorption and transmission of light by chlorophyll as follows: Tear up a few green leaves and place them in a beaker. Cover them with ethyl alcohol. Boil the alcohol until it is deep green. Use a hotplate or water bath. *Do not expose the alcohol to an open flame!* Adjust the positions of a prism, light source, and screen until a spectrum appears on the screen (Fig. 1-21). Insert a rec-

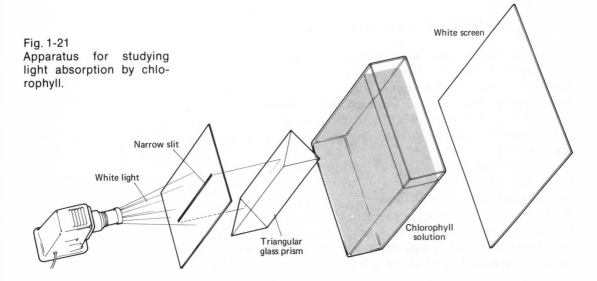

Fig. 1-21
Apparatus for studying light absorption by chlorophyll.

White screen

Narrow slit

White light

Triangular glass prism

Chlorophyll solution

tangular tank in the path of the beam of light. Pour the chlorophyll solution into the tank and observe the effect on the spectrum. Describe and explain the results.

15 a) What effect does organic matter like dead leaves and peat moss have on the water-holding capacity of soil? Why? Design and try an experiment to test your hypothesis.

b) Why are organisms like earthworms important components of soil?

c) Would the soil profile be more clearly defined in a well-drained area that experiences abundant rainfall or in a marshy area? Why?

16 a) In what ways do the trees of a forest help to determine the microenvironments of small communities on the forest floor?

b) Would you expect greater variations in microclimate within a forest or in a grassland? Why?

Recommended Readings

1 *A Guide to the Study of Freshwater Ecology* by W. A. Andrews et al., Prentice-Hall, 1972. Consult Units 3 and 4 of this book for further information on hydrophytic communities.

2 *A Guide to the Study of Soil Ecology* by W. A. Andrews et al., Prentice-Hall, 1973. Consult this book for further information on soil as an abiotic factor in terrestrial ecosystems.

3 *How to Know Pollen and Spores* by R. O. Kapp, Wm. C. Brown, 1969.

4 *Ecology and Field Biology* by R. L. Smith, Harper & Row, 1966. Consult Chapter 5 for interesting material on periodicity (including photoperiodism).

5 *Plants and Environment* by R. F. Daubenmire, John Wiley & Sons, 1967. This text contains thorough discussions of the roles of light, wind, water, soil, and temperature in ecosystems.

6 *The Study of Plant Communities* by H. J. Oosting, W. H. Freeman, 1956. This book also contains detailed information on abiotic factors in ecosystems.

1.4 ENERGY FLOW AND NUTRIENT CYCLING

If you spent a few hours in the middle of a forest in late spring, you would be impressed by the constant activity about you. Squirrels seem to dart everywhere. Birds are constantly searching for food. If you were quiet you might even see a deer nibbling on the saplings or a fox chasing its prey. Activity is the essence of life. And, for activity, energy and nutrients are required.

You may remember that the ultimate source of energy is the sun. Green plants are able to convert solar energy to biochemical energy. In so doing, they support, directly or indirectly, all of the other organisms of the ecosystem. Herbivores lose heat energy as they graze on producers. Similarly carnivores lose heat energy as they prey on herbivores. Thus energy is gradually lost along a food chain. As a result, the flow of energy through an ecosystem is one-way. Little, if any, of the energy trapped by the producers is returned to them.

As green plants convert solar energy into biochemical energy they also absorb, through their roots and stomata, elements and compounds called nutrients. Like energy, these nutrients are passed along the food chain when a herbivore grazes on a green plant, when a carnivore eats a herbivore, and when a carnivore eats a carnivore. Unlike energy, nutrients are not lost along the food chain. Instead, they are returned to the environment at the end of the food chain by the action of decomposers. They are then absorbed by producers and begin the cycle again. Nutrients are recycled. These two processes, *energy flow* and *nutrient cycling,* form the basis for the study of *dynamics* within an ecosystem. Ecologists measure the functioning of an ecosystem by the rate of energy flow and nutrient cycling. Since such quantitative considerations are quite complex, we will avoid them and, instead, limit ourselves to a descriptive approach to energy flow and nutrient cycling within ecosystems.

ENERGY FLOW

Not all of the solar radiation that reaches the earth's surface is absorbed by green plants. In fact, only about 1% of the total incident radiation is converted to biochemical energy. But this seemingly small amount of energy maintains all of the organisms on the earth. Because all consumers ultimately rely on producers for their energy, complex energy relationships exist between the organisms of an ecosystem. Some of these relationships were described in Section 1.1 in terms of *food chains* and *food webs.* Their complexity was simplified by categorizing each organism according to its *niche* — producer, herbivore, first-order carnivore, and so on. Such categories are called feeding or *trophic* levels. The first trophic level is occupied by the producers. What levels do herbivores, first-order carnivores, and second-order carnivores occupy?

Many animals are not easily categorized since they occupy more than one niche. For example, several animals are both herbivores and carnivores. They are called *omnivores.* Can you think of some examples? Clearly the concept of trophic levels is an oversimplification of complex interrelationships between the organisms of an ecosystem. However, trophic levels have been studied extensively and the results of some of these studies are quite interesting.

One of the first studies to be made was a numerical one. The organisms occupying each trophic level within an ecosystem were counted. It was found that, in general, there were successively fewer organisms the higher the trophic level. In other words, a *pyramid of numbers* exists (Fig. 1-22).

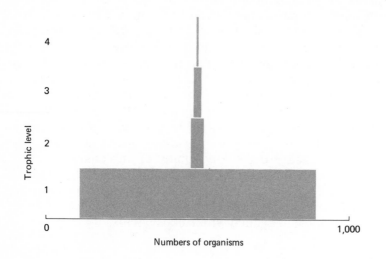

Fig. 1-22
A pyramid of numbers for a hypothetical ecosystem. Notice how many more producers there are than consumers.

A pyramid of numbers is illustrated by this simple food chain:

Wheat → Mouse → Owl

A mouse, restricted to a diet of wheat, must eat several hundred kernels to sustain itself for a day. (Each kernel is essentially a small wheat plant.) Yet, at the next trophic level, an owl needs only 5 or 10 mice per day.

In a few food chains the pyramid of numbers is inverted. That is, there is an increasing number of organisms the higher the trophic level. Can you think of some examples?

Ecologists soon realized that although a pyramid of numbers gives some interesting information, it is not of great importance in understanding the dynamics of an ecosystem. This is because it treats all organisms as though they were the same, totally ignoring size differences. Yet, to a hungry fox, size is important. One rabbit makes a better meal than one mouse! So ecologists decided that a better measure would be the total mass of organisms (biomass) at each level. If you think about this, you will agree. It makes more sense to equate one gram of rabbit with one gram of mouse than it does to equate one rabbit with one mouse. After measuring the total biomass for each level in several food chains, they discovered that, in general, there was a decreasing biomass the higher the trophic level, giving what is called a *pyramid of biomass* (Fig. 1-23). Such a pyramid is clearly illustrated by a food chain of which you are a part:

Grain → Chicken → Man

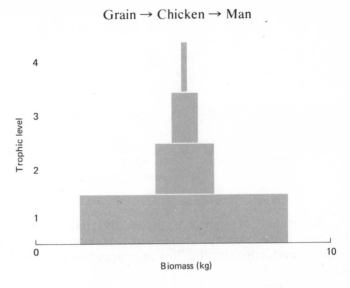

Fig. 1-23
A pyramid of biomass for a hypothetical ecosystem. Although the pyramid of biomass may not look much different from the pyramid of numbers, biomass better represents the value of the fixed energy at any trophic level.

Experienced farmers have now perfected chicken-raising to the point where about three grams of grain will form one gram of chicken (provided that the chicken is in the growing stage). Yet that one gram of chicken will produce only a small fraction of a gram of tissue in a growing human.

Although a pyramid of biomass is a more basic concept than a pyramid of numbers, it has one major fault. It equates unit masses of all organisms. For example, it implies that one gram of rabbit and one gram of mouse will provide a fox with equivalent amounts of energy. Yet experiments have shown that this is not true. Different types of tissue have different energy contents. The most noticeable difference occurs between plant and animal tissue. You can obtain about 20% more energy by eating one gram of animal than you can by eating one gram of plant.

Some animals eat plants to obtain energy for life processes. Some animals eat other animals for the same reason. Basically, then, the efficiency with which energy is passed along a food chain is more important than either the numbers of organisms or their biomasses. Therefore ecologists now concentrate on *pyramids of energy* (Fig. 1-24). Each level in this pyramid represents the sum of the energy tied up in the formation of new tissue and that released by respiration—or, the total energy flow at that level.

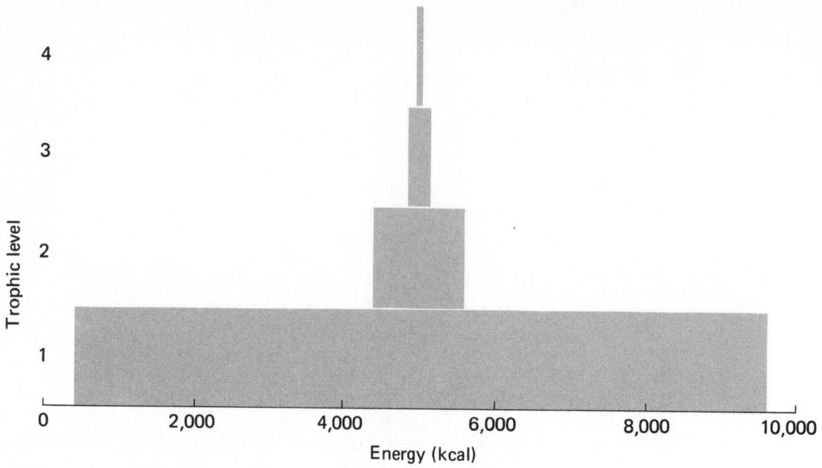

Fig. 1-24
A pyramid of energy for a
hypothetical ecosystem.

A pyramid of energy is never inverted. In order to explain why there is always decreasing total energy the higher the trophic level, consider the flow of energy through this food chain:

Clover → Rabbit → Fox

Study Figure 1-25 carefully as you read this description. Not all of the total energy produced by the clover is available to animals and decomposers. Much of it is lost through respiration. The rabbit consumes part of the net energy produced by the clover. But here, too, part of the energy is lost as the rabbit respires to carry on life processes. The net energy available to the fox is only a fraction of the energy the rabbit obtained from the clover. The fox can utilize only a part of the energy provided by the rabbit. Bones are not digestible, for instance. If the fox has no immediate predators, parasites and decomposers eventually utilize the available energy of the fox. The rest is lost as heat. The fox, too, must use energy for life processes.

As energy is lost at each level in the food chain, so is it lost at each trophic level within an ecosystem. The energy lost as heat cannot be recaptured by any organisms in the ecosystem. Hence the flow of energy is one-way. Energy must enter from the sun to keep an ecosystem operating.

Man is as dependent as any other organism on the flow of energy through ecosystems. His very existence depends on it. However, he can control energy flow and divert it to his own use. For example, he can destroy a natural ecosystem

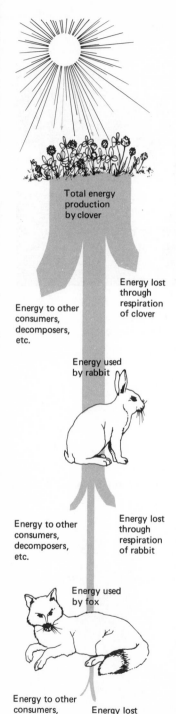

Fig. 1-25
Energy flow along a simple food chain.

Total energy
production
by clover

Energy to other
consumers,
decomposers,
etc.

Energy lost
through
respiration
of clover

Energy used
by rabbit

Energy to other
consumers,
decomposers,
etc.

Energy lost
through
respiration
of rabbit

Energy used
by fox

Energy to other
consumers,
decomposers,
etc.

Energy lost
through respiration
of fox

like a forest and replace it with a grain crop which will yield more energy for him. As the population of mankind increases, more crops will be necessary to supply the increasing food demands, and more natural ecosystems will be destroyed. Fewer niches and suitable habitats will be available for many organisms and the threat of extinction will become real for them. Alternatives do exist, however. What are they?

NUTRIENT (BIOGEOCHEMICAL) CYCLES

As the name suggests, *biogeochemistry* is the study of the exchange of materials between the living and the non-living parts of an ecosystem. And *biogeochemical cycles* show the kinds of exchange that take place. The movement of nutrients through an ecosystem occurs as energy is transferred. But, unlike energy flow, nutrient flow is cyclic. The cycling of nutrients is made possible by the presence of two types of organisms. The *decomposers* (largely fungi and bacteria) break down dead plant or animal matter into simpler organic compounds. Then the *transformers* (bacteria) change those organic compounds into inorganic compounds which can be absorbed by green plants. Elements that were once in a plant can, through a chain of events, eventually be returned to a plant. Let us see how this occurs by considering three of the basic nutrient cycles, those of water, carbon, and nitrogen.

The water cycle (Fig. 1-26). Water vapor enters the atmosphere through transpiration from vegetation and by evaporation from bodies of water and the soil. In the cool upper atmosphere this vapor condenses, forming clouds. In time, enough water collects in the clouds to cause precipitation. When this occurs some of the water falling on the ground is absorbed and some runs along the surface of the ground to a stream, pond, or other body of water. The amount of water absorption and surface runoff depends on the nature of the soil and the amount of precipitation. Some of the water in the soil is absorbed through the roots of the green plants. Thus animals can obtain water by eating green plants. Of course, they can also obtain it directly by drinking it from a body of water. When plants and animals die, they decompose. During this process the water present in their tissues is released into the environment. Some of the soil water percolates to ground water level, only to return to a body of water.

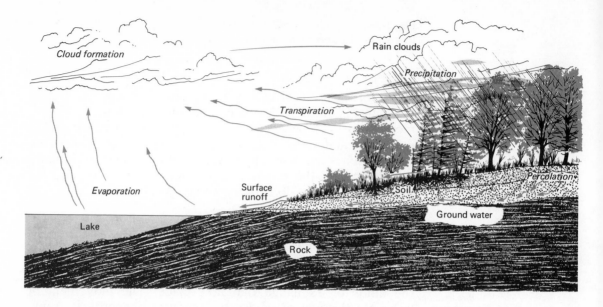

Fig. 1-26
The water cycle.

The carbon cycle (Fig. 1-27). At one time this cycle was considered a perfect one. Carbon was returned to the atmosphere about as quickly as it was removed. Lately, however, the increased combustion of fossil fuels has added carbon to the atmosphere faster than green plants can remove it.

Carbon is present in the atmosphere as carbon dioxide. Plants use carbon dioxide to make organic compounds such as carbohydrates and fats. Animals cannot synthesize

Fig. 1-27
The carbon cycle.

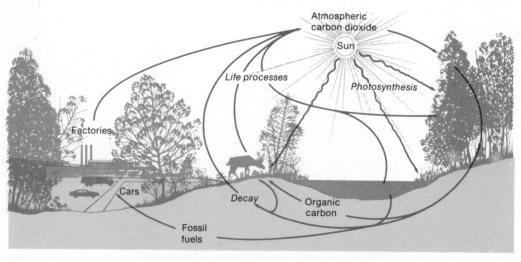

their own organic compounds this way. Thus they obtain the necessary building blocks by eating green plants or other animals. Some carbon dioxide is returned to the air as a by-product of respiration in plants and animals. Still more is released by decay (the respiratory activity of decomposer organisms). Organic matter that does not completely decompose can accumulate and become incorporated into the earth's crust. Oil and coal resulted from accumulation of plant organic matter in the distant past.

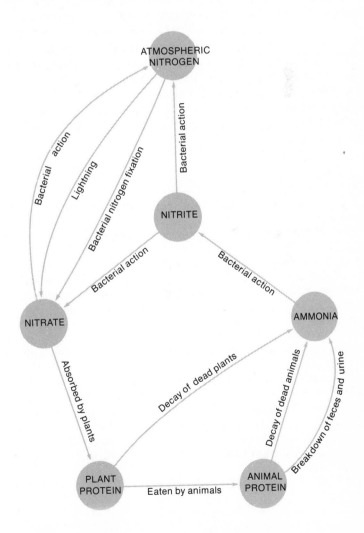

Fig. 1-28
The nitrogen cycle.

The nitrogen cycle (Fig. 1-28). All plants and animals require nitrogen to synthesize proteins. Although almost 78%

of the atmosphere is molecular nitrogen (N_2), neither plants nor animals can use this form directly. Nitrogen must be in the form of a nitrate (NO_3^-) before it can be absorbed by the roots of plants. Lightning flashing through an atmospheric mixture of nitrogen and oxygen can cause this conversion. The bacterium *Rhizobium* lives in nodules on the roots of legumes like clover. It too can convert molecular nitrogen to nitrates. Plants use the nitrates that they absorb to synthesize plant proteins. Animals get the nitrogen that they require for protein synthesis by eating plants or other animals. When plants and animals die, bacteria convert their nitrogen content to ammonia (NH_3) or ammonium (NH_4^+) compounds. The nitrogen in the metabolic wastes (urine) and fecal matter of animals is also converted to ammonia by bacteria. Ammonia, in turn, is converted to nitrites and then to nitrates by bacteria, thus completing one portion of the cycle. Bacteria convert some nitrite and nitrate to molecular nitrogen to complete the total cycle. The nitrogen cycle need not and often does not involve this last step.

Fig. 1-29
A Venus' flytrap. (U.S.D.A. Photo.)

For Thought and Research

1 a) Describe the niches and determine the trophic levels of parasites and scavengers.

b) What niches are occupied by the Venus' flytrap (Fig. 1-29)? Explain your answer.

2 It has been suggested that to make the best use of food on this crowded planet, we should all become herbivores. Therefore, instead of eating cows, pigs, and fowl, we would eat the plants that these animals would normally have eaten. Debate this suggestion in the light of your knowledge of pyramids of energy and energy flow.

3 Use your knowledge of nutrient cycling to develop an argument which should convince a homeowner that he need not fertilize his lawn with commercial fertilizers.

4 Recently many people have suggested diverting the course of several Arctic rivers so that instead of emptying into the Arctic Ocean, they would flow southward. The available water would be used to irrigate arid regions in the American southwest, thereby increasing the productivity of the area.

a) In general, what do you think of this proposal?

b) Use your knowledge of the water cycle to predict some effects of such a diversion.

c) What effects might such action have on the climate of North America?

Recommended Readings

1 *Concepts of Ecology* by E. J. Kormondy, Prentice-Hall, 1969. Consult this book for detailed information on energy flow and nutrient cycling in ecosystems.

2 *A Guide to the Study of Environmental Pollution* by W. A. Andrews et al., Prentice-Hall, 1972. See Unit 2 of this book for more information on nutrients and their movement through ecosystems.

1.5 ECOLOGICAL SUCCESSION

You have probably noticed that a vacant lot or field, left untouched, does not remain in its original state for long. Although it may have started out as a grassy area, it soon becomes overgrown with weeds. As time progresses taller weeds dominate the shorter ones. In a few years shrubs appear. Several years later small trees begin to colonize the area. If you could sit down under one of these trees and observe the area for a few hundred years, you would witness the remainder of one of nature's most remarkable phenomena —*ecological succession*. What is succession? Why does it occur?

A clearly defined succession occurs on sand dunes. Let us examine this environment to gain a clear understanding of the meaning and causes of succession.

Succession on sand dunes. Sand dunes commonly form on the leeward side of large lakes. Wave action piles sand on the beach; the sun dries out the sand; then winds blow it inland, creating large mounds called sand dunes (Fig. 1-30).

Such an area is a harsh environment for any organism. Lack of moisture, few available nutrients, intense light, strong winds, shifting sands, high day temperatures, and low night temperatures are just a few of the problems that confront any organism that attempts to live here. Yet some organisms do establish communities on sand dunes. And, as you know, their presence modifies the environment. The modified environment supports different organisms. These organisms further modify the environment. And on it goes. The interaction of biotic and abiotic factors makes a sand dune a region of

Fig. 1-30
Formation of a sand dune.

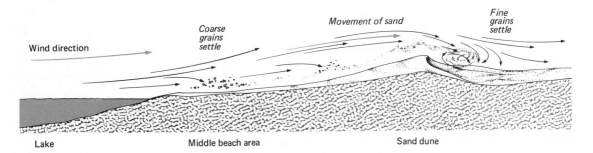

Wind direction

Coarse grains settle

Movement of sand

Fine grains settle

Lake Middle beach area Sand dune

change. Let us take an imaginary trip through time to see exactly what happens. Imagine that you are sitting on a sand dune that has no life on it, other than you (Fig. 1-31). This sand dune is located on the shore of one of the Great Lakes. You are going to sit there for several hundred years to observe and study succession.

With the passage of time, some dead organic matter from the lake is sure to be swept onto the dune. This small amount of organic matter enriches the sand enough that patches of a *pioneer plant,* sand grass, begin to grow around you (Fig. 1-32). This hardy plant is well adapted to the xerophytic conditions of a sand dune. It has an extensive root system that absorbs the small amount of water available and anchors the plant in the shifting sand. Its narrow leaves flex to resist the force of wind-driven sand. The sand grass tends to stabilize the dune. Also, it traps drifting sand, making the dune even larger.

As sand grass dies and decays, humus is added to the soil. This modified soil supports the growth of xerophytic shrubs like the sand cherry. The presence of these shrubs stabilizes the dune still further.

Fig. 1-31
Sand dunes along Lake Ontario.

Next cottonwood trees begin to shoot upward among these shrubs. These characteristic trees are called the *index plants* of this stage in succession. The shade cast by the shrubs and cottonwood trees provides welcome relief to you from the scorching sun. It also helps the soil to retain its moisture longer. In addition, decaying leaves add further to the organic content of the soil. Ants and beetles move busily among the sand grass plants. Birds feed on the sand cherries. The digger wasp, an *index animal* of the cottonwood stage, burrows into the sand at your feet. You notice that the sand is darker in color because of the added organic matter.

The enriched soil now enables pine seedlings to become established in the area. Eventually they become the *dominant species* and, therefore, are called the index plants of this stage. As the pine trees develop, they drop needles about you. The soil becomes still richer. But now, a strange thing happens. Pine trees are sun-loving plants. But the large pine trees cast a dense shade on the soil. As a result young pine trees do not receive enough light to develop. You watch them struggle for survival and die about you. The pines, through living, have brought extinction to the species! For, as the adult trees mature and die, no young pines replace them.

But black oak seedlings grow well in the shade of pine trees. Therefore, if a squirrel or blue jay drops an acorn from a black oak into the pine forest, it will germinate and grow.

Fig. 1-32
Sand grass.

Fig. 1-33
A climax forest, dominated by maple and beech trees.

Eventually black oaks dominate the area. However, the trees are not very large or closely spaced because nutrients and water are still in short supply. This stage may remain for centuries, as the black oaks slowly add humus to the soil in the form of leaves, bark, and fallen branches.

As further humus accumulates, red and white oaks invade the area. They grow well in the shade of black oak trees whereas young black oaks do not. Resting in the shade of the red and white oak trees, you observe that trees still more shade-tolerant invade the area—ash, basswood, and hickory. But they, too, cast a shade too dense for their young to survive. However, young maple and beech trees are very shade-tolerant. They thrive in this environment. Thus, after the passage of considerable time, they dominate the area (Fig. 1-33). Unlike other species, young maple and beech trees can develop in the shade of the parent trees. As a result, the community becomes self-perpetuating. Young trees are always ready to replace dead ones of the same species. Such a community is called a *climax community*.

You have observed a hot, dry, bright environment change to a cool, moist, shady one. The most obvious biological changes were the changing tree species. Looking carefully, you can see still other important biological features. Remnants of previous stages can be seen throughout the climax forest—an occasional oak and basswood tower among the beech and maple trees. In moist areas the hemlock, an evergreen, forms part of the climax community. Also, as the succession of plant communities took place, a succession of animal communities accompanied it. Invertebrates like earthworms, insects, millipedes, centipedes, and snails became more abundant as the climax approached. Toads, salamanders, and a host of mammals and birds appeared.

Now, let us return to the original questions: What is succession? Why does it occur? In summary, living organisms modify their environment. In doing so, they make the environment less favorable for themselves but more favorable for another community of plants and animals. Each stage in succession, except the climax, brings about its own demise. As succession progresses, species diversity, population numbers, and niche availability increase. Also, total biomass and organic matter increase. All of these add to the complexity of the community. It is this complexity that progressively increases the stability of the community. Many plant and animal species mean more food webs. Thus there is less chance of the entire community collapsing because of the extinction of one species.

Obviously it is not possible to wait in one place for several hundred years to observe succession. Fortunately, you don't have to. You can see all of the stages within a period of a few minutes by walking in from the water's edge (Fig. 1-34).

As a dune enlarges and becomes covered with vegetation, a new dune forms closer to the water. As it becomes covered with vegetation, a still younger dune forms between it and the water. Meanwhile the original dune has advanced further in succession. This process can happen again and again. As a result, a young dune with little or no vegetation exists closest to the water. The next dune inland will be further on in succession and the next dune still further on. Thus you can see *in space*, as you walk inland, the stages of a succession that occurred *in time*. And, using suitable study techniques, you can trace the sequence of events that occurred (see Unit 5).

Types of succession. Succession that begins in an area that has not supported life within recent geological times is called *primary succession*. A sand dune succession is in this category. So, too, is the succession that occurs on bare rock. Lichens are the pioneer plants of a rock succession. They attach themselves to rocky surfaces and extract nutrients from the rocks. This weakens the rock surface. Weathering contributes to the breakup of the rocks. Dead lichens add humus to the rock fragments, forming soil. Mosses can now colonize the area. They, too, add humus to the soil as they die and decay. They contribute greatly to succession by trapping wind-blown earth and organic matter. The resulting soil can support plants like ferns and grasses. Later, other herbaceous

Fig. 1-34
Succession on a sand dune in the Great Lakes region.

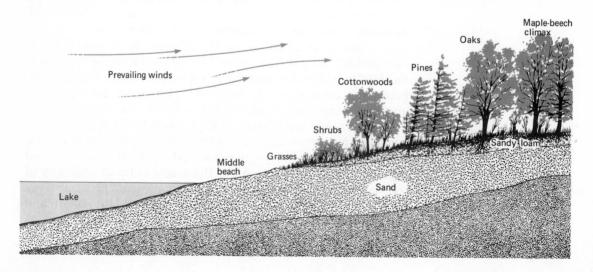

plants and shrubs invade the area. From this point on the succession follows a course similar to that on sand dunes. Thousands of years may be required before the climax is reached.

Succession that begins in a region that once supported life is called *secondary succession*. An abandoned meadow and a forest denuded by fire or lumbering will undergo this type of succession. Secondary succession is generally more rapid than primary succession since soil is already present and, also, some forms of life are already in the area. Grasses usually dominate the early years of secondary succession, but tall weeds like wild asters and goldenrod soon follow. Shrubs like hawthorns quickly invade the area. They are followed closely by sun-loving trees like poplars and pines. Succession then proceeds along the usual path to a climax community.

Both primary and secondary succession are examples of *autotrophic succession*. In both cases succession is dominated by green plants—they are largely responsible for the modification of the environment. However, many interesting examples of *heterotrophic succession* also exist. For example, a fallen log undergoes succession. Bacteria, fungi, and a host of invertebrates succeed one another as they inhabit and feed on the log. The climax is reached when the log has been converted to soil. The climax community is the resulting soil community. Similarly, a rotting carcass undergoes succession. Bacteria are the first to colonize the carcass. Worms follow. Other invertebrates such as flies, beetles, and wasps follow to complete the decomposition of the carcass.

The stages in succession where you live may not be the same as those described here. For example, in the St. Lawrence River valley, the climax consists largely of white spruce and balsam fir. Minnesota has a climax community of maple and basswood. The giant redwoods of the California coast and the Douglas firs of British Columbia dominate the climax forests of their respective regions. But, wherever you live, you are never far from an example of succession.

For Thought and Research

1 a) List, in order, the index plants of a typical sand dune succession.

b) Explain carefully why a succession of plant communities occurs. Be sure to mention all of the abiotic factors involved.

2 Sand dune communities are very fragile. Disturbed topsoil is quickly blown away by the prevailing winds. Vegetation in the area is therefore harmed. The dunes are easily disrupted by natural events like a torrential rain and unnatural events like intrusion by dune buggies and trail bikes. Use your knowledge of

ecology and of succession, in particular, to prepare an argument against the use of motorized vehicles in sand dune regions.

3 Why do earthworms and most other invertebrates become more abundant as succession approaches the climax stage? (Consult *Recommended Reading 3*.)

4 Primary succession occurs in and around a pond or small lake. Consult *Recommended Reading* 4 to find out how this occurs. If possible, visit a nearby pond or small lake to observe this phenomenon firsthand.

5 Find out what the successional stages are in your area. You might begin this investigation by consulting *Recommended Reading* 2.

Fig. 1-35
A reforested dune. (Courtesy of Ontario Ministry of Natural Resources.)

6 Foresters make use of man's knowledge of succession when they are selecting tree species to rehabilitate a sand dune area that has lost its vegetation by fire, wind, or man's intrusion. Figure 1-35 shows an area that has been replanted. What tree species do you think have been planted here? Why did the foresters select them?

Recommended Readings

1 *Ecology and Field Biology* by R. L. Smith, Harper & Row, 1966. Consult Chapter 6 for further information on succession.

2 *The Study of Plant Communities* by H. J. Oosting, W. H. Freeman, 1956. Consult Chapter 10 for a thorough and interesting description of succession. Chapter 11 will help you identify the nature of successional change in your area.

3 *A Guide to the Study of Soil Ecology* by W. A. Andrews et al., Prentice-Hall, 1973. Consult this book to find out the soil preferences of various invertebrates.

4 *A Guide to the Study of Freshwater Ecology* by W. A. Andrews et al., Prentice-Hall, 1972. Consult Section 3.8 for a description of succession in a pond.

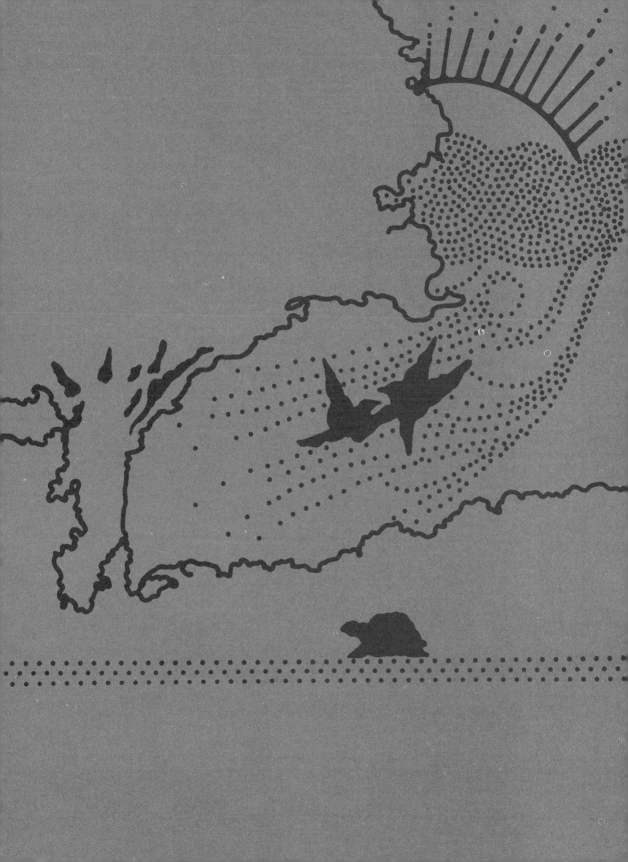

Major Biomes of North America

2

Have you ever awakened in the morning to find a polar bear strolling through your backyard? Have you ever discovered a rattlesnake curled up under a cactus plant by the front porch? Do you have giant redwoods at your doorstep, or a rippling sea of grass as your front lawn? Most of you will answer "No" to all of these questions. Yet if you were to conduct a survey throughout North America, you would get "Yes" answers to all of these. This continent has a tremendous diversity of natural life.

Every living organism is adapted to its environment—a combination of abiotic (non-living) and biotic (living) factors. The earth can be divided into major environmental zones, each determined by a particular geography, and accompanied by characteristic plant and animal populations. These zones are called *biomes*.

2.1   THE DISTRIBUTION OF BIOMES

Broad bands of major climates encompass the earth, roughly parallel to large latitudinal divisions. Oceans disrupt these bands. Mountains and other surface features further alter the climate across each continent. Thus a biome cannot be sharply defined. Ecologists can neither agree on the number of biomes nor on the boundaries which separate them. Certain regions of North America which are regarded as distinct biomes by some people are classed as ecotones (transition zones) by others. Hence Figure 2-1 should be regarded as only a general guide to North American biomes.

A change in altitude can affect environment as much as a change in latitude. As altitude increases, the temperature falls approximately 1C° for every 150 meters. Climbing a few hundred meters up a mountain slope you would detect the same progressive temperature decrease as you would by traveling a far greater distance toward the nearest polar cap. Wind velocity increases at higher altitudes. Mountain soil, eroded by rain, frost, and falling rock, becomes thinner and more deficient in minerals toward the top. As the environment changes, so does the natural life. Northern species project their ranges southward into mountain ridges where conditions

Fig. 2-1
The major biomes of Canada and the United States. Lesser biomes such as the California chapparal and the eastern pine-oak forest are not shown.

Key

Tundra

Tundra—
coniferous forest
ecotone

Coniferous forest

Coniferous—
deciduous forest
ecotone

Deciduous forest

Coniferous forest—
grasslands ecotone

Grasslands

Desert

Sub-tropical forest

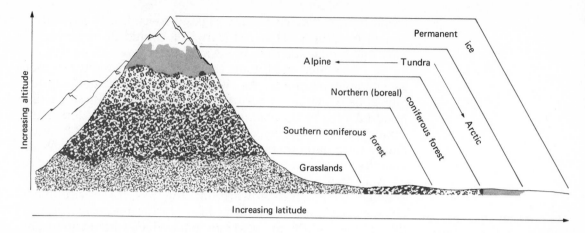

Increasing altitude

Permanent ice

Alpine ← → Tundra

Northern (boreal) coniferous forest

Arctic

Southern coniferous forest

Grasslands

Increasing latitude

match those of more northern latitudes. Less than 6.5 km (4 miles) measured vertically up a mountainside at the equator provides as many different environments as 10,500 km (6,500 miles) measured at sea level between the equator and one of the poles (Fig. 2-2). Hence mountains further complicate the pattern of biomes.

The following sections survey the length and breadth of North America to examine the major biomes of this continent.

Fig. 2-2
Altitude versus latitude. Compare the effect on vegetation in western North America.

2.2   THE TUNDRA

Stretching beyond the forests of the distant north to the edge of the Arctic ice cap lies a vast, treeless plain. This is the land of the *Arctic tundra*. Locate it in Figure 2-1.

ABIOTIC FACTORS

The climate of this region is characterized by low temperatures and cold, dry winds. Even the wettest months in summer yield only about an inch of precipitation. The light winter snowfall is difficult to measure because the snow is swept into shifting drifts by the winds.

Tundra areas north of the Arctic Circle lie in the "land of the midnight sun." Most of you would be startled to find the sun peeping through your window at 2 o'clock in the morning. But if you lived in this part of the world, you would be accustomed to 24 hours of daylight in midsummer when the sun never sets. But you must also endure 24 hours of darkness during midwinter when the sun is too far south to rise above the Arctic horizon. Below the Arctic Circle the photoperiod depends upon the latitude, which is north of 57°N for most of the tundra. Since the sun's rays strike this region of the earth's surface at a very low angle, the radiant energy received by the tundra is never very intense, despite the lengthy summer days.

The long winters are extremely cold. Average January temperatures range from −22°C (−8°F) along the Labrador coast to −29°C (−20°F) in Barrow, Alaska. The soil is completely frozen. Thick fogs prevail wherever the icy land meets the sea. For nine months, tundra lakes lie buried beneath a thick blanket of ice. Shallow ponds freeze to the bottom. When the warmth of springtime finally arrives to melt this frozen wasteland, the short Arctic summer is close upon its heels. In fact, the entire growing season lasts only about 60 days. Although summer brings long hours of daylight, the sun's rays do not generate much heat. June and July in the tundra are usually chilly and raw, much like March or April in southern Ontario or January in Georgia. The warmest month is July, when average temperatures range from a low of 0°C (32°F) to a high of 10°C (50°F). Killing frost can occur at any time. During the short spring and summer interval the surface of the soil thaws to a depth which varies from a few centimeters in some localities to half a meter in others. Below this lies the *permafrost,* soil which never thaws. This permanently frozen layer is 610 m (2,000 ft) deep in spots, preventing proper drainage of the water produced by melting snow in the spring. Instead, the meltwater collects on the flat land surface, producing vast marshy areas called *muskeg,* dotted with ponds and streams. This important water reservoir enables plants to grow despite the low rainfall.

An aerial view of the tundra landscape reveals unique land patterns which resemble a patchwork quilt (Fig. 2-3). These are molded by the constantly active forces of freezing and thawing. Each time the soil freezes, the finer soil and clays, which retain more moisture, expand, only to contract again during the next thaw. This continual process forces larger soil particles above the surface to form patterned ridges in the land. Large boulders can be splintered into rock fragments by similar frost action. The constant heaving and movement of earth greatly limits vegetation. Unstable soil and rocks tend to gradually creep down any slope which forms. Frost is more effective than erosion in wearing down the surface features.

It is interesting to note that a corresponding biome does not exist in the Southern Hemisphere. North of the icefields of Antarctica, most of the land surface within lati-

Fig. 2-3
The patterned land surface shown in this aerial photograph results from repeated freezing and thawing of ice in the tundra soil. (Courtesy of U.S. Fish and Wildlife Service.)

tudes where climate could produce tundra is covered by ocean. However, similar abiotic factors have established separate "islands" of tundra on mountains in high alpine regions. In this *alpine tundra,* permafrost exists only at very high altitudes and on northern mountain ranges. As a result, the ground surface is drier. Yet the combination of frost and wind still produces thin, unstable soils except in small, protected pockets in the mountainsides. The temperature is usually low, but it can fluctuate as much as 32C° (58F°) during a single summer day. Southern slopes are the warmest. The growing season is brief, as in the Arctic, but the alpine tundra is not subjected to the same extreme change in photoperiod. Although summer days are shorter in the mountains, the light intensity is much higher in the thin atmosphere. The clouds and fog which often hide the mountain tops yield more precipitation to the alpine tundra. However, the steep land surface causes rapid water runoff before the moisture can fully penetrate the soil. Low atmospheric pressure and high wind velocity increase the rate of evaporation. Yet humidity remains low because the thin air cannot retain much water vapor. The low density of air (and, hence, reduced concentration of oxygen) is a feature unique to the alpine tundra. How does this affect the plant and, more directly, the animal life of this region?

BIOTIC FACTORS

Life in both the Arctic and alpine tundra presents a fascinating study in adaptation. Although the tundra may appear a rather barren region, its ecology is very important to scientists. The temperature factor alone greatly limits the number of organisms which can adapt and survive in this biome. This makes basic relationships, such as food chains and food webs, simple and easy to determine. Such studies in the tundra may help us to understand more complicated ecosystems in other parts of the world.

Vegetation. At first glance, the summer landscape of the Arctic tundra resembles a grassy plain (Fig. 2-4). Closer examination reveals a complex pattern of vegetation. Grasses, sedges, and herbs stretch between the areas of fine, well-drained soil with woody shrubs such as birch, willow, and heath. Mounds of earth are covered by lichens and blueberry. Wetter hollows are filled with sedges and reeds, typical marsh plants. Clumps of cotton grass rise above a carpet of sphagnum moss, covered with dwarf shrubs. A rich growth of taller shrubs and grasses is found on the steeper southern slopes of hilly areas and in river bottoms. Every nook and cranny which offers shelter is invaded by some vegetation.

Fig. 2-4
Summer in the tundra produces an Arctic grassland. Dwarf woody plants are scattered among grasses, sedges, and lichens. (Courtesy of Ontario Ministry of Natural Resources.)

Fig. 2-5
Compare the growth of this mature dwarf willow with that of its southern counterpart. (Courtesy of U.S. Fish and Wildlife Service.)

You are familiar with the abiotic factors governing this biome. Now consider carefully the characteristics of these tundra plants. For instance, how is growth affected by the low summer temperatures? What type of root system can develop in the thin layer of shifting soil? How do these plants photosynthesize properly in the low light intensity of the Arctic? And how does tundra vegetation manage to propagate during the brief growing season? The answers to these and other related questions reveal the extent of plant adaptation to the tundra environment.

The low soil and air temperatures greatly retard plant growth in both the Arctic and alpine tundra. Hence, plants tend to be small and stunted. A good example is the dwarf willow (Fig. 2-5). If this plant tries to grow vertically in the normal fashion, any terminal buds which form are quickly killed by the chilling winds. Some of the sun's radiant energy which strikes the ground is absorbed by the soil. Thus the soil temperature is generally much higher than that of the air above. In fact, soil temperatures in the alpine tundra can change from 0°C (32°F) to 40°C (104°F) during a summer day. The rest of the heat energy is reflected back into the atmosphere. Therefore, the air temperature immediately next to the soil is higher than the air temperature 30 cm or more above the ground. This means that buds can grow on branches of the plant which spread laterally, close to the warmer soil surface. Growth at this level also affords protection against the constant abrasion from soil and ice particles driven by the wind. As a result, the growth of the dwarf willow is greatly modified from that of related willow species in more southern areas of North America.

Root systems trying to develop in the thin, unstable tundra soil face many of the problems associated with sand dunes. Thus you might expect to find similar plant species, namely grasses and shrubs. If you have ever tried to dislodge a clump of grass, you know how strongly the shallow, branching root network grips the soil. By weaving around soil particles, the root mass can better absorb any available moisture. This is a critical factor in the dry portions of the tundra. Other tundra plants include mosses and lichens which cling to the soil using hair-like rhizoids rather than true roots. Their ability to absorb and retain moisture enables them to grow on the driest surfaces. Yet they also thrive in bogs. These simple plants play an important role by retarding erosion. A dense growth of this vegetation tends to stabilize soil particles. A carpet of moss can slow the rapid runoff of rain water or melted snow. Such moss beds, with their reservoir of water, also provide growth sites for larger flowering plants.

Despite a similar environment, Arctic and alpine tundra have considerably different vegetation. One important cause of this difference is the photoperiod. Arctic species are long-day plants. They are adapted to lower light intensity, but they need longer periods of daylight than alpine plants for proper photosynthesis. Alpine plants are adapted to the high light intensity of the thin mountain atmosphere. The growth of an Arctic tundra plant, transplanted to an alpine location, would be measurably retarded by the shorter photoperiod, despite the stronger sunlight.

The cold climate and brief summer period greatly reduce the action of decomposers. Hence a layer of undecayed vegetation covers much of the tundra. The slow decomposition of organic matter leaves tundra soils deficient in nitrates, phosphates, and other essential minerals. Wherever animal wastes provide these nutrients, plant growth is noticeably improved. Patches of lush green vegetation are signposts for animal burrows, bird cliffs, and the nesting sites of geese.

During the short growing season, Arctic tundra plants must photosynthesize and store enough food to last the entire year. The production of flowers and seeds consumes a great deal of energy. Therefore most tundra plants are perennials. They must grow for several seasons before they have stored enough energy to flower. To attract the limited number of insect and bird pollinating agents, flowers tend to bloom in clusters. These blossoms appear conspicuously large in contrast to the tiny plants which produce them. Different species of herbs generally bloom in succession as if trying to minimize competition with one another. Yet even if pollination does occur, the resulting seeds have little chance of germinating in this hostile terrain. Thus vegetative propagation is predominant among plants of the Arctic tundra. In contrast, alpine tundra plants tend to reproduce by seedlings.

Photosynthesis in alpine vegetation is not limited by low light intensity as in the Arctic. The alpine tundra is also characterized by cushion-forming plants which hug the soil. This blanket of vegetation traps heat and moisture to provide a microclimate for pollinating insects and, possibly, shelter for germinating seeds. Some alpine species are self-pollinating. Others have seeds which begin germination before they are released from the parent plant.

Winter survival for a tundra plant is largely determined by the terrain. Tall shrubs growing in hollows are protected from icy winter gales by insulating snow drifts. Large snowbank formations usually nurture specialized *snowbed plants*. These receive a continuous supply of meltwater from the receding snowbank throughout the growing season.

The small plants of the tundra wage a constant battle for existence in the shifting earth. They can rarely stabilize the ground surface long enough to alter their soil environment. Studies of succession are limited to isolated plant communities which face continual upheaval from the action of frost. A true climax vegetation is unknown.

Animals. What kind of animal life would you expect to find in the Arctic tundra? Because they seldom encounter man, most northern animals do not fear him. But you must search carefully, for several mammal species, both predator and prey, are garbed in white during winter to blend with the snowy landscape. These include the Arctic hare, grey wolf, collared lemming, Arctic fox, and even a few bird species— willow and rock ptarmigans and the snowy owl. In the spring, many of these animals change to darker colors that provide better camouflage in the summer (Fig. 2-6).

How do animals of the tundra endure the severe cold of winter? The larger mammals and permanent bird residents develop an insulating layer of fat. They also have air pockets trapped within long, dense fur or plumage. Ptarmigans and snowy owls grow extra feathers on their legs and tarsi. Yet, consider the exposed body features of such animals—their

Fig. 2-6
The summer and winter at-
tire of a ptarmigan. Tundra
residents which rely on
camouflage must change
color with the seasons.
(Courtesy of Ontario Min-
istry of Natural Resources
[summer] and U.S. Forest
Service [winter].)

nostrils and feet. You could not stand about in the snow in your bare feet for long, but gulls have no trouble walking along an icy shoreline. Nor do caribou and other Arctic animals suffer foot damage. These creatures avoid losing body heat by having two internal temperatures. The main body is kept at a normal temperature, while exposed extremities function at a temperature which varies with that of the surrounding environment. Veins and arteries intermingle in a simple heat-exchange system. Blood from the heart, en route to the extremities, warms the returning cold blood and is, in turn, cooled. The animal's shape and size also affect its ability to retain body heat. A large animal has less surface area per unit volume. Therefore it loses heat more slowly. A spherical shape also helps to conserve body warmth. Thus polar animals tend to be larger and more rotund than their southern relatives. Extremities such as ears, tails, and legs are shorter to further reduce heat loss (Fig. 2-7).

If you were to scan the Arctic landscape, you might discover a snowbank tunnel. A ptarmigan can sometimes roost here for days at a time when it is not busy feeding on buds and tender shoots of shrubs protruding through the snow. This winter food seems to have a higher fat content than the ptarmigan's summer diet. Smaller creatures like lemmings and voles escape the cold and their predators by staying in runways that connect nests beneath the snowdrifts in sheltered hollows. Here they feed on stored seed supplies or nib-

Fig. 2-7
Body extremities become smaller to reduce heat loss by radiation in related species from successively colder climates.

Jack rabbit (desert)

Varying hare (coniferous forest)

Arctic hare (Arctic)

ble at plant growth. Bears shelter in dens where females give birth to cubs in midwinter. The only animal which actually hibernates is the Arctic ground squirrel. It manages to construct a burrow by seeking out sandbanks or hilly mounds where unusual drainage has left a layer of unfrozen soil beneath the frosted surface.

How do smaller organisms survive the winter since refuge below the frost line is limited to such isolated spots? Most invertebrates winter in the larval or pupal stage which resists freezing. Spiders, beetles, and a few other species survive in adult form. Aquatic organisms such as rotifers and midgefly larvae can be frozen in the ice for months or even years. Yet they become active as soon as they thaw!

Arctic travelers frequently spot musk ox pawing the snow to uncover a grassy meal. These wild, shaggy Arctic cattle resemble small buffalo (Fig. 2-8). Their Eskimo name is *oomingmak*, meaning "the bearded one." Dense insulating wool lies beneath the hairy robe so highly prized by hunters. Sleet storms are dangerous, for the freezing moisture forms an immobilizing coat of ice on the animals, making them an easy target for wolves. Yet man, having pushed this species to the brink of extinction, has proven a greater enemy than nature.

Fig. 2-8
Heavy, powerful musk ox weigh from 800 to 900 pounds. They graze continually during the summer to build up winter stores of fat. (Courtesy of U.S. Fish and Wildlife Service.)

Fig. 2-9
Caribou means "shovel-
ler," referring to the way
this animal uses its splayed
hoofs to dig through snow
for winter forage. (Courtesy
of U.S. Fish and Wildlife
Service.)

Another creature threatened by developments in the tundra is the caribou (Fig. 2-9). Its light, air-filled hairy coat provides more than warmth. It also serves as a life jacket! In a land where water is often a barrier to herd movement, the caribou is able to swim faster and more easily than other deer. Broad cleft hooves act like snowshoes in winter and distribute the animal's weight on the soggy summer terrain. The Peary caribou wanders through 3–5 months of continuous night, searching in the snow for reindeer moss and other lichens. This caribou's white winter coat blends well with the snow, just like the white fur of the stealthy wolves which stalk it.

Animals which cannot adjust to the cold and lack of food migrate during the winter. An army of Barren Ground caribou files southward seeking shelter and vegetation below the tree line. The autumn skies are filled with departing birds. Only an occasional hawk, raven, or owl can be spotted in the winter, although marine birds, such as gulls, are found near the open sea. The Arctic fox moves to the edge of the iceflows to scavenge on seal carcasses or the dung left by polar bears.

Huge flocks of snow geese honk their way across the sky as spring heralds the return of many tundra species. Animal activity in the Arctic is geared to the short summer. For example, the ground squirrel surfaces only between May and September. It emerges from the hibernation burrow ready to mate. The young squirrels, born in June, are self-sufficient just a month later. They reach adult size and prepare for hibernation in late September. Certain bird species of the tundra also demonstrate an unusually rapid life cycle. Many of the returning birds have already mated and begin nesting immediately. Others sing out their nuptial proposals or loudly proclaim nesting territories from stations high in the air. There are no perching trees in the tundra. Thus these northern birds tend to lay large clutches of eggs. The young birds also develop much faster than their southern counterparts.

Tundra food chains are remarkably short in winter. They lengthen during the productive summer period, but the total number of species involved remains low. Reptile and amphibian life is rare. Even the insect population is relatively limited, although a plague of mosquitoes, black flies, and deer flies emerges from the swamps. Bumblebees are plentiful, yet the highly adaptable ant is scarce. Songbirds live on seeds, insects, and the August berries. Larger birds of prey seek rodents. Ducks, geese, and shorebirds comprise most of the tundra bird life. These frequent the coast or take advantage of the many ideal nesting sites beside freshwater ponds and lakes, even though the limited period of thaw results in low productivity in these bodies of water. The largely migratory fish are more numerous in the rivers.

The most critical link in the tundra food chain is a stocky little rodent called the lemming. Once each month from April to September, a female brown lemming can produce a litter of 3–11 offspring. Born in a grassy nursery lined with moss, feathers, and fox molt, the babies are weaned within two weeks and soon grow to an approximate length of 15 cm (6 in). Their cousin, the collared lemming, is the only North American mouse to don a white winter robe. Eskimo children value his fluffy fur for parkas for their walrus ivory dolls. When fall arrives, lemmings are busy stocking their underground honeycomb of tunnels and runways with grass, willow catkins, moss, and sedges. Snow insulates the colony from the bitter cold of winter.

Life is full of hazards for lemmings. They are hunted by foxes, weasels, wolves, and bears. Birds of prey deal death from the sky. Even browsing caribou abandon their normal lichen meal to munch lemming victims crushed beneath their broad hooves. Lemmings attempting to swim streams fall prey to large trout. As the lemmings flourish, the predator population grows (Fig. 2-10). But nature seems aware of the dangers posed by unlimited animal activity in the fragile tundra ecosystem. The growth cycle reaches a peak every 3–4 years. Then suddenly the balance is upset. Overcrowding takes its toll as disease and death sweep through the lemming colonies. Sometimes vast hordes of these desperate rodents make a mass migration across the tundra, leaving a trail of devastated vegetation behind. In their frenzied search for living space,

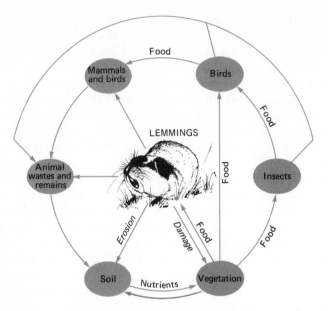

Food

Mammals
and birds

Birds

Food

LEMMINGS

Animal
wastes and
remains

Insects

Food

Erosion

Damage

Food

Food

Soil

Nutrients

Vegetation

Fig. 2-10
Any change in the lemming
population affects, directly
or indirectly, the food supply of many animals in the
tundra ecosystem. Lem-
ming tunnels also modify
soil structure and vegetation.

the lemmings swim across small ponds and streams. But they
cannot distinguish larger bodies of water like the sea, and
countless thousands drown as they seek the other bank. They
even leap from tall cliffs to get into the sea. In the short tundra
food chain a radical change in any trophic level has a violent
effect on other levels. Starvation now haunts the predators.
Northern shrikes, rough-legged hawks, and other birds fly
south. Snowy owls go as far as Michigan. The Arctic fox
becomes a scavenger, following the hunting polar bear. Wolf
numbers drop. Caribou vanish from ranges they have
overgrazed while relieved of attack from wolves. Trappers
note the dwindling number of fur-bearing animals. Until the
lemming population is renewed, many birds, particularly owls
and hawks, will not breed. With fewer predators, lemmings
begin to increase in numbers and the cycle begins again.

Except for the caribou and pipet, animal species of the
alpine tundra are very different from those of the Arctic
tundra. Mammals of the northern mountain ranges include the
collared pika, hoary marmot, singing vole, mountain goat,
Barren Ground caribou, and Dall's sheep. The common pika,
yellow-bellied marmot, and mountain sheep are limited to
southern mountain tundra. Bird life is represented by the
white-tailed ptarmigan, water pipet, and finches. Reptiles and
amphibians are rare. Unlike the Arctic tundra, flies and
mosquitoes are also rare. Yet there is an abundance of certain
insects—grasshoppers, butterflies, spiders, bumblebees, ants,
leaf-hoppers, springtails, mites, and ground beetles.

Fig. 2-11
Tiny mountain haymaker, the pika, dries and stores winter food supplies.

The warm spring sun melts the snow from the southern slopes first. Here, plant and animal activity has a head start over the northern slopes. Growth and reproduction also begin sooner on the lower portions of both slopes. Summer bird residents build their nests on the southern edges of thickets where their young can best benefit from the sun's warmth. These nests seem to be unusually compact, possibly for better insulation against the cold mountain air.

Rather than combat the strong mountain winds, insects and even birds avoid flying, and remain close to the ground. In fact, 60% of alpine insects are wingless. Birds feed and rear their offspring in sheltered crevices or crawl into holes. When in the open, they always face toward the wind. Why?

Summer brings an invasion of bears, coyotes, weasels, badgers, mice, shrews, wapiti, and mule deer. Sandpipers and gulls frequent northern alpine ponds, seeking the scanty aquatic life. The little pikas (Fig. 2-11) which burrow among the rock rubble, work through the summer, drying and storing up stacks of tundra vegetation. A single pika can gather as much as 50 pounds of hay—150 times his own weight—to nourish him through the long winter months.

The pocket gopher spends most of its life in underground burrows where it eventually kills the sedges and cushion plants above by chewing away at their roots. Any remaining growth is smothered by flying soil, scooped to the surface as the gopher tunnels. A different type of plant growth invades the ruins. But this vegetation is not acceptable to the gopher. He moves elsewhere in search of a more favorable residence. The original cushion plants gradually return and the sedges recover. Then back comes the gopher to try again!

Most active winter residents, such as the mountain goat and white-tailed ptarmigan, turn white. The marmots and ground squirrels hibernate. Wapiti, deer, and most of the birds depart to the slopes and valleys far below. Springtails (Fig. 2-12) can often be seen eating conifer pollen on the snow. After freezing at night, these insects thaw out during the day.

The low oxygen concentration of the alpine tundra affects homoiothermic mammals the most. Birds are adapted to fly at high elevations. Invertebrates and plants have a much lower metabolic rate and, hence, a lower oxygen requirement. Increased heart beat and respiration rate can temporarily adjust mammals, including man, to the rarefied atmosphere. But the animals permanently adapted to this high altitude have larger lungs and hearts. They also have an increased number of oxygen-carrying red blood cells.

Fig. 2-12
A lever-like organ called a furcula snaps downward to propel the springtail into the air, throwing the insect forward many times its own length.

In summary, both the Arctic and alpine tundra provide a rigorous environment for plant and animal alike. Yet life has adapted and thrives in seasonal abundance, governed by the laws of nature.

2.3   THE CONIFEROUS FOREST

If you were to follow the migrating geese and caribou southward from the Arctic tundra, you would pass through a transition zone or ecotone. Here, the gradually changing physical factors noticeably alter the plant and animal life. Clumps of dwarf trees, scattered in sheltered nooks, gradually increase in size and numbers as you move south. Finally you reach a fairly distinct tree line that marks the edge of the *northern boreal forest,* the major coniferous forest region of North America. (See Fig. 2-1.)

ABIOTIC FACTORS

This vast coniferous belt, 400–800 miles wide, stretches across North America, largely south of latitude 57°N. Lying closer to the equator, this region receives more of the sun's radiant energy than does the tundra. Average monthly temperatures are higher, ranging from a winter low of −30°C (−20°F) to a summer high of 20°C (70°F). The extended growing season varies from 60 to 150 days. Summer days are shorter but warmer than farther north. More important, the ground thaws completely. The winters are not as long or severe and few areas within this biome are without sunlight. Snowfall is heavier than in the tundra. Yet total precipitation, although greater than in the tundra, is still low. Annual measurements vary from 38 to 100 cm (15–40 in). Summer rains provide most of the moisture.

Centuries ago a massive ice sheet, thousands of meters deep, covered this region. The glacier scraped away topsoil, gouged out countless depressions in the land, and deposited tons of loose rock and earth as it melted. These scars have filled with water to produce the mosaic of lakes and swamps which the Russians call *taiga,* meaning "swamp forest" (Fig. 2-13). The shifting ice cover altered the surface features and hampered the formation of an effective river drainage system. The effect of this has been that water does not drain off readily. The cold air reduces evaporation. Hence most water movement is downward through the shallow soil. As a result, boreal forest soil is usually waterlogged. Melting snow produces spring flooding as rivers overflow.

Fig. 2-13
The great northern woods
abound with lakes and
swamps. (U.S.D.A. Photo by
Freeman Hein.)

Fig. 2-14
Evergreen giants of the
temperate rain forest.
(U.S.D.A. Photo.)

In this cold, wet surface earthworms are rare and the action of bacteria is retarded. Conifer needles and other dead vegetation decompose slowly. They form a peaty surface layer instead of mixing with the soil. Water, filtering through this decaying blanket, becomes acidic and leaches away plant nutrients such as calcium, nitrogen, potassium, and iron. This action leaves a grey, acidic, nutrient-deficient topsoil called a *podsol* —from a Russian word meaning "ashes." (See *Recommended Reading* 1.)

Along the Pacific coast south of Alaska, the effects of climate and topography produce a coniferous forest which differs greatly from the northern boreal growth. Prevailing winds moderate the climate; mean monthly temperatures range from 2°C to 18°C (35°F to 65°F). The ground is frost-free for a period of 120 – 300 days. In winter, moist westerly winds pass over the warm Japanese current. As they move inland from the ocean, they are forced to rise abruptly over the coastal mountains. In the higher, colder atmosphere the condensing moisture is released as rain or snow. Hence the coastal forest receives as much as 635 cm (250 in) of precipitation yearly. In summer, the prevailing northwest winds are cooled by the northern seas. Although they carry little moisture, these colder air masses cause heavy fogs which soak the forest canopy. They contribute, drop by drop, another 130 cm (51 in) or more of water to the soil. This bounty of moisture and high humidity in a warm climate nurtures the *temperate rain forest,* a rich growth of evergreen giants such as the Douglas fir and California redwoods (Fig. 2-14).

BIOTIC FACTORS

As in the tundra, the plant and animal communities of the coniferous forest have more limited structures and relationships than those in warmer regions. One major factor which we should investigate is the dominance of coniferous trees throughout this biome.

Vegetation. The plant life of the boreal forest must cope with a combination of poor soil, low temperatures, and limited rainfall. Although the soil contains enough moisture to support tree growth, it is frozen during much of the year. Humidity is low, summer and winter. Boreal vegetation must be able to tolerate long dormant periods and use to full advantage the available moisture. *Conifers* (cone-bearing trees) thrive in this environment because they are well adapted to dry conditions. Their leaves are modified into needles or scales wrapped in a thick cuticle. This waxy outer skin greatly restricts water loss by evaporation from the inner leaf cells. These needles can also withstand freezing. Such protection helps a conifer survive periods of frost and drought.

The shape and structure of coniferous trees are ideally suited for northern winters. Crushing weights of snow cannot collect on the small surface area provided by the needles. Instead, the flexible branches tend to bend, causing clumps of snow to tumble down the tapering boughs.

The northern summer, which provides the warmth, sunlight, and moisture for growth, is too brief for most deciduous trees. They would lose more stored food when their large leaves were shed in the fall than they could replace during the short growing season. Moreover, deciduous leaves decay quickly. Essential plant nutrients released during decay would be leached from the soil before the trees could reclaim them in the spring.

Most conifers are *evergreens*—they retain their leaves during the winter. Dead needles are gradually shed and replaced throughout the course of the year. The fallen needles decay slowly because their resin content and thick outer covering resist bacterial action. Thus, evergreens can conserve valuable nutrients and are ready to photosynthesize whenever conditions permit. Conifers have an additional defense against the rigors of the north. If the bark is damaged, a sticky resin produced by the tree covers the wound. This safeguard hinders the attack of fungi or bacteria.

The forest floor lies in almost perpetual shade under the dense evergreen canopy. Here vegetation is largely restricted to shade-loving plants like ferns, mosses, and a few

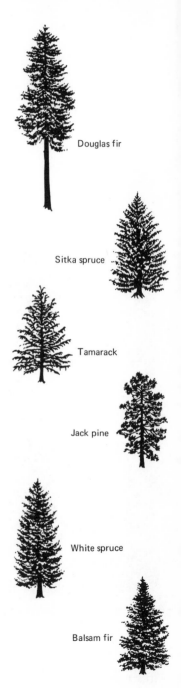

Fig. 2-15
Some common trees of the coniferous forest biome.

Douglas fir

Sitka spruce

Tamarack

Jack pine

White spruce

Balsam fir

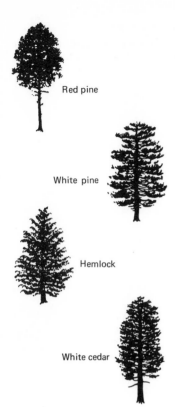

Red pine

White pine

Hemlock

White cedar

Fig. 2-16
The wolverine is a ravenous predator. Its common name, "glutton," is earned from its enormous appetite. (Courtesy of National Museums of Canada.)

herbs. In the absence of earthworms and effective bacterial action, fungi are vital decomposers. Over 1,800 miles of fungal thread may weave through a single cubic foot of needle-laden soil. In autumn, the ground is peppered with the tiny fruiting bodies—spore-bearing "toadstools."

The nature of the coniferous forest changes in different regions of the biome. Across the northern stretches to Alaska, in the Adirondacks, and in the White Mountains, the dominant species are white spruce, black spruce, and balsam fir (Fig. 2-15). Red pine, white pine, eastern hemlock, and white cedar are characteristic of the Great Lakes region. The southern Appalachians are marked by Fraser fir and red spruce. Douglas fir, western hemlock, Sitka spruce, and western red cedar form the temperate rain forest of the northern Pacific coast. Farther south grows the ever diminishing redwood forest. The jack pine is common in dry or fire-scorched areas. This conifer produces a cone which generally will not open to release the seeds until it is subjected to the extreme heat of a forest fire. Thus, in areas where other growing trees and their seeds have been destroyed by fire, the fresh jack pine seeds can pioneer new forest growth. Certain hardwoods, such as birch and poplar, also invade burned over areas of this biome, as well as the moist terrain of riverbanks and wet valleys. The tamarack or larch also frequents moist areas. Unlike most conifers, this species sheds its needles in the fall.

Despite the low seasonal temperatures which affect growth throughout most of this biome, these coniferous forests are very productive and rank high among the great lumber-producing regions of the world.

Animals. Animals of the boreal forest are adapted in structure and behavior to survive the long, cold winter when snow blankets the frozen ground. Foxes, wolves, and moose, wearing thick winter fur, remain active even when the temperature dips to −45°C (−49°F). Like its tundra cousin, the varying hare's coat develops a snow-white camouflage. It also has built-in snowshoes—large tufts of fur which cover its feet. Its predator, the wolverine (Fig. 2-16), is the swiftest mammal in the winter forest. Spreading toes permit this stealthy hunter to chase through deep drifts without sinking. Moose wade through snow as deep as one meter on long stilt-like legs (Fig. 2-17). Normally solitary creatures, moose gather in winter to trample snow into "yards" in order to feed on the tree shoots and brushwood below. They even pack snow into mounds so they can reach twigs on branches above. A grown moose must eat from 3,600 − 4,500 kg (4 − 5 tons) of vegetation in order to

Fig. 2-17
The moose, symbol of the
boreal forest, is the largest
of all deer species.
(U.S.D.A. Photo by Bluford
W. Muir.)

live through this season. Starving moose will even chew conifer bark. By spring, the hungry survivors are gaunt from their
winter ordeal. The blanket of snow protects smaller creatures
from enemies and the cold. Air spaces trapped in plant
undergrowth between the snow and soil create a microclimate
in which the temperature never drops more than one or two
degrees below freezing. Here lemmings, voles, and other
rodents are active throughout the winter, dining on grasses,
mosses, and herbs (Fig. 2-18).

Chattering red squirrels shatter the silence of the
winter forest as they scamper about in search of hoarded food
supplies. Their main diet is conifer seeds, obtained by stripping away cone scales. This activity is very time-consuming.
A squirrel may work away at more than 200 cones but end up
with less than 15 g (½ ounce) of seeds. When the cone harvest
is poor, these saucy characters cause great damage to young
trees by eating conifer buds instead. Another culprit is the
quill-laden porcupine. Strong, curved claws assist him in his
nocturnal climb in search of buds and leaves. During the
winter this rodent damages conifers by eating away the bark,
especially in the uppermost branches.

One of the few hibernating animals, the woodchuck,
may "sleep" as long as eight months in a burrow or hollow

Fig. 2-18
A shrew and larger rodent
neighbor dine on vegeta-
tion beneath an insulating
blanket of snow.

Fig. 2-19
The crossbill's beak can shear through tough cone scales. The bird can then use its long tongue to reach the seeds inside.

Fig. 2-20
Spruce grouse. (Courtesy of Ontario Ministry of Natural Resources.)

log. During this period, the animal's metabolism is reduced to the minimum rate necessary to keep body cells alive. Heartbeat, normally 200 beats per minute, drops to a mere 4–5 beats per minute. The woodchuck may only breathe twice a minute, and stored body fat is consumed very slowly. Accordingly, body temperature falls. However, if outside temperatures drop too much, nervous response rouses the animal and, by resuming activity for a few hours, it restores its normal blood circulation. Chipmunks also hibernate, waking at intervals to feed on stored nuts and seeds. Although bears enter a deep winter's sleep, this is not considered true hibernation because the animal's body temperature falls only slightly.

The choice of food in the coniferous forest is greatly limited, regardless of the season. Only about 50 species of birds can feed on the tough, resinous conifers. Most seed-eaters have strong jaw muscles which control short, sturdy beaks fitted with sharp cutting edges. Some birds have an added advantage. For example, finches do not have to wait for the cones to open because their strong beaks are well designed for extracting the seeds. One type of finch, the crossbill (Fig. 2-19), can penetrate the densest foliage, hanging like a feathered acrobat from any angle while feeding on cones. While the parent gathers nourishment, baby crossbills resist the spring cold by lapsing into a coma. They revive as soon as their protector restores warmth to the nest. The winter diet of the blue grouse consists chiefly of conifer needles which have little nutrient value. To survive on this food, the grouse must eat from morning till night. The spruce grouse (Fig. 2-20) dines exclusively on mature spruce trees. One bird may spend days robbing a single tree of its needles. Grouse chicks cannot live more than a few hours without the insect pupae which they seek independently. These fragile balls of fluff often starve in cold, wet weather because they are unable to leave the protecting warmth of the hen. Hungry chicks which do venture forth quickly perish from exposure.

Very few insect species can feed on coniferous growth. But those which thrive in this habitat virtually rule the northern forest during the summer. Larger animals are driven to distraction by hordes of flies and mosquitoes. Moose escape by submerging in lakes and marshes where they browse on aquatic plants. But more important, every inch of a coniferous tree is prone to attack by some type of insect. Forest areas dominated by one or two tree species are especially vulnerable. Why? Spreading across Canada and the northern states, the larch sawfly has destroyed countless tamaracks over the past 85 years. Outbreaks of spruce budworm have wiped out vast areas of balsam fir and spruce. Bark beetles, wood borers, and long-horned beetles also affect the growth and decay of the forest.

Insects have two main seasons—a short active summer of reproduction and a long dormant period when they winter as larvae or nymphs in bark crevices and beneath the soil. Insect-eaters such as chickadees, woodpeckers, and shrews manage to winter in the forest. Others, such as warblers and bats, migrate until spring.

The birds of prey which patrol the forest sky are equipped with keen vision, deadly talons, and strong, hooked beaks (Fig. 2-21). The owls are silent night hunters which use their sensitive hearing to detect the activity of smaller birds and rodents. Owls have the widest field of binocular vision of all the birds of prey. Some can discern objects in light 100 times less intense than humans require. Hawks, falcons, ospreys, and eagles hunt by day, usually along the forest edge because their large wingspan makes flying difficult in dense forest. Hawks are best adapted. Their rounded wings enable them to hover and turn sharply in pursuit of birds flushed from the treetops.

The smaller carnivores of the boreal forest—minks, martens, weasels, and wolverines—all belong to the weasel family. They hunt rabbits, rodents, birds, and insects. They will also eat most other types of food when the need arises. Since their prey is widely scattered, these predators claim unusually large hunting territories. A single short-tailed weasel may range over an area of 340,000 m² (84 acres). The larger wolverine is chiefly a scavenger. But rather than wait until his host has completed his meal, this vicious intruder will successfully challenge even a bear or a wolf for a fresh kill. Members of the weasel family do not hibernate. Instead they grow protective winter coats which have lured trappers since the earliest settlement. Weasels are the only carnivores in the boreal forest which turn white in the winter. The short-tailed weasel keeps the black tip on its tail. In its white winter robe it is better known as ermine (Fig. 2-22).

Like the lemming in the tundra, the varying hare plays a major role in the coniferous forest food chain. It eats broad-leafed plants, grasses, herbs, and mosses, as do most of the other herbivores of the coniferous forest. A single doe can produce five yearly litters of 3—4 young. Even if only a few survive to reproduce, a ten-year period may result in as many as 4,000 hares for every square mile of forest. Female predators, such as weasels, owls, and hawks, raise large families

Fig. 2-21
This keen-eyed hunter has sharp claws for grasping prey, and a strong, hooked beak for tearing meat.

Fig. 2-22
The short-tailed weasel is called ermine when its red-brown summer coat turns to winter white. (Courtesy of Ontario Ministry of Natural Resources.)

during this time of plenty. Suddenly, the hare population crashes. Factors such as competition for food, increased predation, and the stress of overcrowding are possible causes. The lynx is hardest hit because, in some areas of North America, the hare provides 70% of its diet. In desperation, this stealthy hunter travels afar, seeking squirrels or grouse. But the lynx is so dependent on the hare that its own population cycle trails closely behind the ten-year cycle of its main prey (Fig. 2-23).

You have now met the more prominent animals of the coniferous forest biome. But one adaptation not yet mentioned is most memorable to a spring or summer visitor. Many of these forest dwellers have well-developed hearing and vocal systems. In a habitat where trees limit visibility, vision is often a secondary sense. During nesting season, the air is vibrant with bird songs. The sounds of squirrels, chipmunks, and wolves are also distinguishable. The evening throbs with the calls of frogs and insects. Most of this "music" is designed to attract mates and to proclaim territorial domains. But to the listener it conveys the magic and mystery of the northern woods.

Fig. 2-23
Varying or snowshoe hare populations peak every 10 −11 years and then fall sharply. Records kept by Canada's Hudson Bay Company show that lynx populations have corresponding fluctuations.

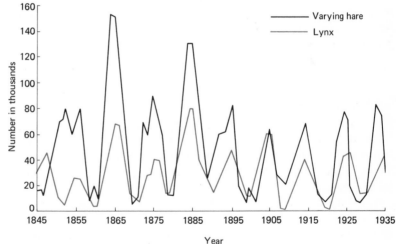

2.4   THE TEMPERATE DECIDUOUS FOREST

Along the southeastern fringe of the boreal forest, deciduous trees invade in ever-increasing numbers, forming a deciduous-coniferous ecotone. This mixed growth gradually blends into the next major biome southward—the *temperate deciduous forest*. (See Fig. 2-1.)

ABIOTIC FACTORS

This region is largely restricted to the eastern half of the continent where the mean annual precipitation varies from 75 to 125 cm (30−50 in). The Gulf states sometimes receive as much as 150 cm (60 in) of rain annually. The four seasons are well developed and precipitation is fairly evenly distributed throughout the year. The winter snow is not as deep or enduring as that of the boreal forest. The climate is moderate. From north to south the temperature ranges from a January high of −12°C to 15°C (10°F to 60°F) to a July high of 21°C to 27°C (70°F to 80°F). Relative humidity is high during the growing season, which may last for more than six months.

The shorter winters are cold enough to reduce greatly both growth and photosynthesis. To increase efficiency, deciduous trees enter a dormant period, shedding their frost-intolerant leaves. A single acre of forest floor may be carpeted with more than 10 million leaves each fall. Along with other decaying matter, the leaves rapidly decompose on the moist ground to produce a rich layer of *humus.* Typical deciduous woodland soil is called "brown earth." It is formed where the downward drainage of rain water (percolation) is balanced by the upward movement of water (capillarity). Capillarity replaces evaporating surface moisture. Therefore, instead of being leached from the soil, nutrients are circulated. Rocky or porous soils support shrubs or conifers. Bogs form in areas where the soil is waterlogged and acidic.

BIOTIC FACTORS

The earliest settlers on the eastern shore of this continent encountered a vast forest so dense that, according to legend, a squirrel could journey through the treetops from the Atlantic coast to the Mississippi River without ever having to set foot on the ground. Today only patches of climax forest remain. Large carnivores like the wolf have largely retreated into coniferous regions. Smaller creatures have adapted to life in small woodlots. What major differences occur between life in this and the coniferous forest?

Vegetation. The long, warm growing season, abundant moisture, and rich soil support a variety of plant species which grow to different levels, or *strata,* within the forest. The taller trees form an upper canopy which receives the full strength of the sun. The broad deciduous leaves permit maximum absorption of light energy. A small oak tree with a trunk diameter measuring 60 cm (24 in) produces more than 100,000 leaves. Their total surface area is about the size of

Fig. 2-24
Some common deciduous trees.

American beech

Sugar maple

Red oak

Black willow

Trembling aspen

Shagbark hickory

Sycamore

two tennis courts. These thin leaves still allow some sunlight to filter through to smaller "understory" trees. Beneath these, a shrub layer grows. And finally, at ground level, ferns, mosses, and other small plants compete for the remaining light. The floor of an oak forest receives only about 6% of the noonday sunlight. Hence most of the smaller plants, growing close to the soil, flower very early in the spring before air temperatures farther above the ground increase enough to stimulate new leaf growth on the trees. By the time a new upper canopy has blocked off the sunlight, these ground plants have stored photosynthesized food in roots or underground stems. After releasing seeds, these plants become dormant until the following spring.

Delicate deciduous leaves are easily injured by frost and quickly dried out by winter winds. Hence they are shed in the fall. Growth is retarded as the trees depend on food reserves stored in roots, trunks, and branches. The long growing season ensures new growth of leaves and seeds each year, although conditions alter the size of the annual seed crop. Some trees, such as the horse chestnut and apple tree, produce colorful, fragrant blossoms each spring to attract pollinating insects. Many trees, like the beech and oak, depend on pollen carried on the wind to fertilize their inconspicuous flowers. The eventual bounty of fruits and seeds is harvested by many animals in preparation for winter.

In autumn, a host of creatures feast upon the fruiting bodies of fungi growing on tree stumps and damp soil. Fungal spores and underground fungal filaments also nourish many soil inhabitants.

Beech-maple forests dominate the north central regions of this biome, while oak and hickory comprise much of the western and southern forest (Fig. 2-24). Before the chestnut blight, the Appalachian mountain chain was covered by oak-chestnut forests. Poplars, willows, and sycamores are also common trees. Elms have been drastically reduced by the Dutch elm disease. As the forest becomes progressively warmer toward the south, the trees become evergreen in nature. Florida and the Mississippi delta support a magnolia-oak forest.

Animals. Forest animals are adapted in structure, function, and behavior to live among trees. Here they find shelter, protection, and nesting sites. From the branches they can sight enemies and proclaim territorial boundaries. Many dwell in the rich humus beneath the trees. Others simply take advantage of the shade, moderate temperatures, and higher humidity of the forest.

Tree-dwellers are well equipped for climbing. Squirrels and woodpeckers have sharp claws with opposing toes for balance (Fig. 2-25). Some squirrels even have a built-in parachute as well as a bushy tail for balance. Tree frogs cling to the bark using suction discs on their toes. Snails and slugs adhere with slimy feet. White-footed mice and opossums use their tails for climbing and grasping, much as monkeys do.

Unlike conifers, deciduous trees are a major source of food which supports a large number of consumers. The largest herbivores include the wapiti (elk) and deer. The white-tailed or Virginia deer is the most abundant North American species. Deer prefer to browse on leaves in woods and thickets bordering meadowland rather than in deep forest. They winter in small herds which can break trails and trample the snow to form a "deer yard." Here they feed on twigs and cedar boughs within reach. Deer often use their weight to bend small trees to the ground in order to reach tender shoots on the higher growing tips.

The most concentrated protein is stored in the buds and seeds of trees. These provide a year-round source of food for finches and other animals. Buds are most valuable during the winter and early spring when other nourishment is unavailable. Autumn produces a rich harvest of seeds which persist far into the winter in the form of berries and nuts. Acorns are a delicacy for larger birds such as jays and woodpeckers.

Rabbits and little rodents form an important link in the forest food chain. Cottontails nibble at herbs, tree bark, and small plant growth along the forest edge. In winter they dare not venture far from the seclusion of the woods. Deer mice are agile climbers which forage in smaller trees or surface litter for buds and seeds to store in their nests. These tiny nut experts use their incisor teeth—which never wear down because of continual growth—to crack open even the toughest shells. Beavers, the largest North American rodents, chew the inner bark on smaller branches of trees such as poplars, birches, and willows growing beside ponds or rivers. Two adult beavers can chisel through a trunk 10 cm (4 in) in diameter in less than 15 minutes!

While larger animals generally cause little damage to deciduous foliage, two major groups of insects are highly destructive. The leaf-chewers, such as caterpillars and beetle and fly larvae, use biting jaws to devour all of the leaf tissue (Fig. 2-26). Some will attack any tree, but most are specialists which strip only trees of a particular species. Oak trees are the target of many such invaders—50,000 caterpillars may share

Fig. 2-25
The woodpecker uses two toes at the back of its four-toed foot to brace itself on the side of a tree.

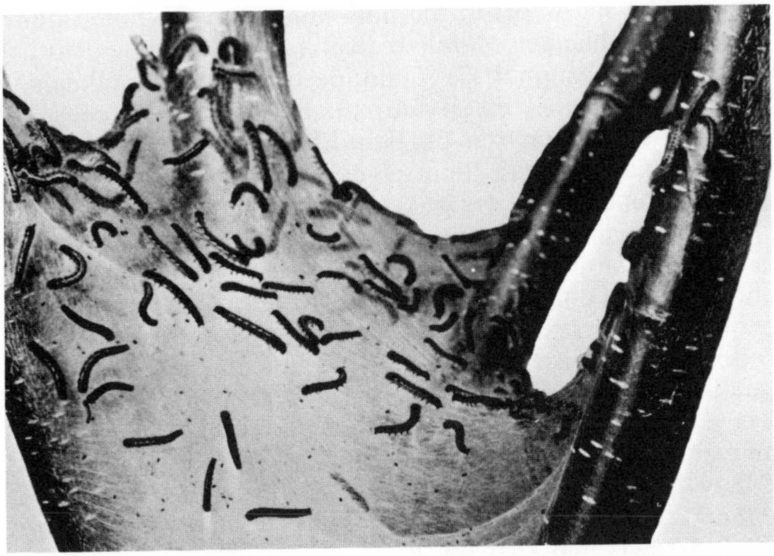

Fig. 2-26
Hundreds of tent caterpillars teem from this nest to strip the host tree of its foliage. (U.S.D.A. Photo.)

the same tree! In self-defense the oak produces new foliage in midsummer. Sap-suckers, such as aphids, have mouth parts which operate like tiny hypodermic needles to reach vital plant fluid. To obtain enough protein to grow, an aphid must gorge itself on the sugary sap. Yet much of this insect activity is beneficial. Excess sap is egested by aphids in drops of "honey dew." Ants and flying insects eagerly lick these liquid feces from the leaves. Ants also store aphid eggs for their winter diet. In return for proteins and sugar, bees and other insects act as pollinating agents for blossoms. The army of caterpillars provides a tasty meal for many forest dwellers such as birds, tree frogs, and insect parasites. Shrews, mice, and toads feast upon those caterpillars which drop to the soil to pupate. Spiders weave a network of sticky death-traps throughout the foliage and insect predators constantly patrol in search of dinner. They, in turn, often fall victim to the many feathered insect-eaters.

This bounty of food disappears with the coming of winter. Some of the birds, such as chickadees and nuthatches, remain. They eat insect pupae, insect eggs, and, in some cases, seeds. Their specialized food preferences allow several wintering species to share the same area without competition. But most birds migrate south to regions of insect activity. Amphibians and reptiles lapse into a hibernating coma when the cold weather arrives. In contrast, the tiny shrew cannot afford to sleep through a single winter day. It must constantly scrounge dormant insects from the soil litter in order to survive (Fig. 2-27).

Fig. 2-27
To match a tiny shrew's appetite, a man would have to consume 500 pounds of food daily.

The shrew is not the only hunter on the forest floor. The yearly blanket of fallen leaves, combined with other organic waste, supports a multitude of plants and animals in warmer months. Essential nutrients, locked in dead cells, are recycled by decomposer fungi and bacteria. The products of decay—and the agents themselves—are consumed by soil organisms such as rotifers and roundworms. Earthworms and other herbivores are constantly preyed upon by the faster, more agile carnivores like centipedes. One square mile of soil litter may be home to more than 300 different species of invertebrates, each one a specialized eater. The surface is alive with a hungry army of spiders, beetles, snakes, toads, and small mammals—all links in complex food chains.

Larger carnivores of the deciduous forest have suffered more from man's intrusion than those in any other zone. Many have retreated into coniferous or mountain forests. Members of the weasel family, bobcats, and birds of prey such as owls and sparrow hawks are still widespread. One which has adapted especially well is the red fox. This crafty nocturnal hunter prefers mice but will settle for birds, large insects, fish, and even berries and grass. When eggs are abundant, foxes bury them, only to dig them up months later when the food supply dwindles. But the fox is not the only versatile feeder. A raccoon's menu includes eggs, fruit, seeds, nuts, and insects as well as aquatic prey. Another omnivore, the skunk, dines on grubs and insects, supplemented by mice, eggs, and an occasional carcass. The Virginian opossum—the only marsupial in North America—eats almost anything from vegetables and fruit to insects and carrion (Fig. 2-28). But the most resourceful eaters of all are the crows. These intelligent, sociable birds are equipped with more than hardy digestive systems. They can adapt feeding behavior to almost any form of nourishment at hand!

Forest activity reaches a peak during the spring and early summer when most of the animals breed. Some, such as deer and bats, mate in the fall. Owls and some squirrels wait until winter. At any time of year, the great diversity and abundance of life in this biome presents a complex study of interrelationships. Yet the same basic principles which govern a simpler biome like the tundra can be applied to deciduous forests to understand and preserve this environment.

Fig. 2-28
The Virginian opossum, an expert climber, is North America's only marsupial, or pouched mammal. (U.S.D.A. Photo.)

2.5 THE GRASSLANDS

If we journey westward, the temperate deciduous forest gradually thins and merges into a *savanna* ecotone. Here, the trees are scattered over an area dominated by grasses and sedges. Eventually all remnants of the forest disappear, leaving miles of rolling prairie. This is the *grassland biome*. (See Fig. 2-1.)

ABIOTIC FACTORS

This region lies between the same latitudes as the deciduous forest. Hence, the seasonal changes and radiant energy supply are similar, although both seasonal and daily temperature fluctuations are more pronounced in the prairies. The critical factor in the drastically altered vegetation is the diminished rainfall. The continental pattern of air circulation from east to west produces *decreasing* and irregular *precipitation* combined with an *increasing* rate of *evaporation* from the soil surface. The annual rainfall, 25 – 75 cm (10 – 30 in), is sufficient for many grass species but is too low for tree growth. Nor can trees survive the frequent droughts which can be severe and prolonged. The intermittent fires kill seedling trees but grasses quickly recover.

The chernozem (Russian for "black earth") soils, characteristic of the prairies, are the most fertile in the world. The short-lived grass plants contribute large amounts of organic material to the soil each year. Rapid decay forms a deep layer of humus. Thus, prairie soil is much darker than that of the forest. Evaporation causes an upward movement of water which deposits calcium and potassium in the upper soil, leaving it rich in nutrients.

BIOTIC FACTORS

Until the nineteenth century, pronghorns and vast herds of bison wandered the prairies (Fig. 2-29). The buffalo, constantly on the move, seldom overgrazed an area. Instead,

Fig. 2-29
Enormous herds of bison —the largest North American animal—once roamed the heartland of this continent. (U.S.D.A. Photo by Leland J. Prater.)

these great beasts moulded the prairies, killing intruding trees by stripping off bark with their horns and by rubbing against them to remove shedding fur. A tasty meal of seedling trees prevented regeneration. Then the white man with his weapons, fences, and agriculture changed the face of the grasslands. Less than 100 years after the first settlers invaded, the buffalo had all but vanished. Longhorns and then modern beef cattle overgrazed and upset the natural balance of the range. The plow produced a dust bowl in the drier plains. Animals such as the badlands grizzly and white plains wolf were hunted to extinction. Now, even the prairie dog is endangered. Today, only a few small areas remain where the earlier grassland ecosystem can be studied. Can man learn from this primitive community how to properly manage the grasslands and perpetuate the continent's "bread-basket"?

Vegetation. The gradient in rainfall produces three distinct types of grassland (Fig. 2-30). Rich soil and moderate rainfall make the eastern prairies a *tall-grass zone*. Here, tall bluestem soars as high as 2.4 m (8 ft), supported by roots buried 1.8 m (6 ft) in the soil. These "sod former" plants develop a solid mat over the ground. Farther west, the drier central grasslands support *mid-grasses*. These species grow from 60 – 120 cm (2 – 4 ft) high. Most are "bunch grasses" which

Fig. 2-30
Soil depth and rainfall combine to produce three distinct types of grassland between forest and desert.

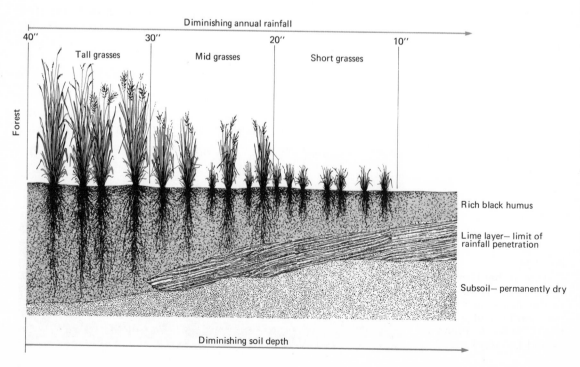

Diminishing annual rainfall

40″   30″   20″   10″

Tall grasses   Mid grasses   Short grasses

Forest

Rich black humus

Lime layer— limit of rainfall penetration

Subsoil— permanently dry

Diminishing soil depth

grow in well-spaced clumps among other species. In the arid western plains, a region of high winds and low humidity, the sod-forming *short grasses* grow no more than 40 cm (16 in) high. Their shallow roots absorb moisture from the upper soil layer but do not penetrate the permanent dry zone beneath. Overgrazing and wheat farming converted this area into the "Dust Bowl." The southwestern desert grassland was produced by fire and is very similar to the short-grass plains.

Throughout the grasslands, herbs and legumes (nitrogen-fixing plants) flourish among the grasses. Tree growth, largely cottonwood, is generally limited to stream valleys and to low mountain ranges like the Black Hills in South Dakota.

There are three strata in grassland vegetation: the roots, the "understory" growth at ground level, and the taller foliage. The deep root layer is very prominent. At least half of the total growth of each plant lies beneath the soil. The roots of healthy plants weigh several times more than the portion above the surface. Many plants also develop underground stems called rhizomes which are used for vegetative propagation and food storage. During the growing season, the plants at ground level are shaded from the sun and sheltered from winds by the taller grasses. A layer of dead vegetation called *mulch* collects on the surface. This mulch must contact the mineral soil before rapid decomposition can begin. As this decaying layer deepens, it soaks up moisture. This creates favorable conditions for the bacteria which convert the mulch to humus. During the growing season, the leaves of grasses continually grow from their bases. As the grass tops are consumed, the crop is renewed.

Animals. Grassland creatures exhibit many fascinating adaptations to the open country they inhabit. Long distance vision is very important for both predator and prey. The eyes of grazing animals are usually located well above the snout to enable the animal to gaze above the grass while feeding. Smaller creatures such as the ground squirrel stand up on their haunches to peer over the vegetation. Others, like the kangaroo rat (Fig. 2-31) hop up and down on well-developed hind legs. There are no trees for concealment or escape. Some animals rely on camouflaging coloration. Sensing danger, they remain motionless in the deep grass to escape notice. If the enemy approaches too closely, these creatures suddenly flee by running, hopping, or flying. By temporarily startling the predator with this flurry of motion, the would-be victim gains a head start. Many prairie animals are built for speed, which they rely on to survive. The pronghorn has sturdy legs, large

Fig. 2-31
The tiny kangaroo rat bounds from the shelter of its underground burrow on powerful hind legs. (Courtesy of U.S. Fish and Wildlife Service.)

lungs and windpipe, and a heart double the expected size. Pronghorns (Fig. 2-32) can race with bursts of speed reaching 60 mph! Jack rabbits propel themselves with long, powerful hind legs. Using 8 m (25 ft) leaps, these long-eared herbivores bound across the prairie at 45 mph, easily clearing obstacles more than 2 m (6.5 ft) high. A number of creatures elude predators by diving into underground burrows. These shelters also protect their smaller, temperature-sensitive residents from the surface heat and cold.

Prairie dwellers seem to believe there is safety in numbers. Life within a herd or colony is typical. Any alarmed

Fig. 2-32
Speed means survival for the pronghorn. When alarmed, the white rump hairs bristle, flashing a danger signal to the herd. (Courtesy of U.S. Fish and Wildlife Service.)

member can alert the others to danger. One vast prairie dog "town" in Texas used to cover 25,000 square miles and was home to more than 400 million of these rodents! Such a community supported badgers, weasels, ferrets, burrowing owls, coyotes, hawks, snakes, and a host of other predators. However, after flourishing amid so many enemies, the prairie dog has finally met his match. Extermination by man has decimated the prairie dog nation, leaving only scattered colonies. How has this affected the great food pyramid of the grasslands (Fig. 2-33)?

Fig. 2-33
A grassland food pyramid. The mass of primary consumers, feeding directly upon the producers, is far greater than that of succeeding trophic levels. The top predators, forming the peak, represent a relatively small mass. Many animals occupy several levels.

Grassland birds must be strong fliers to combat the high winds which sweep the prairies. In the absence of trees, many birds attract mates with flight songs delivered from high in the air. Nests are concealed in the tall grass. The abundant insect population and bounty of seeds attract a variety of birds—sparrows, meadowlarks, longspurs, lark buntings, bobolinks, grouse, and prairie chickens.

The grasslands abound with insect life, notably grasshoppers and their relatives. More than a hundred types of grasshoppers thrived in the northern Great Plains when the early settlers arrived. As farming began, these insects easily adapted to eating cultivated crops. Extensive crop damage has resulted during years when insect populations have reached plague proportions. Ants are also abundant in the drier grasslands. They replace earthworms in the important role of mixing and aerating the soil.

In winter, the grasslands are almost deserted. Although the snowfall is not heavy, it is blown into deep drifts by strong prairie winds. Bison used to move south along with migrating birds. Pronghorns shelter in woodlands and mountain foothills or forage on exposed grass. Many creatures hibernate—rodents in burrows and groups of reptiles in deep holes below the frost line. Most insect life winters in the egg stage or in a dormant, immature form.

The grasslands are vitally important to man. Yet probably no other biome has received greater abuse. Thousands of acres are still being converted into barren desert through man's failure to understand or respect the ecology of this area.

2.6   THE DESERT

Along the western edge of the drier plains lies one of the most arid regions on earth—the desert biome of North America. (See Fig. 2-1.) Yet, despite its inhospitable nature, the desert provides a unique and fascinating study for the ecologist.

ABIOTIC FACTORS

The range of latitudes produces two different types of desert within this biome. The average annual temperature of the more northern "cool" deserts of the Great Basin is about 10°C (50°F), but it is over 20°C (68°F) in the "hot" southwestern desert. If these values seem low, you may be forgetting the winter season which brings snow and cold weather to both types of desert. Summer temperatures in Death Valley have soared as high as 57°C (134°F)—in the shade! But the real impact of temperature lies in the tremendous fluctuations during each 24-hour period. The desert sands receive almost 90% of the total available solar radiation because there are no clouds, water vapor, or canopies of vegetation to absorb the sunlight. But at night, temperatures drop rapidly as 90% of this accumulated surface heat is lost by radiation.

Yet lack of water, rather than heat, produces deserts. They are generally found in regions receiving less than 25 cm (10 inches) of yearly rainfall or where a greater rainfall is sporadically distributed. In North America, the mountains of the western coast are barriers to the moist ocean winds. The deserts are located in the "rain shadow" of these peaks. Long periods of drought are common. Then the rainfall supply for an entire year may fall in one great deluge! This unpredictable moisture usually arrives in the form of thunderstorms or cloudbursts. The ground surface, baked hard by the sun, does not absorb much moisture. Earthworms, which render soil loose and absorbent, cannot endure the dry desert. Many burrowing rodents, which stir up the earth creating underground pathways for water, have been exterminated by pest-control programs. In addition, the scanty desert plant life does not provide a spongy layer of decaying vegetation. Hence, most of the torrent is swept away in surface runoff. The little moisture which does penetrate is quickly evaporated by the hot sun. The relative humidity of desert air averages less than 30% at midday. At times, rain, pouring from black storm clouds, evaporates rapidly as it falls through the blanket of hot, dry air above the sands—and not a single drop reaches the thirsty desert below!

Steady desert winds erode rock into sand and stir up dust storms which scour the land surface. How can any form of life exist in such a harsh world?

BIOTIC FACTORS

Water is the key to desert life. Many plants and animals have endured because they are able to develop and reproduce rapidly during any period of rain. Recent studies suggest that dew formation, common even in the hottest deserts, may provide an important source of moisture for many forms of life.

Vegetation. There are three main types of desert plants—annuals, succulents, and desert shrubs. *Annuals* are plants which live only one season. Hence each generation must produce enough successful seeds to ensure the next generation of the species. Annuals exist as dormant seeds during dry weather. These seeds will only germinate when enough moisture is available to enable the plant to quickly grow, flower, and produce more seeds. The desert brightens with colorful blossoms after the winter and summer rains.

Succulents, or "juicy" plants such as cacti, can survive long droughts by storing water. Most cacti have a rounded shape which minimizes the surface area exposed to the hot, dry air (Fig. 2-34). Some are folded like an accordion and can quickly expand by soaking up rain water. As this stored water is gradually used up, the plant shrivels back to its former shape. Most green plants lose water through the stomata in the leaves. Cacti do not. They are leafless evergreens. (The

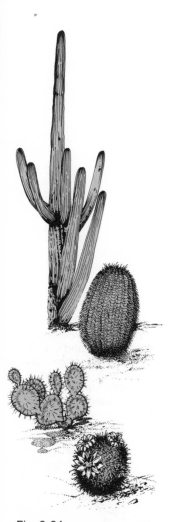

Fig. 2-34
Most cacti have a rounded shape to minimize surface area exposed to the sun. Sharp spines protect fleshy parts from browsing animals.

spines are thought to be the remnants of what were leaves in the early stages of the evolution of cacti.) Their green stems perform the functions of leaves, notably photosynthesis. A thick, rubbery cuticle covers the stem to further protect stored water. Animals seeking the juicy cactus pulp must first maneuver past the sharp, protruding spines. This prickly network also helps to shade the cactus from the direct rays of the sun and reduces water evaporation by surface air currents.

Desert *shrubs* bear small, thick leaves, many with sunken stomata. Waxy leaf cuticles reflect heat and retard water loss. During dry spells, these leaves are shed to help conserve plant moisture, but photosynthesis continues in the chlorophyll-containing stem cells.

The desperate competition for water keeps desert plants well spaced. Most send out shallow, widely branching roots which rapidly soak up any traces of moisture. Others, such as the mesquite, develop long tap roots which reach underground water sources, sometimes more than 30 m (100 ft) deep. The roots of the creosote bush produce toxins which kill any competing plants invading its growth site. The pungent, distasteful juice of this plant also discourages browsing animals.

Yet some plants are actually dependent on animals for their propagation. In June, birds digest the sweet fruit of the saguaro cactus and eliminate the unharmed seeds. Dropping to the shaded ground beneath the nesting sites, these seeds are protected until the next rain stimulates germination. Before the flinty seeds of the mesquite will sprout, they must be eaten. The hard seed covering is removed by animal digestive juices. Moisture can then penetrate and growth begins, after egestion, within the nutrient-rich animal manure.

Animals. The animals of a desert must also cope with the problems of a limited water supply. Desert creatures are adapted to conserving body moisture, which may be lost in any of the following ways:

a)   evaporation from the surface of the body;

b)   exhalation from the lungs during respiration;

c)   elimination through excretion of body wastes.

One obvious precaution is to avoid the intense daily heat. Thus many desert creatures are nocturnal—they confine their activity to the cool desert nights. Some are physically equipped to burrow. Desert scorpions (Fig. 2-35) have

Fig. 2-35
Scorpions are well equipped for digging and capturing prey. They often consume a daily ration of insects equivalent to their own body weight.

enlarged digging claws. Certain snakes and lizards treat sand like water, diving head-first through the surface. Their nostrils are upturned or fitted with valves to keep out the sand. A burrow has many advantages. The surface of the desert sand might register a scorching 65°C (150°F), but an animal burrow only 45 cm (18 in) beneath the surface would remain a cool 16°C (60°F). At night, when surface temperatures drop measurably, the insulating air in the burrow maintains a fairly constant temperature in the underground residence. Moisture from the animal's breath raises the relative humidity in the dwelling. This greatly reduces water loss from the body surface of the inhabitant. Burrows also provide a cool storage site for food and a retreat from many enemies.

Animals which cannot burrow seek refuge from the hot sun in any shady patch. The reptiles and scorpions are suited with a nearly impermeable outer covering to minimize surface evaporation. Lizards and snakes have no glands in their skins. Hence, there is no water loss similar to sweating in mammals. Many desert spiders and insects are protected by a waxy exoskeleton. All desert creatures try to minimize contact between their bodies and the hot sand. While hunting insects during the day, lizards use their legs to lift their bodies and tails off the surface. Some can even stride for short distances with only their hind feet on the ground (Fig. 2-36).

When warm-blooded animals sweat or pant, they are simply using a built-in cooling system to keep their body cells at a functional temperature. If mammals become severely dehydrated in hot, dry air, they suffer "explosive heat death." Body moisture, lost by sweating, is replaced by water from the blood. Eventually the blood becomes so thick that it cannot circulate fast enough to transfer metabolic heat to the skin surface. Soaring body temperature causes rapid death. The body temperature of many animals is regulated by their surroundings rather than by an internal mechanism. Such creatures are often called "cold-blooded"—a highly misleading term. A lizard, basking on a desert rock measuring 38°C (100°F), has anything but "cold" blood! To keep body cells at a functional temperature, such animals must alternate from sun to shade. Most lizards collapse if their body temperature rises above 40°C (104°F). Ten minutes of direct exposure to the hot desert sun can kill a rattlesnake.

Birds are the most active creatures during the day. Perching above the ground, they can easily escape the hot surface as they seek food. During flight, a stream of air cools their bodies. Feathers provide good insulation from the hot rays of the sun, and birds have no sweat glands in their skin.

Fig. 2-36
Some lizard species can stride rapidly for short distances across hot desert sand using only their hind legs. The long tail is raised to maintain balance.

Fig. 2-37
Desert speedster, the road-runner, preys on insects, lizards, and even rattle-snakes. Prey is swallowed headfirst. (Courtesy of U.S. Fish and Wildlife Service.)

Since most birds have higher body temperatures—between 40°C (104°F) and 43°C (108°F)—they can withstand the heat more readily. However, they lose more moisture through panting than small mammals do. Birds of prey (Fig. 2-37) and insect-eaters regain considerable moisture from their food. But many desert birds, especially seed-eaters, must remain within flying distance of surface water. Certain birds, such as swifts and nighthawks, have an added defense against desert rigors. If wind or rain reduces their insect diet for several days, these birds face starvation. To conserve energy, they become torpid—sluggish and inactive—until conditions improve.

Fig. 2-38
Like the desert jack rabbit, the little kit fox displays large ears which are highly sensitive to sound and help to radiate body heat.

Many of the smaller animals use a similar defense during the hottest season when water is desperately scarce. To conserve body moisture, the pocket mouse and ground squirrel enter a deep summer sleep called *estivation*. The animal's body temperature remains just slightly above that of the moist burrow. Larger creatures must simply endure the days, resting as motionless as possible in any spot of shade, until sunset brings relief from the burning heat. Many have conspicuously large ears (Fig. 2-38). Nocturnal hunters and their prey rely upon their hearing for survival. But heat can also be radiated from the body through the many blood vessels in the ears.

Most desert dwellers pass body wastes in a highly concentrated form to further minimize loss of body moisture. The waste product of protein is poisonous and must be eliminated in the form of urea or uric acid. Birds, insects, and most reptiles excrete crystallized uric acid using minute amounts of water. But mammals and some reptiles produce urea which must be dissolved in water before excretion. Some desert mammals have far more concentrated urine than non-desert species. Mammals which eat meat and insects have a high protein diet. They lose more water through excretion than do vegetarian mammals which consume mainly sugars and starches. Thus, insect-eating bats must drink water daily while seed-eating rodents need not do so.

The kangaroo rat is a perfect example of adaptation. On long hind legs, this agile little rodent can spring across the sand like a miniature kangaroo, barely touching the hot surface. The short forelegs dig the burrow used to escape the heat. These remarkable characters live on a diet of dry plant food—and never take a drink! The body mechanism breaks down the food to yield water for the animal. They have no sweat glands and their urine is highly concentrated.

The rainy season brings water. And water brings life to the face of the desert. A throng of hatching insects clamors among the blossoming plants. Birds hasten to mate and rear their young while food and water are plentiful. It is a time of birth for many desert creatures. Nursing mothers must obtain enough moisture to replace the fluid lost in milk production for their offspring. Even tadpoles and shrimp abound in scattered waterholes! All life struggles to perpetuate itself in this endless cycle of moisture and drought. And so life flourishes, even in the face of death, throughout the desert biome.

For Thought and Research

1   Alpine sorrel is a plant found in both the Arctic and alpine tundra. The Arctic growth shows adaptive differences from the alpine growth. Using your knowledge of these two regions, explain each of the following:
    a)   The Arctic growth reaches a maximum rate of photosynthesis at a lower temperature than alpine growth.
    b)   Alpine growth requires a higher light intensity than Arctic growth.
    c)   The Arctic growth requires a longer photoperiod.
    d)   The alpine growth produces a greater number of flowers.
    e)   The Arctic growth develops more rhizomes (underground stems used for food storage).
    f)   The alpine growth reproduces by seedlings; Arctic growth relies on vegetative reproduction.
    g)   Roots of the Arctic growth are short and quickly replaced; alpine growth develops deep, long-lived roots.
2   Many birds return each spring to nest in the Arctic tundra.
    a)   What special problems do they encounter?
    b)   What type of birdlife would find the tundra most favorable? Why?
    c)   Why do many Arctic species lay a larger than average number of eggs?
    d)   What other adaptations do these summer residents exhibit?

e) Compare the Arctic and alpine tundra as a habitat for birds.

3 Soil organisms are essential for the recycling of plant nutrients. What type of decomposers can exist in the Arctic tundra? How do they survive the long, frozen periods?

4 In view of the growing food crisis, is farming of the tundra feasible? Could grains, developed for a short growing season, be successfully cultivated in the Arctic? What major problems do you foresee? Discuss.

5 Conservationists throughout North America fear permanent ecological damage as a result of the development of oil and other natural resources in the Arctic tundra. What are the major problems created by crews surveying or drilling in the tundra? Why is an oil pipeline considered to be an environmental hazard? Compare this hazard to that of huge oil tankers traveling along the Arctic coastline.

6 Why does a tree which can retain its leaves have such an important advantage in the coniferous forest biome? Why is the growth of smaller plants limited beneath the canopy of a coniferous forest?

7 Why are reptiles, amphibians, and smaller invertebrate animals more numerous in the temperate rain forest along the coast than in the boreal forest?

8 Many foresters maintain that mature trees, left undisturbed to age and eventually die, are simply wasted resources. Evaluate this philosophy in terms of the nutrient cycle.

9 Each of the different strata within a deciduous forest supports a certain segment of the animal community. At which level would you expect to find the greatest diversity of wildlife? Explain.

10 Compare a coniferous and a deciduous forest with respect to each of the following abiotic factors (consider seasonal changes in your explanations):

a) Light. Which type of canopy allows greater light penetration to the forest floor? Select the period of greatest illumination for each forest type.

b) Temperature. Where is the highest and lowest daily temperature located within each type of forest? Would this temperature profile change during the night? Explain.

c) Relative humidity. The highest relative humidity is found near a forest floor. Why? Where is the lowest relative humidity found? Is the relative humidity within a forest higher at night or during the day? Explain.

d) Rainfall. During a light rain, leaves tend to capture water which gradually drains down the branches and trunk as "stemflow." This moisture enters the soil around the base of the tree. Which type of forest growth would result in greater "stemflow"? Explain. How would this affect the growth of shade-loving plants colonizing at the foot of larger trees?

e) Wind. Which type of forest would serve as a more effective windbreak? Explain.

11 Compare a coniferous and a deciduous forest as a wildlife habitat. Consider seasonal changes in each forest type and include the following factors:

a) availability and diversity of food;

b) protection from predators;

c) shelter from the elements.

12 The vast herds of buffalo actually helped to maintain the prairies. Yet the cattle which now graze in their place are creating many serious ecological problems such as erosion and competition with wildlife. How do the domestic herds jeopardize species such as elk and bighorn sheep? Compare the life style of the buffalo with that of its modern-day successor to explain the current dilemma.

13 The true extent of man's impact on prairie wildlife can best be understood by researching animal populations, past and present. (See *Recommended Readings* 5 and 8.)

a) The prairie dog. What is its role in the prairie ecosystem? Why is it the target of extermination campaigns? How many interrelated species will vanish with it?

b) Prairie birdlife. How were the ranks of the following species drastically reduced: prairie chicken, whooping crane, trumpeter swan, golden plover, and the Eskimo curlew? What is the greatest threat now facing prairie waterfowl? Why is the bobwhite quail declining in numbers?

c) Why did the white plains wolf and badlands grizzly bear vanish before the turn of the century? Why are each of the following species on the verge of extinction today: the prairie falcon, the black-footed ferret, the tule elk, and the kit fox?

14 a) A brief rainstorm will not stimulate germination of desert annual wildflower seeds. Yet, more than 50% of these seeds begin to sprout after a heavy rainstorm. Furthermore, this water must come from above, not from beneath the soil. Why is this remarkable adaptation so critical to desert plants?

b) Some desert plants, such as the night-blooming cereus, have evolved flower petals which open at night. The blossoms of such plants are usually white and highly fragrant. What purpose could this unusual behavior serve?

15 Desert animals demonstrate many remarkable adaptations. Investigate the habits of some of the following and explain how they are suited to the desert. (See *Recommended Readings* 2, 6, 7, 8, and 9.)

a) The kangaroo rat. Why are these creatures so important to the life of the desert?

b) Desert birdlife. What types of birds are found in the desert? Where do they nest? Does the climate affect their breeding habits?

c) The antelope ground squirrel. How can this mammal remain active during the hot desert day?

d) Desert snakes. When are they most active? How do they locate and capture their prey?

e) The peccary. How do these wild pigs survive in the desert?

16 a) Construct a series of food chains for each of the major biomes you have studied. Consider both the daily and nocturnal activity within each community as well as any seasonal changes in animal populations. Many of the recommended readings provide a more detailed account of the animal species within each region.

b) Combine these food chains to form seasonal food webs for each biome.

Recommended Readings

1 *A Guide to the Study of Soil Ecology* by W. A. Andrews et al., Prentice-Hall, 1973. Consult Unit 2 for soil types.

2 *The Living World of Animals,* The Reader's Digest, 1970. This volume presents a wealth of information supplemented by remarkable photography and excellent illustrations.

3 *The Life of the Mountains* by M. Brooks, McGraw-Hill, 1967. This is one of an excellent series of ecologically oriented books entitled "Our Living World of Nature." Highly recommended resource material.

4 *The Life of the Forest* by J. McCormick, McGraw-Hill, 1966. A fascinating survey of North American forests and their animal inhabitants.

5 *The Life of the Prairies and Plains* by D. L. Allen, McGraw-Hill, 1967. A comprehensive study of prairie life, past and present. This well-illustrated text should intrigue as well as inform any reader.

6 *The Life of the Desert* by A. and M. Sutton, McGraw-Hill, 1966. With the aid of excellent photography, these authors explore the amazing beauty and adaptability of desert life.

7 *Wild Animals of North America,* The National Geographic Society, 1960. This comprehensive resource book contains lively biographies of 138 animal species complete with photographs and illustrations.

8 *Ecology and Field Biology* by R. L. Smith, Harper & Row, 1966. This text includes a fairly comprehensive survey of the major biomes in addition to many related topics.

9 *Animal Ecology* by S. C. Kendeigh, Prentice-Hall, 1961. This text emphasizes the animal life within each biome, while including a general survey of abiotic factors.

10 *Fundamentals of Ecology* by E. P. Odum, W. B. Saunders, 1971. This text includes a brief but descriptive survey of each major biome.

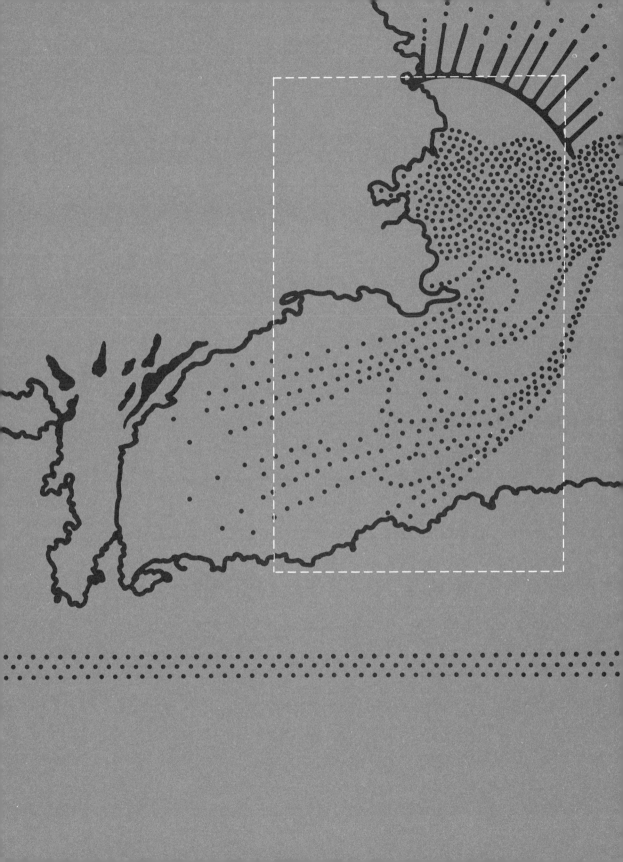

Field and Laboratory Studies: Abiotic Factors

3

Many abiotic factors operate in terrestrial ecosystems. Foremost among these are the topography of the landscape, wind, moisture, light, soil, and temperature. The ways in which these factors interact with one another and with biotic factors is the main topic of the studies in this unit.

3.1   TOPOGRAPHIC MAP ANALYSIS

An invaluable aid to someone interested in outdoor field studies is the supply of topographic maps from various government agencies (Fig. 3-1). These maps are loaded with information and can be obtained at little cost for nearly any area in North America. With a topographic map, you can pinpoint the position (latitude and longitude) and the elevation of your study area. The nature of the surrounding countryside; the location of swamps, dams, mines, and gravel pits; the sources of creeks and streams; the heights of nearby hills; and the extent of surrounding forests can also be determined easily.

The first things to consider in map interpretation are where is north; what is the scale of the map; what do the various map symbols mean; and how old (out of date) is the map?

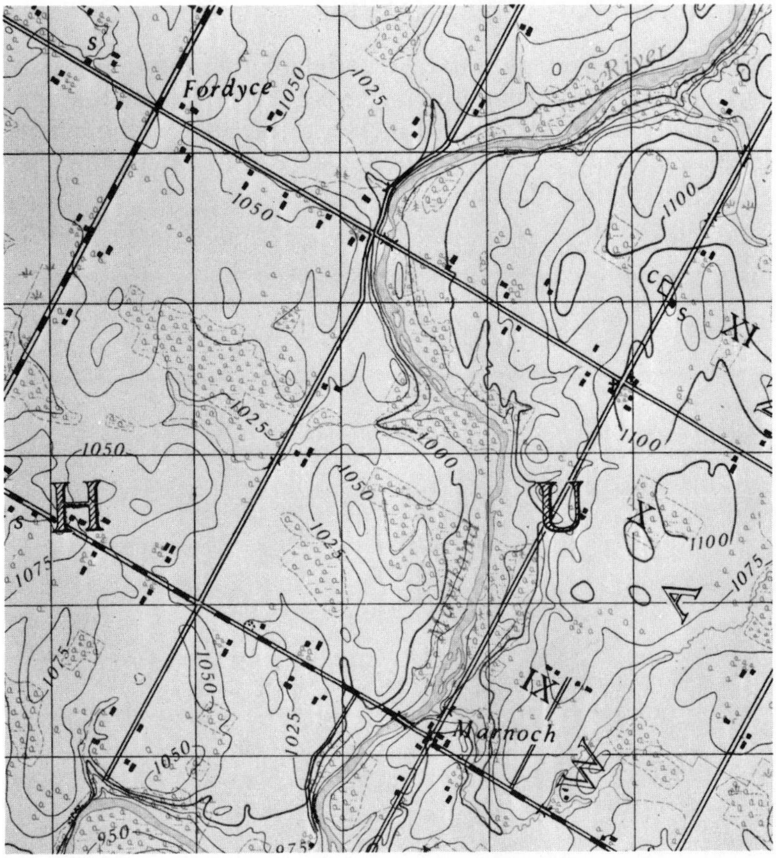

Fig. 3-1
A topographical map supplies information that can be useful in planning a field trip. (This is a section from the topographic sheet 40 $\frac{P}{14}$ west half, scale 1:50,000, published by the Surveys and Mapping Branch, Department of Energy, Mines and Resources, Ottawa. Original in color.)

Procedure

To put the map to good use in your field work:

a)   Locate the study site.

b)   Find its latitude and longitude.

c)   Find the maximum and minimum elevation within the study area.

d)   Determine the proportion of the area forested and the type of forest (deciduous or coniferous, if listed).

e)   Locate the sources of streams running through the study area.

f)   Find the position of the study area in terms of distance and direction from the nearest important town or landmark (for example, 3.5 kilometers, N.N.E. of the intersection of highways #110 and #42).

3.2 AERIAL PHOTO ANALYSIS

Aircraft have been used to take aerial photographs of much of
the North American continent (Fig. 3-2). These photographs
commonly have a scale of 4 inches to the mile, although en-
largements with a much greater scale can be obtained. They
show a great deal of detail.

Fig. 3-2
An aerial photograph re-
veals many of the features
of the site and the sur-
rounding terrain. (Courtesy
of Ontario Ministry of Natural Resources.)

If a government agency can supply you with aerial
photos of your study area, they can be used to predict many
things about conditions in the study area before you go into
the field. What types of trees exist? Where are the hills,
valleys, streams, houses, and roads? Where will the ground be
moist? Where will it be dry? As you search for answers to
such questions, you should get an idea of the kinds of studies
that can be done in the area.

Procedure

If aerial photos have been obtained for your use, spend at least one period in class examining them. Working in groups, determine what you can from them. Answer the questions prepared by your teacher which are pertinent to your studies. Try predicting the conditions mentioned previously.

Take particular note of the scale of the photograph; where north is on the photograph; any landmarks that will be useful in locating the boundaries of your study site in the field; and the exact points where your field exercises will be carried out.

You can trace a map from the photograph without harming it if you place a pane of glass over it. If your school has an electronic stencil cutter, excellent copies of the map are cheaply available.

By covering a copy of the map with a grid system (a series of evenly spaced vertical and horizontal lines), you can determine accurately the locations of landmarks and study sites. If you have trouble finding these when you arrive at the study area, you can pace off the distances that you determined with your grid system. You must, of course, know the scale of the photograph. A grid system can also be used to calculate the proportion of open space to forest and the proportion of water to dry land. Try these with your aerial photograph. Compare your results with those of others in your class.

3.3 DETERMINING SLOPE WITH A CLINOMETER

Animals and plants living on flat ground encounter different conditions than those living on gently or steeply sloping sites. There are both positive and negative factors associated with slope. Hundreds of variations are caused by slope at different sites. For example, in the Northern Hemisphere in winter, north-facing slopes get less of the sun's warming rays than do south-facing slopes. In the spring, after the melting of the snow and the appearance of spring rains, mice, moles, and even worms may have their burrows flooded on poorly drained, flat land. During summer storms, surface runoff may carry away seeds and topsoil from steep slopes and leave the roots of many plants exposed to the drying air.

The degree of slope has varying effects on the inhabitants of different sites, and should not be overlooked, especially when studying communities living on hilly terrain.

Materials

a) protractor

b) fine thread

c) small weight (metal washer)

d) nails

e) two wooden poles (1.5 meters in height)

Procedure

a) Construct the clinometer shown in Figure 3-3. First drill a hole through the *center* of the half-circular protractor. Nail the protractor to a 1.5 meter long pole, within 1 cm of the end. The nail should be left protruding 0.5 cm from the protractor. The protractor must be free to rotate. Tie a 20 – 30 cm piece of fine string to the protruding end of the nail and tie the washer to the end of the hanging string.

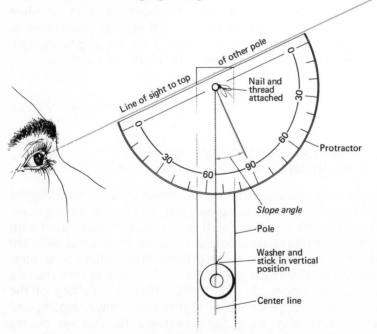

Fig. 3-3
Clinometer and sighting technique used to determine angle of slope.

b) To make a slope reading, one person must take a second pole (of equal height) to the top of the slope that is to be measured. This pole must be held vertically.

c) Two people at the bottom of the slope take the reading. One keeps the pole still and vertical (using the hanging washer as a guide). The other person rotates the protractor to sight along the upper edge until the straight edge points directly at the top of the pole up the hill. The person holding the clinometer pole reads the slope angle as shown in Figure 3-3.

d) To determine slope at particular spots, make a clinometer as shown in Figure 3-4. It is similar to the one described previously, except that the protractor is tacked so it cannot move on the frame.

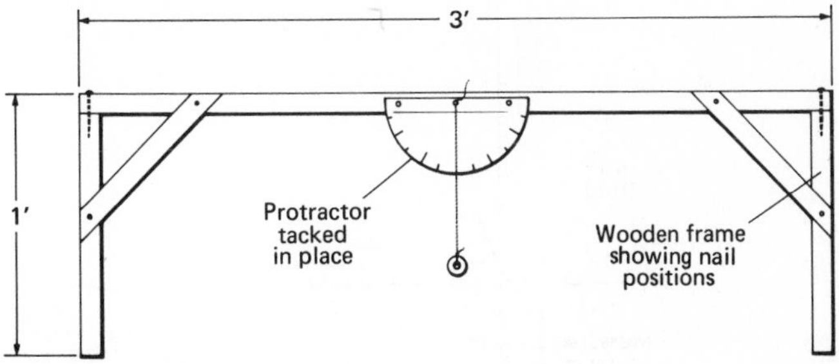

Fig. 3-4
Clinometer used to take spot slope angle measurements.

e) Spot slope angles can be read simply by placing the wooden frame upright on the side of the hill with the one leg directly downhill from the other. The angle of slope can then be read by one person looking from the side.

f) Many types of commercially manufactured clinometers are available. If your school has any of these, you should compare the accuracy of your homemade one against that of the commercial ones.

3.4 DETERMINING PERCENT SLOPE

When you are comparing one area with another, it is often useful to have slope measurements expressed in percent. These can be found for given spots on the side of a hill using the following method.

Materials

a) two meter sticks

b) carpenter's level

Procedure

a) Draw a line on one meter stick at the 80-cm mark.

b) Place this meter stick horizontally as shown in Figure 3-5, with the zero end touching the ground. Use the level to keep it horizontal.

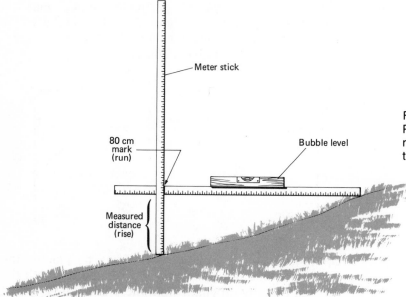

Fig. 3-5
Percent slope can be determined using this apparatus.

c) Use the second meter stick to measure the vertical distance to the ground from the bottom edge of the horizontal meter stick.

d) Multiply this distance by 10 and divide by 8 to get the percent slope. Suppose that you obtain a vertical measurement of 20 cm. Then the percent slope is $\frac{200}{8}$ %, or 25%. Percent slope can also be expressed as

$$\frac{\text{rise}}{\text{run}} \times 100$$

Refer to the figure to determine why you multiply by 10 and divide by 8.

3.5 A HILL PROFILE FIELD SURVEY

Some very simple survey techniques can be profitable in studies of hilly areas. If a study involves comparing communities at various points on the side of a hill, then a hill profile will be useful in mapping what you find, where you find it. Keep in mind that this technique will help in contour mapping later.

Materials

a) surveyor's level

b) stadia rod

c) measuring tape (50 feet or more in length)

d) 2 wooden stakes

e) pencil and note paper

Procedure

a) Select the hill site for the study. Place marker stakes *A* and *B* at the bottom and top of the hill site, so that both *A* and *B* are visible to worker 1 (Fig. 3-6).

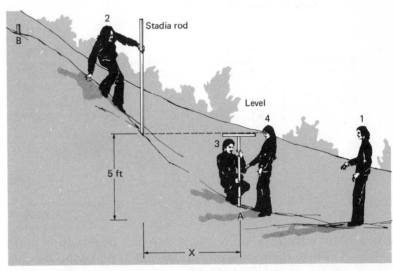

Fig. 3-6
A team of four students making the first 5-foot contour sighting and, later, the distance measurement (*X*) on the hillside. The numbers given to the various workers correspond to the text.

b) Duties are as follows: Worker 1 remains at the bottom of the hill about 10 meters behind stake *A*. His job is to make sure that the other workers make all measurements along the line between stakes *A* and *B*. (If a long rope or string is available, stretch it between *A* and *B*. Then no one is required for this task.) Worker 2 carries the rod up the hill. Worker 3 stands to the side of the level, keeping the base vertical using the leveling mechanism. This person also records all data. Worker 4 sights along the level.

c) To start, place the surveyor's level at stake *A*. Worker 4 sights into the side of the hill in the direction of stake

B. He also directs the stadia rod carrier (worker 2) to the sighting point.

d) The person lining up stakes *A* and *B* (worker 1) motions the rod carrier (2) to left or right if he has strayed to one side or the other of the line.

e) Worker 4 should check the position of the stadia rod, while, at the same time, worker 3 makes sure that the level is aiming horizontally.

f) Measure the horizontal distance *X*, from the top of the level at the center of the sighting board, to the bottom of the rod, as shown in the diagram.

g) Prepare a data table similar to Table 2. Enter the first elevation (+5 feet) and the measured sighting distance (*X*) in your table. This is observation point 1.

TABLE 2 SAMPLE SURVEY DATA

Observation point	Elevation from stake *A*	Sighting distance (*X*)	Distance from stake *A*
Stake *A*	0	Start	Start
1	+5	22'6"	22'6"
2	+10	18'6"	41'0"
3	+15		

h) Move the level up to the position of observation point 1. Move the rod farther up the hill to make the sighting on the next 5-foot elevation. This will be observation point 2.

i) Repeat, up to or beyond stake *B*, recording all data along the way.

Notes

a) You should practice as a team at the school before going into the field. It is wise to have a good working knowledge of the level and rod before you attempt important studies.

b) Rotate duties after every two readings so everyone gets a chance to perform each duty.

3.6 GRAPHING HILL PROFILE FIELD DATA

A hill profile can be helpful in summarizing the positions where various organisms or conditions are encountered in the field. The hill profile graph that can be drawn from the field data represents a miniature cross-section of the hill.

Materials

a)   graph paper

b)   ruler, pencils, eraser

c)   field data

Procedure

a)   Turn the graph paper on its side. Select vertical and horizontal lines about 2 – 3 cm from the left and bottom edges of the page. Draw them to meet at the point labeled "Stake *A*" in Figure 3-7.

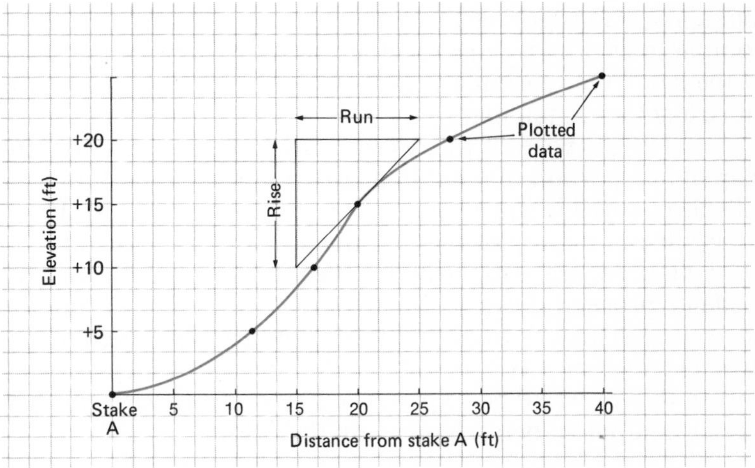

Fig. 3-7
Method of placing axes to graph field data for hill profiles. Some representative data are shown along with the way of measuring the slope at a given point on the hill.

b)   Since the graph is a miniature drawing of the actual hill, some scale must be selected so the drawing will fit on the page. If you let 2 cm on the graph paper equal 10 feet for the actual hill, will the data fit? If your data will not fit on the graph, select another scale such as 1 cm equals 10 feet.

c)   Label the vertical axis as the elevation in feet.

d)   Label the horizontal axis as the distance from stake *A* in feet.

e)   Plot your field data.

f)   The *slope* at any point on the hill can be found by drawing the tangent to the curve on the graph and measuring the *rise* and *run* shown in Figure 3-7.

$$\text{percent slope} = \frac{\text{rise}}{\text{run}} \times 100$$

3.7   CONTOUR MAPPING IN THE FIELD

One of the initial steps in a detailed study of a particular site is contour mapping of the area to show differences in elevation. A contour map is made up of lines joining points of equal elevation. If you were to look at the side of a hill slightly more than 20 feet in elevation, on which all points with elevations of 5, 10, 15, and 20 feet were painted, you would see something resembling Figure 3-8A. If you could then get into a helicopter and hover over the hill, your view would be that shown in Figure 3-8B. This latter view is what a contour map looks like. Considering these two views, what do you think contour lines drawn close together mean in terms of the slope of the land? On reasonably flat land, will the contour lines be close together or far apart?

The purpose of this exercise is to contruct a contour map of one portion of a hill in a fairly open area (preferably a hillside covered in grass, and having few obstructions). From a base line at the top of the hill, the boundaries of the area to be contoured are established. Then teams of four or five students proceed down parallel transect lines, measuring the horizontal distances to each 5-foot contour point (each 5-foot drop in elevation). It is recommended that all students taking part in this exercise be experienced at working with the surveying equipment before going into the field.

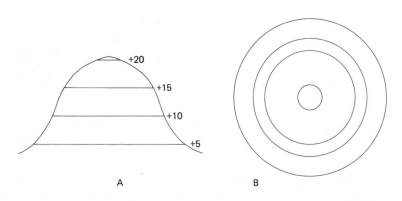

Fig. 3-8
Diagram representing a simple hill on which 5, 10, 15, and 20 foot elevations (contours) are shown. (A) represents a side view. (B) represents an aerial view, the view seen on a contour map.

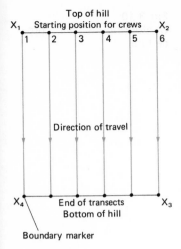

Top of hill

Starting position for crews

X_1 X_2

1   2   3   4   5   6

Direction of travel

X_4 End of transects X_3

Bottom of hill

Boundary marker

Fig. 3-9
Contouring a hill: general layout.

The general layout of the exercise is shown in Figure 3-9. The size of the study area is quite variable. It depends on the size of the class, available equipment, type of hillside, and time available. Data collected in the field are used to construct a contour map. This can be done back in the lab, as described in Section 3.8.

Materials

a) long rope or strong cord to mark the base line and the boundaries of the study area. It should have knots every 10 meters, the distance between transects.

b) surveyor's levels

c) stadia rods

d) measuring tapes

e) marker stakes

f) ropes or string to mark contour lines (optional)

g) ditto master

h) data tables

Procedure

a) Two students act as "foremen." They must meet with the teacher beforehand to organize equipment, become familiar with the sequence of events, and organize working groups.

b) Four students are assigned to locate boundaries (with marker stakes) of the total area to be contoured; to locate and mark the starting and ending position of each transect with stakes; and to provide any assistance needed by a transect crew.

c) Each transect crew consists of four students with jobs similar to those outlined in Section 3.5.

d) Figures 3-9 and 3-10 illustrate the positions of the various activities. The base line is established by pulling a rope or cord in a straight line along the top of the hill. It should have knots every 10 meters, to locate the transect starting positions.

e) Insert marker stakes at X_1, X_2, and each transect starting position.

f) The foremen should now organize equipment and crews at their proper starting positions.

g) The students marking the boundaries should pull out strings or ropes at 90° from the base line to points X_3

Fig. 3-10
Contouring a hill: pro-
cedure.

and X_4. (Sighting along the level with it tilted on its side should help in forming 90° corners.)

h)   Before inserting marker stakes at X_3 and X_4, use the rope for the base line to make sure the distance between X_3 and X_4 is the same length as the base line.

i)   Place stakes at X_3, X_4, and the other transect end points.

j)   While the boundaries are being established—steps d) to i)—the transect crews, under the guidance of the foremen, should determine which stake on the base line is at the highest elevation. (This isn't difficult to do. Can you figure out how?)

k)   This stake will now be referred to as stake A at elevation zero. All further elevations recorded will be less than this.

l)   One foreman will hold a stadia rod at this stake to start off all the transect crews, who do steps m) through t).

m)   The first objective is to find the −5 foot point on the transect line. The two students operating the level should move down their transect. Keep sighting back to the base of the rod at stake A (even if this stake is not on your transect). When the sighting hits the ground at the base of the rod, you are at observation point 1, 5 feet below stake A.

n) Measure the horizontal distance from the start of the transect to this point. Enter the measurement on a data sheet similar to that shown in Table 3.

TABLE 3

Observation point	Elevation from stake A	Distance measured
1	-5	
2	-10	
etc.	etc.	

o) The person carrying the stadia rod proceeds down the slope to make the next reading. He is guided along the transect by the observer at the top of the hill who lines up the rod with the marker stakes at top and bottom.

p) The level operators must sight on the stadia rod and tell the rod carrier when the -5 foot mark is sighted.

q) When the rod carrier is in this position, the stadia rod will be at observation point 2, 10 feet below marker A.

r) The distance from the level to the rod is measured and recorded.

s) The level is moved to observation point 2 and the stadia rod is moved down the hill for the next reading.

t) This process continues to the bottom of the hill.

u) Data sheets should be turned in to the foremen. They will then compile the data of all groups on a single ditto master to make copies for everyone.

v) (Optional) If each group places a stake at each 5 foot drop in elevation, the four students originally involved in setting out the boundaries of the study area could use ropes or cord to connect stakes of equal elevation. In so doing, a life-size contour map will result, in which each rope or cord represents a contour line.

3.8 MAPPING CONTOUR FIELD DATA

A contour map, just like a hill profile graph, can be extremely useful for summarizing conditions found in the field.

Materials

a) graph paper
b) ruler, pencils, eraser
c) field data

Procedure

a) The scale of the map depends on the length of the base line and the length of the individual transects. An appropriate scale will normally have 2 − 3 cm on the graph paper equal to the distance between the transects.

b) First draw the base line ($X_1 X_2$) across the top of the page. Then mark the transect lines in place (2 − 3 cm apart if you use the scale recommended above). They should run parallel to one another, at 90° to the base line.

c) Label the position of stake A. Number each of the transects according to the numbers used in the field.

d) Use a copy of the results compiled in the field study. Convert field distances along each transect into distances in cm along the graph lines.

e) Label each point along the lines as to its elevation.

f) After all transects have been completed, join points of equal elevation to obtain contour lines as shown in Figure 3-11.

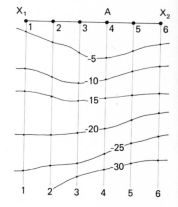

Fig. 3-11
A contour map plotted from the field data of six transect crews.

3.9 MAPPING: THE BEARING-INTERSECTION METHOD

This section describes a simple technique for obtaining a map of your study site.

Materials

a) 360° protractors (2) (Fig. 3-12)
b) straight pins

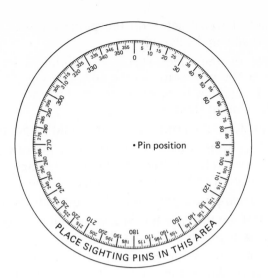

Fig. 3-12
Calibrated cardboard disc
(protractor) used to take
bearings.

c)   2 pinning boards
d)   1.5 m stakes (2), hammer and nails

Procedure

a)   Select two vantage points 30 to 50 meters apart which
        have unobstructed views of the area to be mapped.

b)   Place a tall stake at point *A*. Then accurately measure
        a base line to point *B*.

c)   Note the length of the base line on a data sheet similar
        to the one shown in Figure 3-13.

d)   Nail a pinning board to the top of each stake.

Map Title:	Names of Recorders:	
Schoolyard		
Length of Base Line	**Sighting Position**	**Date**
50 meters	B	8/10/74
Observation Number	**Description**	**Bearing Sighted**
1	Position A	180°
2	Field goal post	82°
3	etc.	
4		

Fig. 3-13
Sample data sheet for bearing-intersection method.

e)   Place the protractor on the pinning board. Put a pin vertically in the center.

f)   Sight on the other stake. If sighting from point *A*, rotate the protractor so the zero bearing aims at stake *B*. If sighting from point *B*, rotate it so that bearing 180° aims at stake *A*.

g)   Tack down the protractor so it can no longer rotate.

h)   In cooperation with the workers at the other sighting position, select different objects to map, entering a description and bearing for each observation.

i)   Final mapping of the data is best done in the lab.

j)   First draw the base line at a scale and position suitable to plot all points sighted in the field.

k)   Using a protractor, plot each of the angles for sighting point *A*. Mark the angle with a pencil, and number each according to the observation number.

l)   With a ruler, draw straight lines from point *A* through each of the measured angles.

m)   Repeat k) and l) for data from sighting point *B*.

n)   The points where lines with the same number cross represent the positions where certain objects were located in the field. Label each spot as to what was present at that position.

o)   *Note*: compasses can be used in place of the protractors for this exercise. You are advised to select a north-south base line, if possible, for your first trial using compasses.

3.10   WIND VELOCITY AND DIRECTION

Wind velocity and direction are abiotic factors that you should measure on virtually every field trip to a terrestrial environment.

A.   WIND VELOCITY

This exercise indicates how you can determine the relative wind velocity at different elevations and in different environments, to show how wind velocities vary over the landscape.

Materials

a)   anemometer

b)   rubber stopper

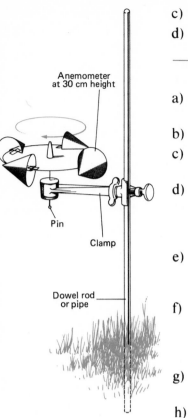

Anemometer
at 30 cm height

Pin

Clamp

Dowel rod
or pipe

Fig. 3-14
Mounting an anemometer
for wind velocity studies.

Fig. 3-15
Data sheet for recording
wind velocities.

c)   test tube clamp

d)   dowel rod or metal pipe, 1 cm in diameter, at least 2 meters long

Procedure

a)   Fasten the anemometer to a dowel rod or pipe as shown in Figure 3-14.

b)   Set up the apparatus at the site to be studied.

c)   Stand 3 or 4 meters away from the anemometer and downwind from it. Why?

d)   Count the number of revolutions of the anemometer over a 30-second interval. This is done by noting each time the red-colored cup spins around. One person should count while the other keeps time.

e)   Make 30-second counts in the first trial for heights of 15 cm, 30 cm, 1 meter, and 2 meters. Record the counts on a data sheet similar to Figure 3-15.

f)   Repeat the trials a second, third, fourth, and fifth time. (Do not make all five readings for one elevation consecutively. Move the anemometer to a different height after each reading. Why?)

g)   Find the average for each height and the average for the site for all four heights.

h)   Compare this set of data with that obtained at other sites. Some interesting comparisons can be made by recording wind velocity data in a completely exposed site free of vegetation; in a grassy "jungle" or weedy field; under a tree; in a valley; on top of a hill; behind

Environmental Description:						
Height above Ground	**Number of Revolutions in 30 Seconds**					
	Trial Number					**Average**
	1	2	3	4	5	
15 cm						
30 cm						
1 m						
2 m						
			Site Average for 4 Heights			

dense shrubs; at different points around any major obstruction or topographic feature (a large rock, a building, or a car).

i) There are a number of ways of determining what a particular number of revolutions means in terms of actual wind velocity in miles per hour. Have you figured out a calibrating method yet? If possible, check your calibration against a commercial anemometer or other wind gauge.

Discussion

a) Does there appear to be any difference in the wind velocity at different heights above the ground? Plot your data on a graph relating height and the mean number of revolutions per 30 seconds.

b) On a windy day, where will delicate insects find greatest security? Why?

c) How is the vegetation in exposed habitats adapted to strong winds?

d) What types of trees offer larger wildlife the greatest protection from the elements? Why?

e) Under what conditions does wind erosion occur? What factors prevent wind erosion? What techniques are or could be employed to prevent wind erosion?

f) How have plants adapted to make use of beneficial effects of the wind? What animals have made use of the wind in a positive manner?

B. WIND DIRECTION

Wind direction should be recorded in any field study even if, at the time, this information seems of little use. If you or someone else were to return to the same site on a day when wind directions were different, the chances are many other aspects of the environment would also be different.

Commercially produced weather vanes are available. Alternatively, you can make your own. Ask your teacher for instructions. A moist finger and a compass will also do the job.

3.11 MEASURING RELATIVE HUMIDITY

The theory of evolution is widely accepted as an explanation for the variety seen in present-day life. According to this theory, life originated in the sea. At some stage in history, some organisms became chance invaders of the terrestrial environment. Most perished, but some survived, and heralded the beginning of the terrestrial ecosystem.

Because air is not saturated with water, the biggest problem for these early land dwellers was drying up. Water evaporated from their surfaces into the unsaturated air. At first, only those terrestrial environments with permanently near-saturated atmospheres were successfully used by the displaced ocean organisms. Even today, many organisms can survive only in areas where the *relative humidity* is high. On the other hand, some plants and animals have *adapted* very well, and live under conditions of very low relative humidity. For example, desert plants and animals have evolved many modifications that enable them to live in what humans, probably the most adaptable of all organisms, consider to be intolerable conditions.

To determine relative humidity, we employ a simple phenomenon noted by physicists. When a fluid evaporates, it cools. When you get out of a hot shower, the water covering you starts to evaporate. Immediately you feel the cooling effect, especially if you stand in a drafty spot. The less saturated the air is, the faster the rate of evaporation and the greater the cooling effect.

A device called the *hygrometer* uses this phenomenon to determine the relative humidity. Two thermometers are necessary, one with no moisture on the bulb (the *dry bulb*), and the other with a wet piece of cloth wrapped around the bulb (the *wet bulb*). The wet bulb is soaked with distilled water. In unsaturated air, evaporation from the wet cloth cools the bulb, giving a temperature lower than the actual air temperature measured with the dry bulb thermometer. By consulting tables, or, in the case of some hygrometers, by using a device on the hygrometer, you can determine the relative humidity if you know the wet and dry bulb temperatures. If the difference in readings is 0C°, there was no cooling; no evaporation took place; the air was saturated, or had a relative humidity of 100%. If the difference was 3C°, some cooling took place; a moderate amount of evaporation occurred; the air must have been rather humid, but not saturated. If the difference was 10C°, there was a large cooling effect due to a great deal of evaporation; the air must have been rather dry.

Practice using the hygrometer in and around school since you will be using it in many of your studies.

Materials

a)   sling psychrometer—a hygrometer that can be whirled (Fig. 3-16)

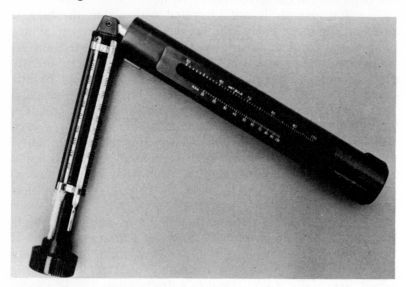

Fig. 3-16
A sling psychrometer.

b)   small vial filled with distilled water

c)   relative humidity chart

Procedure

a)   Moisten the wet bulb cloth with distilled water.

b)   Stand in an unobstructed place. Whirl the hygrometer through the air for at least 2 minutes. Keep clear of any objects that might shatter the thermometers.

c)   Check the wet bulb thermometer reading every 15 – 20 seconds to observe if the temperature is decreasing.

d)   After no further decrease is noted, record the wet bulb reading and then the dry bulb reading.

e)   Use these two readings to calculate the relative humidity. (The method depends on the make of hygrometer used.)

Discussion

Predict how the relative humidity will differ between two environments. Then check your predictions. You could compare classroom air to outdoor air at the same time of day; early morning air to late afternoon air; classroom air before and after the room has been occupied by people; a wooded area with an open area; and a stand of coniferous trees with a nearby stand of deciduous trees.

3.12 RELATIVE HUMIDITY AND POPULATION STRUCTURE

The physical environment influences the growth of most species of animals. Here you study the influence of relative humidity on the pattern of development of the flour beetle *Tribolium confusum* when light, temperature, food supply, and space are optimal.

Materials

a) flour beetles, *Tribolium confusum*

b) flour

c) bolting silk no. 5xx (hole diameter 0.25 – 0.28 mm), for sieving flour

d) 2 jars of about 300-ml capacity

e) 2 battery jars or other transparent containers large enough to cover the 300-ml jars and other materials shown in Figure 3-17

f) 2 evaporating dishes

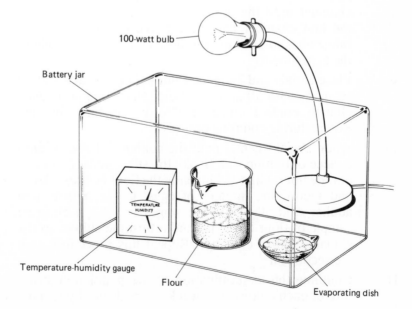

Fig. 3-17
Climate control chamber.

100-watt bulb

Battery jar

TEMPERATURE
HUMIDITY

Temperature-humidity gauge

Flour

Evaporating dish

g) 2 bulbs (100 watt)

h) forceps with sponge pads glued to the tips

i) 2 thermometers and 2 humidity gauges (or 2 combined temperature-humidity gauges)

j) dissecting microscope or pocket magnifier

k) balance

l) desiccant, preferably silica gel

m) blotting paper

n) petroleum jelly

Procedure

a) Research the life cycle of the flour beetle, *Tribolium confusum*. Be sure you can distinguish male and female beetles by the *elytra* pattern.

b) Set up two climate control chambers (Fig. 3-17). Put desiccant in the evaporating dish of one chamber and moist blotting paper in and around the evaporating dish of the second chamber. Seal the lines of contact between the battery jars and the counter-top with petroleum jelly.

c) Adjust the position of the lamp and the amount of desiccant in the first chamber until the temperature is as close as possible to 29°C and the relative humidity is in the range 20–40%. Adjust the position of the lamp and the amount of moist blotting paper in the second chamber until the temperature is the same as that in the first chamber and the relative humidity is in the range 60–80%. Maintain these conditions throughout the experiment.

d) Place 2 male and 2 female flour beetles in each 300-ml jar along with 50 grams of flour. Place one jar in each climate control chamber. Do not disturb the jars except during counting periods.

e) After 2 weeks gently pour the contents of one jar onto a piece of bolting silk. Shake the silk carefully to sieve out the flour without damaging the flour beetles. Count and record the number of eggs, larvae, pupae, and adults. Add all of the life stages to a fresh 50 gram sample of flour in the jar and return the culture to the climate control chamber. Repeat this procedure with the second jar.

f) Continue this determination of the population structure of each colony at 2-week intervals until you have arrived at definite conclusions regarding the effects of humidity on the pattern of development of *Tribolium confusum*. If the population in either jar becomes high enough that crowding or lack of food might become a controlling factor, add more flour.

g) Plot graphs of time versus number of eggs, larvae, pupae, and adults for each jar.

Discussion

a) List and explain the conclusions that you derived from this experiment.

b) What factors do you feel are more important than relative humidity in influencing animal populations? Why?

c) A forest community has a gradient of relative humidity which decreases from the ground upward. What effect would this gradient have on the diversity of insects in the forest?

d) Why is low relative humidity often a barrier which limits the distribution of moist-skinned animals?

e) How would you adapt this investigation to determine the effects of temperature on population structure? If time permits, try your adaptation.

f) The scope of this investigation may be extended if some groups use another species of flour beetle such as *Tribolium castaneum*.

3.13   PRECIPITATION MEASUREMENTS

All living organisms require water, and each species has its optimal moisture conditions. Since precipitation varies over the surface of the earth, it has a direct effect on the distribution of plants and animals. Even in small areas precipitation can vary considerably from place to place. The windward and leeward sides of a steep hill may receive different amounts of precipitation; the ground stratum in one type of woodlot may receive more precipitation than the ground stratum in another type of woodlot nearby.

This exercise describes a technique that you can use to determine precipitation. It also suggests some studies of precipitation as an abiotic factor.

Materials

a) rain gauges (Fig. 3-18)

b) boards, $2'' \times 2'' \times 3'$

c) light mineral oil

Fig. 3-18
A standard rain gauge.

Procedure

a) Mount a rain gauge on one end of each of the boards.

b) Add a few drops of mineral oil to the collecting tube of each gauge. This oil will float on any water that collects in the tube, preventing its evaporation.

c) Select a large open area, away from obstructions like trees and buildings. Place 4 or 5 of the rain gauges throughout the area.

d) Note the accumulated water after each rainfall. The average for the 4 or 5 gauges is the control against which you can compare measurements from other areas.

e) At the same time that you place gauges in the open area, place some under coniferous trees and some under deciduous trees. Some of the gauges could be placed close to the trunks of trees, others at the edges of the downward projections of the crowns, and still others in between these two extremes. Again, take readings after every rainfall.

f) Note the soil conditions and the characteristics of the vegetation every time you visit the gauges.

g) Determine the direction of the prevailing winds in your locality. (See Section 3.10.)

Discussion

a) Describe and account for any differences in precipitation that you observe among the various areas.

b) Compare the findings in your control area with those reported by the official weather agency in your area. (Consult the newspaper or weather office for daily and seasonal records.)

c) Describe and account for any effects that precipitation appears to have on soil conditions and vegetation characteristics.

d) Predict other sites where variations in precipitation might occur. Set out rain gauges to check your predictions.

3.14 EFFECTS OF MOISTURE ON PLANT GROWTH

Too little water can affect the growth of many plant species. Too much water can also harm some plants. This investigation looks into the effects of too much or too little water on several species of plants.

Materials
a) 3 sets of potted plants of various plant species
b) trays
c) balance
d) centimeter ruler
e) bucket
f) knife or scissors
g) drying oven
h) crucibles or similar containers
i) plastic bags and ties (optional)

Procedure
a) Obtain 3 sets of equally developed plants. The same species should be represented in each of the sets.
b) Put one set of plants in a tray containing 5 to 10 cm of water. The soil should become saturated with water.
c) Beside this tray, set up the second set of pots. Water all of these plants on a normal schedule.
d) Place the third set in the same growing conditions, but water the plants only intermittently and lightly. Wait until they begin to wilt before you water them.
e) Grow the plants for a week or two under these conditions.
f) Working with one species at a time, carefully invert the pots, tap the bottom, and remove the soil.
g) Scoop or scrape 50 to 100 gm of the bottom soil from each pot into a weighed crucible or similar container.
h) Weigh the container and this small amount of soil.
i) Place the container and soil in an oven at 105°C for 48 to 72 hours. Find the dry weight of the container and soil.
j) Calculate the percent water content:

$$\frac{\text{total wet weight} - \text{total dry weight}}{\text{total dry weight} - \text{container weight}} \times 100$$

k) Fill a bucket with water. Carefully separate the soil from the roots of each plant by gently agitating the roots in the water. Do not pour the muddy water into the sink nor wash the roots in the sink!

l) For each species, measure the height of the upper growth and the greatest root length for each of the three growing conditions. Enter the information in a data sheet similar to Table 4.

TABLE 4

Species	Upper growth						Root growth					
	Length			Wet weight			Length			Wet weight		
	wet	normal	dry	wet	normal	dry	wet	normal	dry	wet	normal	dry

m) Cut up the root material. Determine the total root weight for the members of each species growing under the three conditions.

n) Do the same for the upper growth. Enter all measurements in your data sheet.

o) (Optional) Do percent water content analyses on each species for both root and upper growth using the material just weighed above. This can be done by using the same procedure as you used for the soil. (Note: you can store the plant material in sealed plastic bags in the refrigerator if time is not available to complete all of the work on a single day. Label all plant samples carefully.) See also Section 3.16.

Discussion

a) What do the percent water content determinations for the soil tell you about availability of minerals in the soil; availability of water for transpiration; and aeration of the root cells?

b) Do some species seem to be more tolerant than others of the saturated or low water content conditions? Why?

3.15 EFFECTS OF ABIOTIC FACTORS ON TRANSPIRATION RATE

A *potometer* is an instrument which measures transpiration rates of plants. Although many variations of the potometer apparatus exist, the one used in this investigation can be easily assembled using standard laboratory materials.

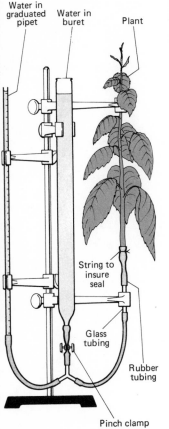

Fig. 3-19
Measuring transpiration rate.

Materials

a) a small branch from a woody-stemmed plant, possessing many leaves

b) ring stand, clamps, graduated pipet, buret, T-tube, glass tubing, and rubber tubing as shown in Figure 3-19

c) razor blade or sharp knife

d) string

e) stopwatch or watch with second hand

Procedure

a) Set up the apparatus as shown in Figure 3-19.

b) With the clamp pinched off, fill the buret with tap water.

c) Open up the clamp slightly until water flows over the top of the rubber tubing into which the plant will later be inserted.

d) Take a freshly cut branch. Hold the end under water and make a sharp-angled cut across the end.

e) Keep a drop of water on the tip at all times. Insert the end into the rubber tubing. (Air bubbles will otherwise clog the conducting tissues in the plant.)

f) Clamp the plant gently into position. If necessary, tie a string around the rubber tubing just tightly enough to prevent leaks.

g) Release the pinch clamp to fill the pipet. Then close the pinch clamp.

h) Record the pipet reading. After 5 minutes, record the water level again.

i) Calculate the transpiration rate in ml per minute.

j) Repeat the experiment for at least one more 5-minute reading and average the results. If the rates do not correspond closely, keep repeating the experiment until the rate becomes constant. Use the last two readings.

k)   When the level of water gets low in the pipet, release the pinch clamp to refill the pipet. Close the pinch clamp and continue taking recordings.

l)   Determine the relationship between transpiration rate and various abiotic factors by placing the apparatus in a variety of conditions such as different relative humidities, different air temperatures, various light intensities, and various wind velocities (created by an electric fan placed at various distances).

m)   Remove some of the leaves, a few at a time. Recalculate the transpiration rate each time.

n)   Remove all leaves and recalculate the transpiration rate. Note: The apparatus can be left overnight by placing a plastic bag over the branch and leaving the pinch clamp open. Why put a plastic bag over the apparatus?

Discussion

a)   What conditions tend to increase the transpiration rate and therefore the water requirements of the plant tested? Why?

b)   From your results, is it possible to determine the transpiration rate per square cm of leaf surface area?

c)   What types of adaptations have plants developed to prevent excessive water loss?

3.16   WATER CONTENT OF PLANT TISSUES

Water makes up a large percentage of the weight of a plant or animal. Some examples in animals of the percentage of water are 59% in flour beetles, 65% in mammals, 80% in earthworms, and 95% in jellyfish. These percentages reflect the degree to which these animals are dependent on water. Ultimately, every animal will perish without adequate water. But it is quite obvious that the jellyfish cannot tolerate water shortages as well as a flour beetle. Although it is only a rule of thumb, percent water content is a measure of *water dependence,* which may be useful in ecology studies.

In the following exercise, the percent water content is determined for a number of plants and plant parts to get an estimate of water dependence. The types of plant tissues you collect in the field will determine what comparisons you can make. Some things to consider collecting are leaves from plants of the same species growing in different habitats; leaves from plants of different species growing in the same habitat; leaves of the same species shaded and exposed to sunlight; leaves of evergreens and of deciduous trees; woody stems and herbaceous stems; various plant tissues from the same plant such as roots, stems, leaves, fruits, and seeds.

Materials

a) pruning shears or a sharp knife

b) plastic sandwich bags and ties

c) labels

d) drying oven

e) balance

f) watch glasses, petri dishes, or other containers suitable for drying

---

Procedure

a) Clip samples of about 100 gm in the field for each type of plant tissue for which a percent water content measurement is to be made.

b) Place the leaves or clippings in plastic sandwich bags with a label describing the date, sample number, plant species, plant tissue, and habitat type.

c) Tie the top of the bag to prevent drying on the return trip to the lab.

d) Make a chart with the following headings: sample number, plant species, plant tissue, habitat type, sample weight before drying, sample weight after drying and percent water content.

e) Weigh the containers in which the plant samples are to be dried.

f) Weigh the containers again with about 40–60 gm of the sample. Calculate and record the weight of the sample alone.

g) Place the container and sample in an oven at 105°C.

h) Reweigh at 24 and 48 hours and at each successive 24-hour interval until a constant dry weight is reached.

i) Record the sample weight after drying.

j) Calculate the percent water content and record the value.

Discussion

a) Account for the variations in percent water content of the different plants tested.

b) Do plants living in moist habitats have greater or lesser percent water contents than those in dry habitats? Why?

c) What conclusions can be reached for any other comparisons you made in your studies?

d) Give reasons for differences seen in percent water content for the various parts of a single plant.

3.17 LIGHT INTENSITY

Few abiotic factors surpass light intensity in importance, since it plays a key role in determining the rate at which producers store energy for an ecosystem.

Within even a small community, light intensity can vary considerably from place to place. You should be able to notice corresponding changes in the vegetation. Plants that are constantly exposed to low light intensities should show adaptations to that environment. For example, they may have broad leaves to trap the little light that reaches them. Watch for such variations as you perform this study.

Materials

a) light meter with a scale that gives intensity (Fig. 3-20)

b) sheet of grey, non-glossy paper, preferably about 1 m × 1 m

c) strong cord

Procedure

a) To measure directly the intensity of the light striking a surface, set the light meter on the surface with the window pointing directly upward. This method can, on occasion, give erroneous results. For example, a small beam of sunlight filtering through the leaf canopy of a tree could strike the meter and cause a high reading that is not representative of the immediate surroundings.

b) If you do not require a direct measurement but only wish to compare light intensities in various areas, you

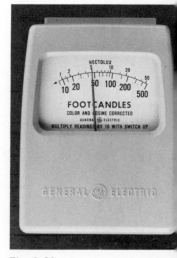

Fig. 3-20
A light meter suitable for intensity studies.

can reduce the chances of error as follows: Place the sheet of grey paper on the ground. Hold the light meter vertically above it at a distance of 1 meter and take a reading off the paper. Be sure that your shadow does not interfere with the reading.

c)   Select an area where the light intensity changes rapidly over a short distance. The ecotone between a grassy area and a woodlot is suitable. Lay out a line 50 meters long from the grassy area into the woodlot. At regular intervals along the line (for example, 5 meters) measure the light intensity using either or both of the methods described. Record your results.

d)   At each site examine the vegetation carefully, looking particularly for adaptations to the light conditions at that site. Shape, size, thickness, and arrangement of leaves are some factors that should be studied. Record your results in tabular form.

e)   Record also any evidence of the effects of light intensity on the distribution of animals in the area.

Discussion

a)   Why was grey paper chosen for this study? What particular disadvantages are offered by black, white, and green paper?

b)   Describe and account for your observations.

c)   Design and test a method for measuring light intensities in the various strata of a woodlot. For safety reasons, tree-climbing is not an acceptable method.

3.18   EFFECT OF LIGHT DIRECTION ON PLANT GROWTH

Microscopic examination of cross-sections of leaves usually reveals that the chloroplasts are found in greatest numbers close to the upper surface of the leaf. Thus the greatest amount of photosynthesis takes place there. This assumes, of course, that the leaves are properly oriented toward the sunlight. Can plants change the orientation of their leaves to get the maximum amount of sunlight hitting the upper surface? This experiment tests the ability of various plant species to orient toward a light source.

Materials

a) corn or oat seeds and a variety of other seeds

b) potting soil

c) flats or planting pots

d) aluminum foil

e) petroleum jelly

f) light source

g) copper wire

h) centimeter ruler

Procedure

a) Plant 4 – 5 corn or oat seeds in each of 4 or 5 small pots filled with sand. Be sure to plant the seeds close to the surface—about 0.5 cm deep.

b) Place the pots in a dark chamber. (Cover them with brown paper bags, if necessary, to help keep out all light.)

c) When the plants have grown to 3 or 4 cm in height, do steps d) to g).

d) Leave 3 seedlings untouched.

e) Make 3 small aluminum foil caps, each 1 cm long, to fit over the tops of 3 seedlings.

f) Make 3 aluminum foil caps 0.5 cm long and place them over a second set of 3 seedlings.

g) Cover 3 other seedlings with petroleum jelly.

h) Place all seedlings in a position where light is received from only one side of the plant.

i) Cut pieces of copper wire to serve as markers. Insert them beside the seedlings (on the lee side of the plant so as not to create a shadow). Their tops should point at and nearly touch the tip of the sprout.

j) After 24 hours, re-examine the plants. Note any increase in height and any lateral movement (bending) of the tip from its original position.

k) Average the results for each set of plants. Do not include measurements of diseased plants.

l) (Optional) Reposition the markers and repeat your measurements after another 24 or 48 hours.

m)   Repeat the entire investigation with two or more other species of plants.

Discussion

a)   Do the seedlings orient in some manner with respect to the light source?

b)   Does covering the tip of a seedling affect its growth? Account for your answer.

c)   Does covering the tip have any effect on orientation of the seedling?

d)   What was the purpose of covering 3 seedlings with petroleum jelly?

3.19 EFFECT OF LIGHT DURATION ON PLANT GROWTH

A plant flowers when it is exposed to a certain number of hours of light and darkness in a 24-hour period. This sequence of light and dark is called the plant *photoperiod*. Plants are called *long-day, short-day,* or *day-neutral,* according to the duration of light that makes them bloom. This investigation should indicate why different plants bloom at certain seasons of the year.

Materials

a)   4 short-day plants (chrysanthemum, soybean, poinsettia, aster, cosmos)

b)   4 long-day plants (radish, red clover, barley, oats)

c)   4 day-neutral plants (tomato, corn, cucumber)

d)   100-watt bulbs

e)   growing box

f)   thermometer

g)   black cloth

Procedure

a)   Grow or purchase 4 chrysanthemum plants, 4 red clover plants, and 4 tomato plants (or other plants of each type). Select species that are local to your area and use plants that are about 4 weeks old.

b) Place 2 of each of the 3 types of young plants in a growing box (a wooden box that will hold 6 plants and which admits light from the top only). Place the other 2 of each of the 3 types in a second growing box.

c) Expose each group of 6 plants to similar soil, moisture, temperature, and other physical factors. Only the duration of light exposure is to be varied.

d) Expose one group to 8 hours of daylight and 16 hours of darkness. Cover the growing box with the black cloth during the dark period so no light can enter.

e) Expose the second group of plants to 16 hours of light and 8 hours of darkness. The first 8 hours of light should be daylight (the same as group one), while the remaining 8 hours of light should be provided by 100-watt light bulbs.

f) Continue the light-dark cycle until the plants have flowered or shown indications that they will not flower.

Discussion

a) Summarize in chart form the effects of different photoperiods on *long-day, short-day*, and *day-neutral* plants.

b) Suggest why the photoperiod of a plant might be an important consideration for a greenhouse owner.

c) Why is the latitude an important factor to be considered if one is trying to determine which species of plants will grow in a certain area?

d) How can farmers use a knowledge of photoperiodism to improve their crops?

e) How could the nightly exposure of plants to artificial lights in cities make the plants more vulnerable to winter frost?

3.20 LIGHT PHOTOPERIOD: EFFECT ON ANIMALS

The daily and seasonal movements of the sun have profound effects on the patterns of activity in animals. Even under artificial light, many animals time their actions according to the duration of light to which they are exposed. In this investigation, we study this *biological clock* of animals using an insect, the fruit fly *Drosophila*.

Materials

a) *Drosophila* culture bottles with medium
b) *Drosophila* larvae and pupae
c) a dark room (or light-proof containers)
d) graph paper
e) incandescent light
f) thermometer

Procedure

a) Establish a colony of fruit flies. Expose the culture to a definite cycle of 8 – 10 hours of light followed by 14 – 16 hours of darkness. Keep the temperature at 20 – 22°C. Allow a few days for the fruit flies to develop a rhythm of pupal emergence.

b) For the next few days, study the colony closely every 3 hours until you have found the daily pattern of emergence. Plot the number of flies which emerge in each 3-hour interval on a histogram.

c) Leave some flies in the colony on the original light-dark cycle as a control group. Expose the remaining flies to a continuous dim light. Leave the colony untouched for 2 days. Then study the pattern of emergence every 3 hours for the next 2 or 3 days. Plot your results on a histogram.

d) Allow adult fruit flies to lay eggs in continuous darkness. Maintain this colony in darkness for a few days to allow larvae to hatch. Now, for the next 3 days, expose the larvae to 2-minute periods of bright light during each 24-hour period of darkness. Again, study the pattern of emergence every 3 hours for the next 2 or 3 days. Plot your results on a histogram.

e) Expose the original control group to a different photoperiod and determine the effects that the change has on the pattern of emergence.

Discussion

a) Summarize the effects that the photoperiod appears to have on fruit fly behavior patterns.

b)   Many species of animals tend to maintain their original pattern of activity even when exposed to continuous dim light. Others quickly lose the old rhythm. Describe the effect of continuous dim light on the fruit fly population. Does this mean that the rhythm is inborn or that it is caused by environmental stimuli? Explain.

c)   Account for the pattern of emergence which resulted when fruit flies in complete darkness were exposed to brief periods of light. What does this indicate about the influence of light on rhythm patterns in fruit flies?

d)   How do different periods of light and darkness influence migration in birds?

e)   Most plants and animals set their activity patterns in time with the rhythm of the annual light cycle. Discuss a few ecological problems which might occur if organisms did not synchronize their activities to the same biological clock.

f)   If you were isolated from the outside world, without any idea of time, how long would you continue your present activity cycle? Why is this important in space travel?

3.21   RESPONSE OF ANIMALS TO LIGHT INTENSITY

In this investigation animals are offered a choice between light and dark conditions. You are to determine the preferences of various animals. You should be able to relate your findings to the light conditions present in the natural habitats of the animals.

Materials

a)   at least 10 large petri dishes

b)   black paper

c)   several 25-watt bulbs

d)   10 specimens of each of several types of arthropods (for example, sow bugs, fruit flies, houseflies, millipedes, centipedes, flour beetles, small spiders, ants)

Procedure

a)   Cover half of the lid of each petri dish with black paper as shown in Figure 3-21.

Fig. 3-21
Determining the light intensity preferences of various arthropods.

b)   Mount a 25-watt bulb about 25 cm above each dish.

c)   Place 10 sow bugs in one dish, 10 spiders (same species) in another, 10 millipedes (same species) in another, and so on. Set up at least 10 petri dishes, each containing a different species of arthropod.

d)   Allow the dishes to remain undisturbed for 5 minutes. Then count the number of individuals in the uncovered portion of each dish at 1-minute intervals for 10 minutes.

e)   Turn the lid through 180° so that the portion of the dish previously lit is now dark. Wait 5 minutes and again count the number of individuals in the uncovered portion of each dish at 1-minute intervals for 10 minutes.

f)   Combine your results with those of other groups. Then calculate the percentage of each arthropod found in the light portion of the dish. Enter your calculations in a table with the following column heads: Arthropod; Percent in light area; Natural habitat.

Discussion

a)   Account for the results summarized in your table.

b)   What other variables could affect the distribution of the arthropods in the dishes? Explain.

c)   If larger containers such as laboratory trays are used, your results will generally be more reliable. Larger containers will also permit you to study the responses of larger animals such as earthworms, crayfish, and gerbils.

d)   Instead of offering the animals a choice of a light or a dark environment, you can give them several light intensities to choose from. Use a glass tube at least 26

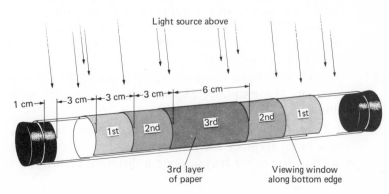

Fig. 3-22
A method of offering arthropods four choices of light intensity.

cm long and 2 cm in diameter. Cut strips of paper 0.5 cm less in width than the circumference of the tube. Then, when the paper is taped to the tube, a "window" 0.5 cm wide will be present on the bottom. The first strip is 18 cm long, the second 12 cm, the third 6 cm. When taped as shown in Figure 3-22, the darkest area will be in the center. Place 10 individuals of the same species in the tube. Wait 5 minutes and then count the number in each light zone.

3.22 RESPONSE OF ANIMALS TO LIGHT QUALITY

Do animals prefer a particular color of light?

Materials

a) at least 5 rectangular trays (laboratory trays 40 cm × 25 cm × 5 cm are desirable)

b) at least 5 daylight lamps (optional)

c) black paper

d) 30 or more specimens each, of at least 5 types of arthropods (for example, sow bugs, fruit flies, houseflies, millipedes, centipedes, flour beetles, ants)

e) filters of several colors (preferably the gelatine type used by photographers)

Procedure

a) Cover the base and sides of each tray with black paper.

b) Place strips of colored filters across the top of each tray as shown in Figure 3-23. Use a light meter or the known exposure factors for the filters to determine the relative intensity of the light that passes through each of the filters. Add extra layers where necessary to make all filters transmit light of the same intensity. Why is this necessary?

c) Mount a daylight lamp the same distance above each tray or, alternatively, expose each tray to the same intensity of daylight.

d) Lift a filter at one end of a tray and insert 30 or more sow bugs. Replace the filter. Repeat this procedure for each of the other trays, using a different arthropod in each case.

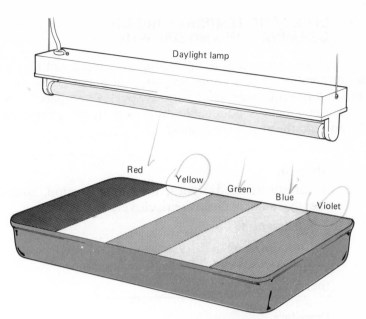

Fig. 3-23
Determining the color of light preferred by organisms.

Daylight lamp

Red Yellow Green Blue Violet

e) Wait at least 10 minutes for the arthropods to distribute themselves.

f) Count the number of arthropods in the different regions of each tray. Tabulate your results.

g) Combine your results with those of other groups.

Discussion

a) What color of light, if any, is preferred by each of the arthropods?

b) Do those arthropods showing a preference for a particular color show this same preference in their natural environments? Why?

3.23 THE SOIL FACTOR

Most of your field studies should involve the consideration of soil factors. Foremost among these are moisture content, water-holding capacity, percolation rate, capillarity, pore space, organic content, pH, temperature, the main minerals—nitrogen, phosphorus, potassium, and calcium—and the nature of the soil profile.

Consult *A Guide to the Study of Soil Ecology* by W. A. Andrews et al., Prentice-Hall, 1973, for the significance of these factors and for the techniques used in investigating them.

3.24 EFFECT OF TEMPERATURE ON GERMINATION AND GROWTH

You probably know that temperature is an important factor in the germination of seeds and the growth of plants. How do the temperature requirements of various species compare? Will a few degrees make a noticeable difference in the germination of seeds and the growth of plants?

Materials

a) a variety of seeds (corn, lima bean, melon, squash, radish, spinach, pea, wheat, clover)
b) 2 flats (planting boxes)
c) potting soil
d) centimeter ruler
e) thermometers

Procedure

a) Prepare 2 flats so they contain soil of the same type, depth, compactness, texture, and moisture content.

b) Plant identical sets of the various seeds in each flat. Use the same layout of rows, same planting depth, same spacing of seeds, and so on. Plant at least 5 seeds for each species.

c) Expose both flats to identical light conditions and water them, when necessary, with the same amount of water.

d) The only abiotic factor that is not to be kept identical is the temperature. Keep one flat at a relatively cool temperature—15° to 20°C. Keep the other one at a relatively warm temperature—25° to 30°C. Thermostatically-controlled soil heating coils are available. Or, the flats can be heated from beneath by 2 or 3 light bulbs. You should make sure you can maintain the desired soil temperatures before you do any planting. In warm weather you may have to place one flat on a cool basement floor to attain the lower temperature.

e) Check the flats at 24-hour intervals for 2 or 3 weeks. Note *for each species* the following: the percentage of seeds that germinated; the average time required for germination; the average heights of the plants. Record your data for each flat in a separate data table.

Discussion

By comparing the results in the two flats, draw conclusions regarding the effects of temperature on germination and growth for the various species studied.

3.25   TEMPERATURE AND ANIMAL RESPONSE

In this investigation several species of arthropods are exposed to a wide range of temperatures in a closed container. You are to observe and interpret the behavioral responses of the arthropods to the temperature gradient.

Materials

a)   brass plate about 60 cm × 6 cm × 3 cm

b)   glass container about 50 cm × 6 cm × 5 cm

c)   hot plate

d)   cold packs (or ice)

e)   thermometer

f)   20 or more arthropods each, of several species (sow bugs, ants, mealworms, flour beetles)

Procedure

a)   Draw parallel lines 2 cm apart across the brass plate. Number the lines. Drill a hole on each line. The holes should be 2 cm from the same edge and 2 cm deep. Make them slightly larger in diameter than the thermometer bulb. Put 2 or 3 drops of odorless mineral oil in each hole.

b)   Construct the glass container using sheets of glass and epoxy glue.

c)   Assemble the materials as shown in Figure 3-24. The cold packs should be at 0°C or colder and the hot plate at about 40°C.

d)   Allow at least 15 minutes for a temperature gradient to be established in the brass plate.

e)   Adjust the temperature control on the hot plate until the temperature ranges from about 15°C at the cold end to 40°C at the warm end.

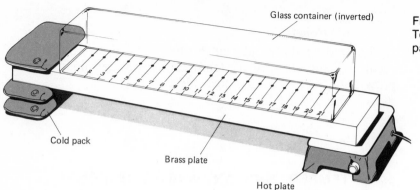

Fig. 3-24
Temperature gradient apparatus.

f) Remove the glass container and measure the temperature at each of the lines by inserting the thermometer bulb into the hole. Replace the glass container. Wait 10 minutes and repeat the temperature measurements to ensure that the gradient is steady.

g) Prepare a data table with column headings for the line number, temperature, and number of arthropods. Record the temperature at each line.

h) Place 20 or more arthropods of the same species under the glass container. Distribute them as evenly as possible along the brass plate.

i) Observe and record the behavioral responses of individuals that were placed in regions that were obviously too hot or too cold for them.

j) When at least 75% of the arthropods appear to have selected a preferred temperature region, count and record the number in each temperature region. For example, if 5 arthropods are closer to line 2 than they are to either line 1 or line 3, assign them to line 2 in your data table.

k) Repeat the investigation for several other species of arthropods.

l) Plot graphs with temperature on the horizontal axis and number of arthropods on the vertical axis.

Discussion

a) Use your results to explain what is meant by the terms *optimum temperature* and *temperature tolerance range*.

b) Account for the differences in behavioral response of the various arthropods tested.

c)   What role might temperature play in making it possible for a large number of arthropod species to inhabit the same locality? Could temperature affect interspecific competition in any way? Explain.

d)   How do insects survive the winter?

3.26   INTRODUCTION TO NUTRIENTS AND PLANT GROWTH STUDIES

Plant tissue is made up of a wide variety of basic elements. The three most abundant—carbon, oxygen, and hydrogen—are supplied by the carbon dioxide of the air and water from the soil. All of the other elements basic to plant growth are divided into two groups. The first group consists of seven elements called the *essential elements* because of their relatively large use in most plants. The second group consists of a host of *trace elements* which, although important, are required only in very small amounts.

As a result of the practical needs of gardeners and farmers, nutrient solutions have been devised to supply plants with all of their basic mineral requirements. By altering these solutions and omitting certain elements from a plant's "diet," the relative importance of single elements can be tested. If an element has any importance at all, stunted growth will likely result from its absence.

The seven essential elements are nitrogen, phosphorus, potassium, sulfur, calcium, magnesium, and iron. Some of the trace elements are boron, copper, zinc, and manganese. These various elements can be "fed" to plants by dissolving certain soluble salts in distilled water and letting the roots absorb the prepared brew. This practice has been carried out in gardening for many years. It has long been recognized, for example, that soils may become depleted of certain elements. These elements are wisely replaced by the knowledgeable gardener. Other soil factors such as the acidity can also be controlled through the addition of chemicals. Manipulation of the soil's chemistry by agriculturalists has been a major reason for the present food bounty in North America.

The following instructions outline the ingredients for making a commonly used nutrient solution.

Materials

a)   potassium chloride, KCl

b)   primary potassium phosphate, KH_2PO_4

c)   magnesium sulfate, $MgSO_4 \cdot 7H_2O$

d)   calcium nitrate, $Ca(NO_3)_2 \cdot 4H_2O$

e)   iron(III) tartrate, $Fe_2(C_4H_4O_6)_3$

f)   6 one-liter flasks

g)   6 clean rubber stoppers

h)   balance

i)   distilled water

j)   graduated cylinder (1 liter or more)

k)   glass marking pencil

l)   (optional) $MnCl_2$, $ZnCl_2$, $CuCl_2$, H_3BO_3 and an additional 1-liter flask

Procedure

a)   Clean all glassware and stoppers. Rinse them with distilled water.

b)   Measure out the following amounts of each compound: 6.0 gm of KCl; 6.0 gm of KH_2PO_4; 9.0 gm of $MgSO_4 \cdot 7H_2O$; 10.0 gm of $Ca(NO_3)_2 \cdot 4H_2O$; 0.6 gm of $Fe_2(C_4H_4O_6)_3$

c)   Add 1 liter of distilled water to each of 5 flasks.

d)   Add one of the compounds to each flask. Label each flask as to the type of solution present.

e)   Stopper each flask and shake it to dissolve the salt.

f)   Measure out 50 ml of each stock solution of the salts. Mix these together in another 1-liter flask.

g)   Add 750 ml of distilled water to make 1 liter of the nutrient solution. Label the flask.

h)   (Optional but recommended) Trace elements are sometimes available in sufficient quantity in the seed or as impurities in the salts. You can be sure they are present in sufficient quantity. Mix the following in an additional 1-liter flask: 0.10 gm $MnCl_2$; 0.05 gm $ZnCl_2$; 0.01 gm $CuCl_2$; 0.05 gm H_3BO_3; 1 liter of distilled water. Add 10 ml of this solution to 1 liter of the nutrient solution in step g).

Discussion

a)   Which of the seven essential elements did each salt listed in b) contribute to the nutrient solution?

b)   What trace elements were contributed by each of the substances listed in h)?

3.27 NUTRIENT DEFICIENCY TEST: NITROGEN

In this investigation and the next, one common procedure for mixing solutions, growing plants, and making measurements is used. Therefore, the deficiency test for nitrogen is dealt with in detail, where only the variations that exist in the later tests are covered in detail.

Materials

a) stock solutions prepared in Section 3.26
b) seeds of tomato, wheat, corn, barley, or oats
c) calcium sulfate, $CaSO_4 \cdot 2H_2O$
d) 2 one-liter flasks and clean stoppers
e) balance
f) distilled water
g) 3 – 4 petri dishes
h) blotting paper
i) glass marking pencil
j) a commercial fungicide (optional)
k) 3 large beakers or clean clay pots
l) washed quartz sand

Procedure

a) (Optional) Soak several dozen seeds in a commercial fungicide to prevent fungal infections.

b) Germinate several dozen seeds in petri dishes containing blotting paper moistened with distilled water.

c) Prepare a new stock solution with the following ingredients: 1.8 gm of calcium sulfate ($CaSO_4 \cdot 2H_2O$) in 1 liter of distilled water.

d) Stopper the flask and label it. Shake and give the salt time to dissolve.

e) Prepare a *modified* nutrient solution (lacking nitrogen) using the following ingredients: 50 ml KCl stock solution; 50 ml KH_2PO_4 stock solution; 50 ml $MgSO_4 \cdot 7H_2O$ stock solution; 200 ml $CaSO_4 \cdot 2H_2O$ stock solution; 50 ml iron(III) tartrate stock solution; 10 ml of trace elements stock solution; 590 ml of distilled water.

f) Fill 3 large beakers or clean clay pots with washed quartz sand. Carefully transplant 4 seedlings, all of approximately the same development, into each of the containers.

g)   Pour a measured quantity of distilled water into one pot to moisten the soil thoroughly. Label this pot "distilled water." Pour an equal amount of complete nutrient solution into the second pot and label it. Pour an equal amount of modified nutrient solution (in this case, lacking nitrogen) into the third pot. Label it.

h)   Place the plants in a proper growth chamber. Check the plants every 24 hours. Add *distilled* water to maintain adequate soil moisture in all containers. Add 20 – 30 ml of the nutrient solutions to the respective test plants every 3 – 4 days.

i)   Continue the experiment for 4 – 8 weeks. Record each day the average height of the plants in each culture and total water transpired during the experiment for each culture (keep daily records of water added).

j)   At the end of the experiment carry out the measurements listed in Table 4, Section 3.14, page 116.

Discussion

a)   Use your observations and measurements to describe the effects of the absence of nitrogen on the growth of the plants.

b)   Are there any other ways that nitrogen can enter plants? Do plants obtain nitrogen from the air?

3.28   ADDITIONAL NUTRIENT DEFICIENCY TESTS

This investigation follows the method outlined in Section 3.27. Carry out measurements, calculations, and a discussion similar to the ones there.

A.   PHOSPHORUS

Phosphorus is eliminated by replacing the KH_2PO_4 stock solution with KCl solution.

Materials

As in Section 3.27, except that KH_2PO_4 and $CaSO_4 \cdot 2H_2O$ stock solutions are not required

Procedure

a) Repeat the procedure outlined in Section 3.27, except that when preparing the modified nutrient solution, use the following ingredients: 77 ml KCl stock solution; 50 ml $MgSO_4 \cdot 7H_2O$ stock solution; 50 ml $Ca(NO_3)_2 \cdot 4H_2O$ stock solution; 50 ml $Fe_2(C_4H_4O_6)_3$ stock solution; 10 ml trace elements stock solution; 763 ml distilled water.

b) Make observations and measurements as outlined in Section 3.27.

Discussion

Summarize and account for the effects of phosphorus deficiency on the plants.

B. POTASSIUM

Potassium is eliminated by altering the two solutions which contained it in the original complete nutrient recipe. The KCl stock solution is replaced by a NaCl solution, and KH_2PO_4 stock solution is replaced by $NaH_2PO_4 \cdot H_2O$ solution.

Materials

a) stock solutions prepared in Section 3.26, except for KCl and KH_2PO_4

b) equipment listed in Section 3.27

c) sodium chloride, NaCl

d) primary sodium phosphate, $NaH_2PO_4 \cdot H_2O$

e) 2 one-liter flasks and clean stoppers

Procedure

a) Make two new stock solutions using the following ingredients: 4.7 gm NaCl and 1 liter of distilled water; 6.1 gm $NaH_2PO_4 \cdot H_2O$ and 1 liter of distilled water.

b) Repeat the procedure outlined in Section 3.27, except that when preparing the modified nutrient solution, use the following ingredients: 50 ml NaCl stock solution; 50 ml $NaH_2PO_4 \cdot H_2O$ stock solution; 50 ml $MgSO_4 \cdot 7H_2O$ stock solution; 50 ml $Ca(NO_3)_2 \cdot 4H_2O$ stock solution; 50 ml $Fe_2(C_4H_4O_6)_3$ stock solution; 10 ml trace elements stock solution; 740 ml distilled water.

C. MAGNESIUM

Magnesium is eliminated by replacing the $MgSO_4 \cdot 7H_2O$ stock solution with $Na_2SO_4 \cdot 7H_2O$ solution.

Materials

a) stock solutions except for $MgSO_4 \cdot 7H_2O$
b) equipment listed in Section 3.27
c) sodium sulfate, $Na_2SO_4 \cdot 7H_2O$
d) one-liter flask and clean stopper

Procedure

a) Make up a new stock solution using 9.8 gm of $Na_2SO_4 \cdot 7H_2O$ and 1 liter of distilled water.
b) Repeat the procedure outlined in Section 3.27, except that when preparing the modified nutrient solution, use the following ingredients: 50 ml KCl stock solution; 50 ml KH_2PO_4 stock solution; 50 ml $Na_2SO_4 \cdot 7H_2O$ stock solution; 50 ml $Ca(NO_3)_2 \cdot 4H_2O$ stock solution; 50 ml $Fe_2(C_4H_4O_6)_3$ solution; 10 ml trace elements stock solution; 740 ml distilled water.

D. CALCIUM

Calcium is eliminated by replacing the $Ca(NO_3)_2 \cdot 4H_2O$ stock solution with $NaNO_3$ solution.

Materials

a) stock solutions, except for $Ca(NO_3)_2 \cdot 4H_2O$
b) equipment listed in Section 3.27
c) sodium nitrate, $NaNO_3$
d) one-liter flask and clean stopper

Procedure

a) Make up a new stock solution using 7.2 gm of $NaNO_3$ and 1 liter of distilled water.
b) Repeat the procedure outlined in Section 3.27, except that when preparing the modified nutrient solution, use the following ingredients: 50 ml KCl stock solution; 50 ml KH_2PO_4 stock solution; 50 ml $MgSO_4 \cdot 7H_2O$ stock solution; 50 ml $NaNO_3$ stock solution; 50 ml $Fe_2(C_4H_4O_6)_3$ solution; 10 ml trace elements stock solution; 740 ml distilled water.

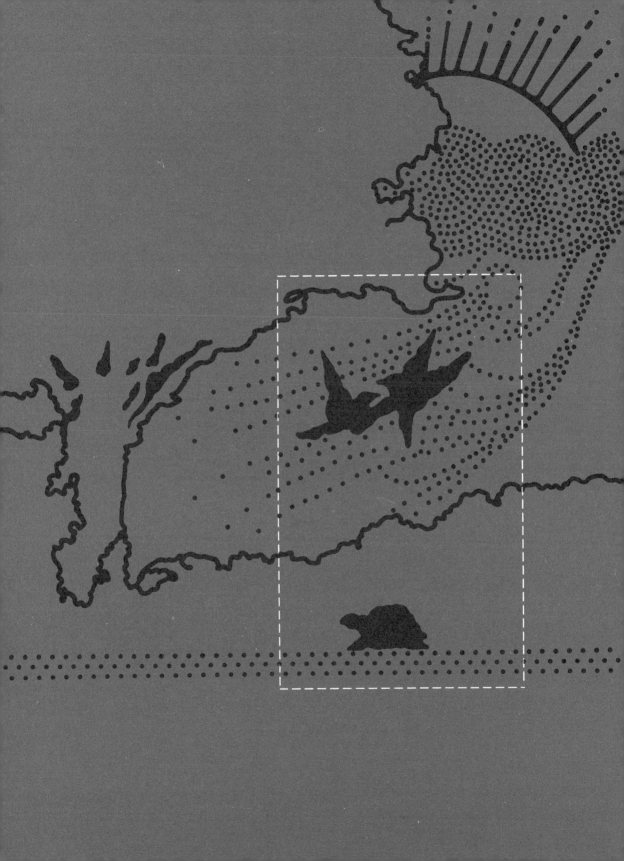

Field and Laboratory Studies: Biotic Factors

4

The studies in this unit deal with the many interesting ways in which the biotic components of terrestrial ecosystems interact with one another and with the abiotic components.

4.1 THE WOODLAND TERRARIUM

You can make a miniature woodland ecosystem by transferring some plants and animals from a woodlot to a container in which you have duplicated most of the physical environment of the woodlot. Close observation of this ecosystem for an extended period of time should reveal many interesting aspects of the ecology of the ground stratum of a woodlot.

Materials

a)   terrarium case (Fig. 4-1) or an aquarium or large jar

b)   gravel

c)   sand

d)   humus

e)   a compatible group of plants and animals

Procedure

a)   Place 2 or 3 cm of gravel in the bottom of the terrarium case to act as drainage material.

Fig. 4-1
A 5—10 gallon terrarium case is the best container for a small indoor terrestrial ecosystem.

b) Prepare a soil mixture consisting of 1 part sand to 3 parts humus. Place this mixture on top of the gravel to a depth of at least 5 cm. The terrarium will look more natural if the soil is deeper at the back of the case than it is at the front. Also, hills and hollows, stones, and pieces of wood increase the natural appearance.

c) Moisten the soil so that it clings together when squeezed but does not cake. A soil mixture that is too heavy or one that is poorly drained or poorly aerated will not support much plant life.

d) Visit a woodlot and collect a variety of plants that appear to require the same physical environment. For example, lichens, mosses, liverworts, ferns, and club mosses usually grow well together. Note the soil, light, and humidity conditions that the plants seem to prefer so that you can duplicate these conditions in your terrarium. Retain a clump of soil on the roots of each plant to lessen the shock of transplanting.

e) Moisten the roots of the plants and plant them in the terrarium. Place tall plants near the back and spreading plants near the center. (Leaves that touch the sides of the terrarium case usually die.) Avoid overcrowding. Carefully remove dead leaves and stems.

f) Small animals that inhabit the forest floor can be added to your woodland terrarium. Before doing this, research the life cycles, feeding habits, and physical needs of the animals you wish to use. Summarize this information in a booklet and leave it near the terrarium. Earthworms, snails, slugs, beetles, centipedes, millipedes, and other invertebrates are common inhabitants of the litter layer of the forest floor. If you transfer some of the litter (decaying leaves and wood) to your terrarium, the invertebrates will require no further care. Many small vertebrates will thrive in your terrarium if they are properly cared for. Small toads, tree frogs, and the common newt feed on mealworms and small insects. Woodland salamanders like the red-backed salamander and slimy salamander feed on earthworms and will even eat liver dangled on a string. Small garter and green snakes feed on mealworms and earthworms. Be sure to provide suitable cover and a small pan of water for the vertebrates.

g) For best results, place the terrarium in an area where the temperature remains within the range 18°–22°C (65°–72°F).

h)   Expose the terrarium to light conditions comparable to those of the forest floor from which the plants came. For example, the plants listed in d) will do well in a north window since they do not require direct sunlight.

i)   Spray the plants with a fine mist of water. Place the glass cover on the terrarium. Adjust its position from time to time until you achieve a relative humidity comparable to that of the natural environment. The cover should never fit tightly enough to prevent circulation of air.

j)   Water the plants and feed the animals when required. Observe the animals carefully. Note their preferred habitats and behavioral traits associated with feeding, movement, and other activities.

Discussion

a)   List the food chains that exist in the terrarium. Are they long or short? Why?

b)   Explain the behavior patterns that you observe.

c)   Which plants thrive best in your terrarium? What adaptations do they possess that make this possible?

d)   What changes would have to be made if you wished to make this terrarium a closed system (one with nothing but light and heat energy going in and out)?

4.2   THE DESERT TERRARIUM

Because desert ecosystems are, in general, simpler than most other ecosystems, a desert terrarium is easier to establish, maintain, and interpret than other terraria. Concentrate on the unique adaptations of desert plants and animals as you perform this exercise.

Materials

a)   terrarium case

b)   fiberglass screening

c)   coarse sand

d)   fine sand, preferably real desert sand

e)   wood and stones from a beach or desert

f)   several species of cacti

g)   2 or 3 desert animals

h)   100-watt bulb

Procedure

a)   Place 3 – 4 cm of coarse sand in the bottom of the terrarium case. Moisten this sand by sprinkling it lightly with water.

b)   Cover the coarse sand with 1 – 2 cm of fine desert sand. Do not moisten this layer.

c)   Add a few small stones and pieces of weathered wood to provide cover for animals and to increase the aesthetic value of the terrarium.

d)   Add a shallow pan of drinking water for the animals. Bury it so that the sand is level with its top edge.

e)   Moisten the roots of the cacti and plant them in a scenic arrangement. Lightly sprinkle the sand around each cactus with water.

f)   Add 2 or 3 desert animals. Horned toads, small desert snakes, and collared lizards thrive in a desert terrarium and require little care. Feed them live insects and mealworms. They will often eat raw liver and earthworms dangled on a string. Sprinkle the animals once a week with water if they appear not to be drinking.

g)   Cover the top of the terrarium case with fiberglass screening. Do not use the glass cover. The relative humidity must remain low in a desert terrarium.

h)   Place the terrarium in a bright area—either in direct sunlight or under one or more 100-watt bulbs.

i)   The best temperature range is 20° – 30°C (68° – 85°F). Close placement of the lamps will help maintain this temperature in cool weather.

j)   Water the sand around each cactus lightly about once a month.

Discussion

a)   What adaptations do the plants have which permit them to live under xerophytic conditions?

b)   What adaptations do the animals have which permit them to live under xerophytic conditions?

c)   Name two mammals which can live under xerophytic conditions for long periods of time. What unique adaptations or behavior do they display?

d)   Describe and account for any unique behavioral traits of the animals in the terrarium. Include habitat selection, feeding habits, response to your presence, and response to periods of light and dark.

e)   Could this terrarium be made into a closed ecosystem? Explain.

4.3   THE BOG TERRARIUM

A bog ecosystem has many interesting features. Its soil is acidic and contains low concentrations of many nutrients. Its atmosphere is cool and moist. It contains many unique plants, including fascinating insectivorous plants like the Venus' flytrap. If you carefully duplicate the natural conditions, you will find the bog ecosystem easy to maintain and interesting to study.

Materials

a)   terrarium case

b)   gravel

c)   coarse sand

d)   acid soil (from a bog)

e)   sphagnum moss or peat (partially decomposed sphagnum)

f)   bog plants (sundew, pitcher plant, Venus' flytrap, mosses, ferns, small cranberry and Labrador tea plants, seedlings of tamarack and black spruce)

g)   moisture-loving animals (toads, newts, frogs, salamanders)

h)   pond water or dechlorinated tap water with a pH of about 7

Procedure

a)   Arrange gravel in the bottom of the terrarium case so that it is 5 cm deep at one end and slopes to a depth of less than 1 cm at the other end.

b)   Cover the gravel with a 2-cm layer of coarse sand.

c)   Cover the sand with sphagnum moss (living or dead). Soak the sphagnum and pack it down. Continue to do so until a 5-cm layer covers the sand. Alternatively, you can use a 5-cm layer of soil mixture consisting of 1 part sphagnum and 2 parts acid soil.

d)   If bogs are common in your area, collect a few bog plants. Retain soil around the roots and put the plants in polyethylene bags to prevent dehydration. Do not collect orchids and other rare species. If bogs are uncommon in your area, purchase the plants from a biological supply house.

e)   Transplant the plants as quickly as you can to the terrarium. Pack sphagnum firmly around the roots of the plants. Be sure to plant them to the same depth at which they grow naturally. Venus' flytraps and pitcher plants should be planted deeply. The shallow-rooted sundew should have its roots placed just under the surface. Mosses can be used to hold dead sphagnum in place. Feed the insectivorous plants every 2 or 3 weeks. They will eat fruit flies. The larger ones will eat mealworms and small pieces of lean ground beef.

f)   Add 2 or 3 suitable animals (newts, toads, frogs, salamanders). Feed them as described in Section 4.1.

g)   Water the bog until the gravel layer contains 2 – 3 cm of water. Maintain this level. Siphon off the water every month or so and replace it with fresh water. Why? Test the pH of the water each week.

h)   Keep the glass cover on the terrarium, allowing a slight space for circulation of air.

i)   Place the terrarium where it will receive indirect sunlight and where the temperature is $18° - 22°C$ ($65° - 72°F$).

Discussion

a)   What unique adaptations do bog plants have in common?

b)   The insectivorous plants are photosynthetic. That is, they can make their own food. Why is it necessary for them to "eat" insects? (Hint: What are the characteristics of the soil?)

c)   Describe and account for the changes in the pH of the water over a one-month period.

d)   What is the main role played by sphagnum in a bog?

e)   How does a bog differ from a swamp or a marsh?

f)   Find out why most orchids will not survive if transplanted from a bog to a terrarium.

g)   Could this terrarium be made into a closed ecosystem? Explain.

4.4 VEGETATION ANALYSIS: THE QUADRAT METHOD

Many questions come to mind as we set out to study the importance of a particular species of plant in a community: How widely distributed is this species? How many plants of this species are present in the community? How much of the total available space does this species occupy? If you can answer these questions, you can conduct some interesting and important studies. For example, you can compare the vegetation in one region with that in another; you can study seasonal changes in vegetation within a given area; you can determine the relationships between plant populations and abiotic factors; you can investigate ecological succession.

If you require only a rough idea of the contribution of each plant species to a community, a qualitative study is often sufficient. For example, to estimate the abundance of each species you simply prepare a list of the species present and categorize each species as *abundant*, *frequent*, *occasional*, or *rare*. It is difficult, however, to remain objective when using such an approach. The observer may list a species as abundant because its height or color makes it quite easy to spot when, in actual fact, other less obvious species are more abundant. Thus, for precise work, quantitative methods must be used.

Very accurate quantitative information could be obtained if a team of observers went into the study area and identified, counted, and measured every plant. In large areas this would obviously be impractical, if not impossible. Besides, it is unnecessary, since ecologists have developed sampling techniques that give equally valid results in much shorter time periods. The most commonly used techniques are described in this section and the next three.

Although these studies yield interesting information on their own, they are best performed in conjunction with such things as animal population studies, soil studies, and measurement of the appropriate physical factors. The approach to use in such combined studies is outlined in Unit 5. The methods of vegetation analysis are described separately so that you can conveniently select and study the most suitable method to use on a field trip. Where possible, you should rehearse the method near the school before you go on an outing.

The quadrat method is one of the most widely used means of obtaining quantitative information about the composition and structure of plant communities. In principle, the

Fig. 4-2
A square quadrat frame can be made from four meter sticks.

method appears quite simple. You merely sample the study area at several sites using *quadrats* (plots of standard size). You then assume that these sample plots give a reliable picture of the vegetation over the total study area. This assumption is true only if you have picked the proper size and shape of quadrat and if you use a suitable number and arrangement of quadrats. The following description of the quadrat method considers these factors.

Shape of Quadrat

As the word "quadrat" implies, a square plot is often used in this method of vegetation analysis (Fig. 4-2). However, circular and rectangular plots are also used. The choice of shape depends largely on the nature of the vegetation being investigated. Circular plots generally give more valid results with low vegetation than will a similar number of square plots of the same area. Also, circular plots are easier to lay out. If small plots are required, a series of hoops can be tossed in random directions from a central point. Larger circular plots can be laid out as shown in Figure 4-3. Circular plots can be used effectively only in areas of low vegetation.

Fig. 4-3
Laying out a large circular plot. Markers are required in areas where the peg does not leave an easily identifiable scratch in the earth.

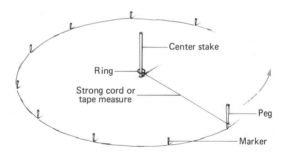

Center stake

Ring

Strong cord or tape measure

Peg

Marker

Square and rectangular plots can be used in vegetation of any height. Rectangular plots usually give more accurate results than an equal number of square plots of the same area. This is because rectangular plots sample a greater length of the vegetation and are, as a result, more likely to detect variations in it. Because of this, they are particularly useful in areas such as sand dunes where a gradient in environmental conditions and vegetation types occurs. In such cases the long axis of the plot should be oriented parallel to the direction of the gradient. Rectangular quadrats having a width-to-length ratio of 1:2, 1:4, and 1:8 are commonly used.

Small square and rectangular quadrats can be formed with meter sticks. Larger ones (suitable for studying shrubs and trees) can be marked out with four stakes and some rope. The first step in laying out such a quadrat is to form a right angle for one of the corners. You can do this by placing two stakes in the ground 9 meters apart. Then use tape measures to find a point that is 12 meters from one stake and 15 meters from the other. Drive in a third stake at this point. These three stakes form a right-angled triangle. By sighting over pairs of stakes you can determine the direction in which each side of the square or rectangle should proceed from that corner. (See the green arrows in Fig. 4-4.) Lay out a tape measure in each of these directions and drive in stakes to indicate the positions of the second and third corners of the quadrat. For example, if the quadrat is to be 2 m × 10 m, drive in a stake at the 2-m mark on one tape and at the 10-m mark on the other. The final corner of the quadrat can be located by running lines from the second and third corners that are equal in length to the original two sides (in our example, 2 m and 10 m). Drive in a fourth stake where these two lines intersect.

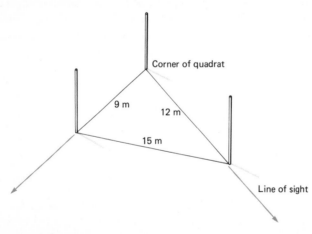

Fig. 4-4
Establishing a right angle for the corner of a square or rectangular quadrat.

Size of Quadrat

Both the height and the density of the plants in the study area should be considered when you are deciding what size quadrat to use. The quadrat must be large enough to contain a significant number of plants yet small enough to permit you to identify, count, and measure the plants in a reasonable length of time, without omissions or repetitions. In general, the following quadrat areas are satisfactory:

Mosses and lichens	0.1 square meter
Herbs (including grasses) and tree seedlings	1 square meter
Shrubs and saplings (up to 10 feet)	10 – 20 square meters
Trees	100 square meters

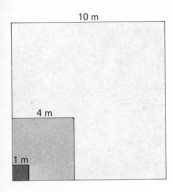

10 m

4 m

1 m

Fig. 4-5
Nested quadrats for sampling the vegetation in the main strata of a forest.

Therefore, if you are sampling the vegetation of a forest using square quadrats, you could use plots 10 m × 10 m for the trees, plots 4 m × 4 m for the shrubs and saplings, and plots 1 m × 1 m for grasses, other herbs, and tree seedlings. What dimensions would you use for the moss and lichen quadrat? You can reduce considerably the work involved in setting up the quadrats for a forest study by "nesting" them as shown in Figure 4-5. If you plan to use rectangular or circular plots you will have to do a little arithmetic to determine the length and width of the rectangle or the radius of the circle that will give you the desired area.

If you are sampling in an area where certain species of plants are quite abundant, you can save time by sampling those species with smaller quadrats. For example, in prairies or artificial grassland regions you can effectively sample the grasses with quadrats 10 cm × 10 cm instead of 1 m × 1 m. Rather than guess at the best size of quadrat to use, you can determine this experimentally by plotting a *species-area curve*. Your teacher has information on how to do this.

Number of Quadrats

The number of quadrats required to sample an area effectively can range from fewer than 10 for small areas to over 100 for large areas. Some ecologists suggest that your sample plots should make up about 10% of the total area being studied. You can often find out if you have used enough quadrats by walking through the area after sampling has been completed, looking for plant species that are abundant but missed by your sample plots.

You can determine more objectively when you have used enough quadrats by plotting a *species-area curve* as you proceed with your sampling. Again, your teacher can tell you how to do this.

Arrangement of Quadrats

a) **Random.** For your results to be statistically valid, the plots should be randomly located within the study area (Fig. 4-6). If you are working in an area of low vegetation, you can locate the plots randomly by closing your eyes, turning in a circle three or four times, and then throwing the quadrat. This procedure obviously will not work in a forest. Studies have shown that although this procedure is supposed to locate the quadrat randomly, human error often interferes. Apparently the thrower tends to toss the quadrat in the direction of species that have not been previously encircled.

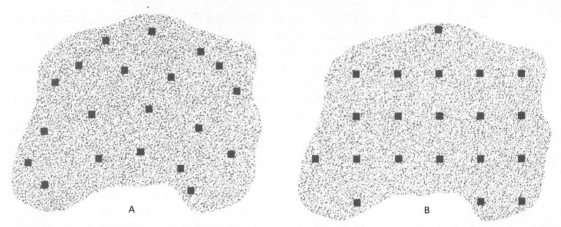

Fig. 4-6
Quadrats may be located randomly (A) or systematically (B).

You can avoid such human error quite easily. Lay out a series of grid lines on a map or aerial photograph of the study area. Number the grid lines on both the horizontal and vertical axes. Now record these numbers on small pieces of paper of identical size. Place the numbers for the vertical axis in one container and those for the horizontal axis in another. Mix each set of numbers thoroughly. With your eyes closed, draw a number from each container. These two numbers give the location of the first plot. Repeat this procedure until you have located the desired number of plots.

b) Systematic. Systematic sampling uses quadrats that are spaced as widely and evenly as possible through the study area. This can be accomplished satisfactorily by a combination of measurement and pacing. A series of evenly spaced transects are run through the study area using a compass. Then plots are located at equal intervals along these lines. Pacing off a predetermined distance is usually sufficient. You need not measure accurately the distance between each plot, provided you resist the temptation to shift the location of the plot a few feet one way or the other to include some feature that you find attractive.

Systematic location of plots is generally easier than random location. It is particularly useful when you are studying an area where successional changes occur.

Kinds of Quadrats

Once quadrats have been selected, various types of information can be sought within them. Quadrats are named according to the type of information sought and the uses to which it is put.

a) List quadrat. In this type of quadrat the plants within the frame are identified and listed by name. No count of numbers is made. If sufficient list quadrats are used over the study area, you can calculate the *frequency* of occurrence of each species, that is, the number of quadrats in which each species occurs.

b) Count quadrat. Here the *number* as well as the name of each species is noted. Information such as height and diameter is also commonly recorded. The count quadrat is widely used in woodlot surveys where the objective might be to determine the monetary value of the woodlot.

c) Cover quadrat. In ecological studies it is often desirable to know what percentage of the land surface in the study area is "covered" by a certain species. A cover quadrat study is performed to determine this.

d) Chart quadrat. A chart quadrat is a map to scale of the plot, showing the positions of the various plants. Although this is a very time-consuming thing to do, the chart quadrat is useful if you plan to conduct studies of the same area over a long period of time. Changes in vegetation patterns with time are best followed with the chart quadrat.

Materials

The materials required for a quadrat study depend on the shape, size, arrangement, and kind of quadrat to be used. In other words, your equipment list depends on the purpose of the study. Listed here are items commonly used in quadrat studies. Some are used only in forest studies, others only in meadow studies. From this list you can select the items required for your particular study.

a)   tree calipers

b)   diameter or basal area tapes (or conversion tables)

c)   measuring tapes

d)   string and pegs

e)   hammer

f)   identification guides

g)   data sheets

Procedure

a)   Define the purpose of the study. Then decide upon the shape, size, number, arrangement, and kind of quadrat.

b)   Make up a class rule regarding whether you include plants on the plot boundary as being in the plot. For example, you may decide to include in your plot any plant whose rooted base lies more than halfway inside the boundary.

c) Go to the study area and locate the quadrats. For large areas or when time is limited, this step is best performed by a small group in advance of the main field trip.

d) Identify the species within your quadrats and make any required measurements of the plants and their positions.

e) Record your results. A table similar to Table 5 can be used to record the results of most quadrat studies. For frequency studies, simply tick the appropriate box if the species is present. For count quadrats, place a tally mark in the appropriate box every time you see the species in a particular quadrat.

TABLE 5

Plant species	Quadrat number									
	1	2	3	4	5	6	7	8	9	10

f) Using the collected data, make the appropriate calculations.

Calculations

The data from a quadrat study can be used to calculate many factors of importance in ecological studies.

a) The **frequency** is the percentage of quadrats occupied by a given species. It is calculated with this formula:

$$\frac{\text{number of plots in which species occurs}}{\text{total number of plots}} \times 100$$

Thus, if 20 plots were used and oak trees were found in 5 of these, the frequency of occurrence of oak trees would be $\frac{5}{20} \times 100$, or 25%. In general, the higher the frequency, the more important the plant is in the community. A better idea of the importance of a species can be obtained by comparing the frequency of occurrence of that species with the frequency of occurrence of all of the species present. The result is called the *relative frequency*. It is calculated as follows:

$$\frac{\text{frequency of a species}}{\text{total frequency of all species}} \times 100$$

b) The **abundance** of a species compares the number of plants of that species with the total number of plants of all species in the study area. It is calculated with this formula:

$$\frac{\text{number of plants of a certain species}}{\text{total number of plants}} \times 100$$

Suppose that, during a study of trees in a woodlot, 550 white pines and a total of 2,500 trees of all types were counted in the quadrats. The abundance of white pine is $\frac{550}{2,500} \times 100$, or 22%.

Although a high frequency value means that the plant is widely distributed through the study area, the same is not necessarily true for a high abundance value. (Why is this so?) Thus abundance is not always an indicator of the importance of a plant in a community.

c) Density. Closely related to abundance but more useful in estimating the importance of a species is the density. It is defined as the number of plants of a certain species per unit area. It is calculated as follows:

$$\frac{\text{number of plants of a certain species}}{\text{total area sampled}}$$

If 25 quadrats, each 1 m² in area, were studied and a total of 125 dandelion plants were counted, then the density of dandelion plants would be $\frac{125}{25}$ or 5 per m². This means that, on the average, the study site contains 5 dandelion plants on every square meter of ground.

A better idea of the importance of a species can be obtained by calculating the *relative density:*

$$\frac{\text{density of a species}}{\text{total density for all species}} \times 100$$

d) Cover. In areas inhabited by both small plants like grasses and large plants like trees, frequency, abundance, and density values could suggest that the more numerous grasses are more important than the trees. Yet, because of their size, the trees probably determine the character of the community and are, as a result, more important than the grasses. Thus a further factor needs to be considered when the importance of a species is being calculated. This factor is the *cover*, the proportion of the total area occupied by the species. Since many ecologists use cover as a means of identifying the dominant species, it is also commonly called *dominance*. It is calculated with this formula:

$$\frac{\text{total area covered by a species}}{\text{total area sampled}}$$

If 35 quadrats, each 1 m² in area, were studied and sand grass covered a total of 7 m² within these quadrats, the cover of sand grass would be $\frac{7}{35}$ or $\frac{1}{5}$. This means that sand grass covers, on the average, $\frac{1}{5}$ of the total area.

Relative cover, like relative frequency and relative density, gives a better indication of the importance of a species than does the absolute value. It is calculated as follows:

$$\frac{\text{cover for a species}}{\text{total cover for all species}} \times 100$$

The method used to determine cover depends on the type of plant. If the plant is a circular one that hugs the ground, you simply measure its diameter and then use arithmetic to determine the area that it covers. If the plant is a tall herb or shrub, you can measure the diameter of its crown directly or you can measure the downward projection of the crown on the ground (the diameter of its shadow, if the sun were directly overhead). Again, you convert diameter to area. For trees, you obviously have to determine cover by using the downward projection of the crown. If you are studying *only* the trees of a forest, you can assume that the cross-section area (*basal area*) of the trunk gives as good a measurement of *relative* cover as would the downward projection of the crown. Much time will be saved if you do this. Foresters commonly measure the diameter of a tree trunk 4.5 feet from the ground. This value is called the *dbh* (diameter, breast height). *Tree calipers* measure *dbh* directly (Fig. 4-7). *Diameter tapes*, wrapped around a tree, give the diameter. Regardless of how you obtain the diameter, you convert it to area and use the area to calculate cover. Tapes are available that read basal areas directly. You merely wrap the *basal area tape* around a tree at the 4.5 foot level and read the basal area directly.

e) Importance value. Relative frequency, relative density, and relative dominance each indicate a different aspect of

Fig. 4-7
Tree calipers are used 4.5 feet from the ground to determine the *dbh*.

the importance of a species in a community. Therefore, the sum of these three values should give a good overall estimate of the importance of a species. This sum is called the *importance value*. You can summarize all of the calculations performed during a quadrat study in a table with column headings for species of plant, frequency, relative frequency, abundance, density, relative density, cover, relative cover, and importance value.

Discussion

There are many interesting quadrat studies you can do in and around the schoolyard. For example, you can compare the plant populations in trampled and untrampled areas of the lawn or football field. You can compare plant populations on north and south slopes of a hill in a park or greenbelt area. Farther afield, you can compare plant populations in grazed and ungrazed portions of the same meadow. You can determine the effects of cows on a woodlot by comparing the vegetation in an area to which cows have access with a nearby area from which they are excluded. Many other ideas for quadrat studies will come to mind as you examine potential study sites. Keep in mind that the most meaningful exercises are those which combine vegetation studies with other studies.

Regardless of the type of study you undertake, go into the field with carefully prepared data tables. With the data organized in tables, it will be easy for you to rank the plants according to importance value. Also, it will be easier for you to determine the reasons for the ranking.

4.5 VEGETATION ANALYSIS: THE LINE INTERCEPT (LINE TRANSECT) METHOD

The line intercept method differs from the quadrat method in that, instead of laying out plots, you run several lines through the plant community. You then identify, count, and measure the plants that intercept (touch, overlie, underlie) each line. Using the data obtained, you can calculate most of the same quantities as in a quadrat study. Density cannot be obtained by this method but relative density can. Frequency and abundance are not as reliable when obtained with this method. On the credit side, the line intercept method is usually more rapid and more objective. It is widely used in sampling non-forest vegetation like grasslands and low shrub areas. Although it has been used successfully in forests, other methods are generally easier to use and more accurate. (See Section 4.7.) This method is particularly useful in studying successional changes such as those which occur on sand dunes, from the flood plain of a river to the adjacent upland area, or from the margin of a pond to the surrounding forest. It is also useful for studying ecotone regions.

Materials

a) long tape measures (at least 20 m) or lengths of strong cord or rope

b) meter sticks or short tape measures

c) compass

d) identification guides

e) data sheets

Procedure

a) Define the purpose of the study.

b) Lay out a transect line. The length of the line depends upon the conditions. Usually a length of 20–30 m is sufficient. A shorter line will do if you are studying the transition from one small plant community to another. A line 200–300 m long might be required to study succession from a lake margin to the surrounding forest. If you wish to determine the direction of the line randomly, close your eyes, rotate two or three times, and toss a stick. Then lay out the line along the direction in which the stick points, beginning at a marked end of the stick. To adequately sample an area, 20–30 lines are usually sufficient. All lines should be of the same length.

If the purpose of the study is to investigate succession, the transect lines should run parallel to one another and to the direction of the environmental gradient. (Use a compass.) They should be spaced evenly throughout the study area.

A long measuring tape makes an effective transect line. However, strong cord or rope that is marked off in equal intervals of known length is a good substitute.

c) Consider the line to be a strip 1 cm wide along one side of the tape or cord.

d) To calculate frequency, divide the transect line into several intervals of equal length. Then record whether or not a species occurs in each of these intervals by using a table similar to Table 6.

TABLE 6

Species	Interval											
	1	2	3	4	5	6	7	8	9	10	11	12

BLE 7

Stratum Ground	Transect line #5
Species	Intercept length
Dn	1.7 cm
Hv	2.9 cm
Hv	2.5 cm
Th	5.5 cm
Dn	1.2 cm
St	15.5 cm
Ae	6.5 cm
Ae	7.0 cm

e) Now move along the transect line with a meter stick or short tape. For each plant that touches, overlies, or underlies the 1 cm strip, record the name and the distance along the line that is intercepted by the plant. It is usually best to study each stratum of vegetation separately. Study the ground stratum first so that it will not have been trampled by your movement through the area. The distance intercepted by the species in this stratum can be measured directly. For tall herbs, shrubs, and trees, the distance intercepted must be determined by measuring the downward projection of the crowns onto the strip.

Record all data as they are obtained. Thus your data sheet for a transect through the ground stratum might look like Table 7. The use of symbols for species names will speed up your work.

Calculations

a) Determine the number of intervals in which each species occurred, the total number of individuals of each species, and the total intercept length for each species. Enter your results in a table similar to Table 8.

TABLE 8

Species	Number of intervals containing species	Total number of individuals	Total intercept length

b) Using the information in Table 8, perform the following calculations:

$$\text{frequency} = \frac{\text{number of intervals containing the species}}{\text{total number of intervals}} \times 100$$

$$\text{relative frequency} = \frac{\text{frequency of a species}}{\text{total frequency of all species}} \times 100$$

$$\text{relative density} = \frac{\text{total number of individuals of a species}}{\text{total number of individuals of all species}} \times 100$$

$$\text{cover} = \frac{\text{total intercept length of a species}}{\text{total length of transect(s)}} \times 100$$

$$\text{relative cover} = \frac{\text{total intercept length of a species}}{\text{total intercept length of all species}} \times 100$$

importance value =
relative frequency + relative density + relative cover

c) Summarize the calculations in a table with column headings for species, frequency, relative frequency, relative density, cover, relative cover, and importance value.

Discussion

a) Consult Section 4.4 for the meanings of terms.

b) If you are working in dense vegetation, the counting and measuring of the plants can become quite tedious. In such a case you can study 5 m, skip 5 m, study the next 5 m, skip the next 5 m, and so on. You may shorten or lengthen the intervals to suit your particular situation but be sure to be consistent for all transects.

c) Interpret the results of your vegetation analysis in the light of any measurements of abiotic factors that were made. (See Unit 5 for more details.) Graphs of various abiotic factors vs. distance, compared with graphs of the frequency of occurrence of the plant species vs. distance, are helpful where successional changes occur.

d) Would importance values be of more use to a person studying a site where a vegetation gradient occurs or where the vegetation is relatively uniform? Explain.

e) What relationships exist between vegetation patterns and soil conditions?

f)   What relationships exist between vegetation patterns and animal populations?

VEGETATION ANALYSIS: THE BELT TRANSECT METHOD

A belt transect is a long, narrow, rectangular plot that is divided into regular blocks for the purpose of studying the vegetation and its associated biotic and abiotic factors. It is, in effect, an elongated quadrat. Thus the belt transect method has most of the advantages of the quadrat method. Since the length far exceeds the width, a belt transect also has most of the advantages of the line intercept method. It can be used to study changes in vegetation from one point to another.

This method is widely used to study the vegetation changes that occur because of some gradual change in environmental conditions. For example, it is used to study successional changes. It is also used to study vegetation changes that occur because of a change in wind velocity, air temperature, or soil temperature from one point to another. Such changes occur between cut and uncut regions of a forest or meadow. A belt run from a sunny to a shady area gives interesting information regarding the light preference of plants. A belt run up the south slope of a hill and down the north slope will detect great changes in vegetation. Where a marked chemical gradient occurs, a belt transect gives rich results over a very short distance. In all of these cases, the belt must run parallel to the environmental gradient if you are to gather meaningful data.

Materials

a)   long tape measure
b)   strong cord or rope
c)   stakes
d)   hammers
e)   meter sticks or short tape measures
f)   compass
g)   identification guides
h)   data sheets

Procedure

a) Determine the compass bearing for the direction in which the belt is to run.

b) Lay out a belt transect by placing 2 lines, each 20 – 30 m long, parallel to each other and 1 m apart. Close off each end with a 1-m length of cord. (This is an average size for a belt transect. Obviously you would not use one of this size to study mosses on a rock. You must adjust its dimensions to suit the vegetation being studied. Consult Sections 4.4 and 4.5.)

c) Lay out further belt transects of the same size until the study area has been adequately covered. In general, the total sample area should be about 10% of the total study site.

d) Divide each belt into equal-sized plots by running cords from one main cord to the other at the 1-m, 2-m, 3-m,...marks (Fig. 4-8). Identify the plots as A, B, C, ... This permits different groups of students, working along the same belt, to coordinate their results at the end of the study. If one pair of students is going to study the entire belt, marking the belt off into 1-m² plots is not necessary. The pair need only lay a meter stick across the belt at the 1-m mark and study the vegetation up to that point. Then they place a second meter stick at the 2-m mark and study the vegetation between the two sticks. The first stick is now moved to the 3-m mark. This process is continued down the belt.

e) Study the plants in each plot. Record the name and numbers of each species encountered. Organize your data in a table with one column for species, and columns for each of the plots. (It will be similar to Table 6 on p. 157.)

f) Back in the laboratory, plot graphs of your data, with "Number of plants" on the vertical axis and "Plot" on the horizontal axis. If your belt transect followed accurately the direction of the environmental gradient, you should get graphs similar to Figure 4-9. Such graphs facilitate the interpretation of your data.

g) If environmental measurements have been made (for example, light intensity, wind velocity, organic content of the soil), you can plot graphs with the environmental factor on the vertical axis and "Plot" on the horizontal axis. Relationships can now be spotted

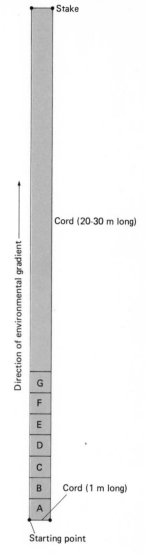

Fig. 4-8
Laying out a belt transect.

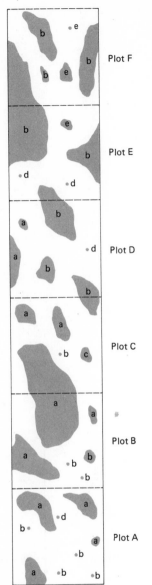

Fig. 4-10
Vegetation mapped to scale along a belt transect. Changes in cover can be observed along the belt. This map will be used at a later date to reveal changes that occurred. The symbols *a* to *e* represent different plant species.

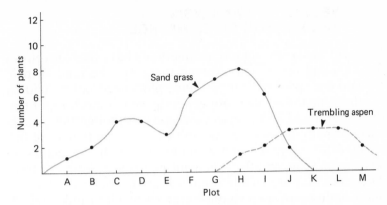

Fig. 4-9
Line graph of number of plants (two species) against plot for a study of succession on a sand dune.

between environmental conditions and plant populations by comparing these graphs with those plotted in f).

h)   The data collected up to this point permit you to calculate frequency, abundance, density, relative frequency, and relative density. If you wish to calculate cover, relative cover, and importance value, you should treat each 1 m² plot as a quadrat and make the required measurements and calculations. (See Section 4.4.)

i)   If you plan to study the same area at a later date or if your school wishes to keep an ongoing record of vegetation changes in the area, you should map the location of the vegetation along the belt (Fig. 4-10).

j)   For long transects that have a gradual change in vegetation, you can speed up your study by investigating only every second or third plot along the belt. You must, however, be consistent in all belts across the study area.

Calculations

Usually the graphs of f) and g), combined with the mapping suggested in i), are sufficient to enable you to interpret your data. In some instances, however, you may find it helpful to calculate density, cover, and other factors for each plot along a belt.

4.7 VEGETATION ANALYSIS: THE RANDOM PAIRS METHOD

In recent years several plotless methods have been developed for sampling vegetation. Among these are the random pairs method and quarter method. Since plots need not be laid out for these methods, they are generally much more rapid than the quadrat and belt transect methods. Although they can be used in many types of communities, these methods are best adapted for sampling communities in which the plants are spaced far apart and the dominant plants are shrubs or trees. Therefore they are widely used in studying the trees of forests and woodlots. In such studies, only trees with trunks over 10 cm (4 in) in diameter are considered.

The random pairs method uses two-tree samples, selected at each of a number of points spaced along compass lines through the forest or woodlot. From measurements made on these samples, you can calculate the same quantities that you can with the quadrat method.

Materials

a) compasses

b) tree calipers (diameter tapes; basal area tapes)

c) tape measures

d) tree identification guides

e) data tables

Procedure

a) Determine the compass line pattern to be used by the class for this study. Although either a regular or zigzag pattern can be used, it is suggested that you use a regular pattern consisting of a set of evenly spaced lines running parallel to the long axis of the woodlot. Space the compass lines far enough apart that two adjacent groups will not sample the same trees.

b) Each pair of students should now proceed into the woodlot, following its designated compass line.

c) Choose your first point (P_1) so that it is well within the woodlot (Fig. 4-11).

d) Select the tree nearest to you that has a *dbh* over 10 cm (tree A). Record its species and *dbh* (*dbh* = diameter, breast height—the diameter 4.5 feet from the ground).

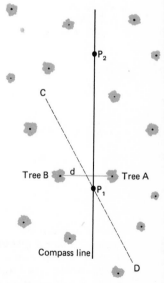

Fig. 4-11
The random pairs method for sampling the trees of a woodlot.

e) Facing tree A, raise your arms straight from your sides to make an 180° angle with the tree (line CD).

f) The tree that you select as the second tree of the pair will be behind your arms. It is the closest tree that is on the opposite side of CD from tree A (tree B). It must also have a *dbh* over 10 cm. Record its species and *dbh*.

g) Measure the distance, *d*, between the *center* of tree A and the *center* of tree B.

h) Continue to the next point (P_2) and repeat the entire procedure. The distance from P_1 to P_2 must be great enough that the same tree is not sampled twice. Generally 10 – 20 m is sufficient, but it is best to determine the distance at the site by inspection. Once determined, the same distance must be used consistently by all groups.

i) Repeat the procedure at further points along your compass line until you have reached the end of your study area. At least 50 (preferably 100) pairs should be studied for a woodlot. If fewer than 30 trees of a particular species are sampled, you cannot rely on your calculations of relative density.

j) Tabulate your data as shown in Table 9.

TABLE 9

Point	Tree A		Tree B		Distance (*d*) between A and B
	Species	*dbh*	Species	*dbh*	
P_1					
P_2					
P_3					

Calculations

Since no measurements of area are made in this method, the calculation of density and dominance (cover) must be done indirectly. Be sure to think through the following instructions carefully before you attempt the calculations.

a) Total the distances (*d*) for all points. Divide by the number of points to get the average distance between trees in the woodlot. (Experiments have shown that a more accurate estimate of the average distance is obtained if you multiply this answer by 0.8.)

average distance between trees $(D) =$

$$\frac{\text{sum of all distances}}{\text{total number of points}} \times 0.8$$

b) Square the answer obtained in a) to determine the average area occupied by a tree.

average area occupied by a tree $= D^2$

c) Divide the result of b) into the unit area in which you want density expressed. This gives the total density of all species (number of trees per unit area, regardless of species).

$$\text{total density of all species} = \frac{\text{unit area}}{D^2}$$

For example, if the average area occupied by a tree is 25 m² and you wish to express density as number of trees per 100 m², then

$$\text{total density} = \frac{100 \text{ m}^2}{25 \text{ m}^2} = 4 \text{ trees per unit area}$$

Foresters commonly express density as number of trees per acre. Since there are 43,560 ft² in an acre, the following formula can be used to calculate the average number of trees per acre (d must be measured in feet):

$$\text{total density (trees per acre)} = \frac{43,560}{D^2}$$

d) Determine the number of individuals of each species of tree.

e) Using the *dbh* values and conversion tables, calculate the basal areas for all of the trees.

f) Total the basal areas for each species. Divide by the number of individuals of the species to obtain an average cover for the species.

average cover for a species $=$

$$\frac{\text{total basal area for the species}}{\text{total number of individuals of the species}}$$

g)   Summarize your calculations in a table with column headings for species of tree, number of individuals, and average cover.

h)   Using the original data and the table in g), calculate the following:

$$\text{frequency} = \frac{\text{number of points at which a species occurs}}{\text{total number of points}}$$

$$\text{relative frequency} = \frac{\text{frequency of a species}}{\text{total frequency of all species}} \times 100$$

$$\text{relative density} = \frac{\text{number of individuals of a species}}{\text{total number of individuals of all species}} \times 100$$

$$\text{density} = \frac{\text{relative density of a species}}{100} \times \text{total density of all species}$$

$$\text{cover} = \text{density of a species} \times \text{average cover for the species}$$

$$\text{relative cover} = \frac{\text{cover for a species}}{\text{total cover for all species}} \times 100$$

$$\text{importance value} = \text{relative frequency} + \text{relative density} + \text{relative cover}$$

i)   Summarize your calculations in tabular form with column headings for species of tree, frequency, relative frequency, relative density, density, cover, relative cover, and importance value.

Discussion

a)   The method by which density is calculated assumes that the species of tree is randomly distributed through the woodlot. If you have evidence which indicates that this is not so, use another method to analyze the tree population.

b)   If possible, compare the results of this method with those obtained by a quadrat study of the same woodlot. Compare the efficiency of the plot and plotless methods.

c)   The ground and shrub strata can be sampled at the same time, if desired, by setting up suitable quadrats at each of the points used for random pair selection.

d)   This method can be used to estimate crayfish populations in a wetland area, anthill numbers in a meadow, and the number of bird nests in a shrubby area. How?

4.8   NETTING TECHNIQUES FOR INSECT SURVEYS

The classic pose of the butterfly collector with net in hand is considered by some to be a laughable sight. Nevertheless, the use of nets to catch various animal types has been going on for centuries and will continue simply because it works. An *entomologist,* a person who studies insects, employs a wide variety of nets designed for sampling from different types of environments.

Sweep net. This type of net is designed for grassy or weedy areas. It is swept back and forth through the upper parts of the vegetation. The net must be made of heavy-duty material which can take punishment. Light canvas or muslin is suitable. The only trick to the operation of this net is that it requires quick wrist action to keep the net moving from side to side with the opening always forward. Sweeping is done in

Walking direction

Fig. 4-12
Procedure for side-to-side sweeping and final trapping of collected insects in the end of a sweep net.

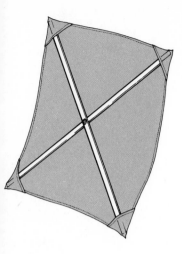

Fig. 4-13
A beating net.

front of the operator as he walks forward through the field. To prevent the insects from escaping at the end of a sweep, quickly twist the handle to flip the end of the bag over the rim of the metal frame. This seals the insects in the tip of the bag. Figure 4-12 shows how this technique is performed.

Aerial net. This net is designed mainly for capturing butterflies and moths. Therefore it must be made of light material, such as marquisette, which will not injure their delicate wings. Use the same procedure as above to trap the insects in the tip of the bag after you have encircled them with the net.

Beating net. Many insects live on leaves and twigs in trees and shrubs. The only practical way of taking large scale samples from this type of environment is to dislodge the residents. One common practice is to beat or otherwise jar the branches. Exercise care to avoid damaging the small twigs, leaves, and buds. Dislodged insects are caught in a horizontally held beating net (Fig. 4-13). The fabric in this net is light canvas or some other heavy-duty cloth. To make comparisons valid, all nets used in a study should be of the same shape and area. Nets 1 meter by 1 meter are commonly used.

4.9 TRAPPING INSECTS AND DETERMINING THEIR ENVIRONMENTAL PREFERENCES

By odor. Many insects, especially night flyers, are attracted to food sources by the smells given off. The following potions are designed to attract insects that seek sweet foods:

a)   finely ground fruits such as bananas, peaches, pears, and prunes, allowed to ferment, then mixed with thick sugar solution;

b)   stale beer mixed with concentrated sugar solution;

c)   rum flavoring in a molasses or honey solution.

Prepare enough solution to allow you to paint small sections (about 10 cm in diameter) of 20 – 30 trees, which then represent your collection sites. The selected trees should be about 20 meters apart. Paint the trees at the beginning of a field trip to give the insects plenty of time to find the liquid food. Paint only on the shaded side of a trunk. Why? Return to the "traps" at the end of the field trip. Flick any visiting insects into a collecting or killing jar. This technique works best as a night-time exercise but can also be useful in daylight.

Various experiments can be designed using this technique. You can

a)   compare the numbers of insects caught at two different heights by placing potion at 2-meter and 20-cm heights on the trees;

b)   compare the insects attracted to two different potions;

c)   compare the insects of different forest habitats;

d)   compare the insects of exposed (windy) sites with those of sheltered sites. Use an anemometer to measure the wind velocities.

When you find differences between catches from different sites, ask yourself why. Close examination of the insects will often answer the question. Use a 10X hand lens.

By lights. On warm humid nights, most outdoor lights attract a variety of night-flying insects. Specially designed light traps can easily be constructed (Fig. 4-14). Easier still, just hang a white sheet in some exposed place. Suspend an electric bulb a few feet in front of it. Leave 0.5 to 1.0 meters of the bottom edge of the sheet on the ground. Then insects falling from the light source can be spotted and scooped up with a collecting or killing bottle. Car headlights can also be used to light the sheet. Being brighter, they often attract more insects. They also permit you to work in areas without electricity.

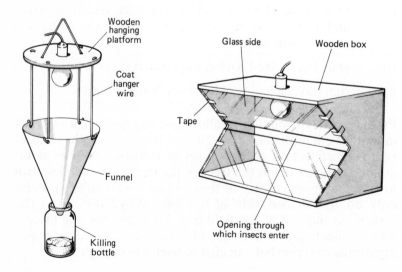

Fig. 4-14
Light traps.

Keep a record of such things as the relative humidity, temperature, wind velocity, and wind direction. Make collections over a period of about five nights. Make collections at the same time and for the same interval each night. Try to determine under which conditions these night prowlers are most active.

By sunken ground traps. By burying tin cans (do not use glass jars) in the ground at a variety of sites, estimates of the relative populations of ground-dwelling insects living in various areas are possible. Ground traps usually take many days to collect appreciable numbers of insects. Therefore you should return to them every 24 hours for a number of days to collect each day's catch. Two usual baits are used for ground traps:

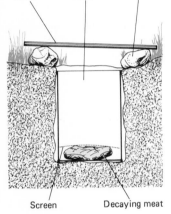

Wood   Can   Stone

Screen   Decaying meat

Fig. 4-15
A ground trap.

a)   the fermented liquid potions mentioned earlier. Usually a solution that is 2 parts molasses and 1 part water, poured to a depth of 1 cm, is best. Sieve out insects trapped in the fluid and carefully wash them with water. This can be done back in the laboratory.

b)   decaying animal products such as a piece of fish, hamburger, or dog food. Such material attracts carrion feeders. This type of trap should be covered with a small board as shown in Figure 4-15.

Discussion

The most successful trapper or collector is usually the one who is most familiar with the behavior of the sought-after species. List the factors in the environment that most insects require at some or most stages of their life cycles. What special types of behavior might be used to trap insects? How? Where are the most ideal sites for collecting a wide variety of insects a) within 100 meters of the school; b) in North America; or c) in the world?

4.10 TECHNIQUES FOR INSECT COLLECTION AND HANDLING

To fully exploit field studies that include capturing insects and other arthropods, you should be familiar with a number of techniques. This section describes a few of the methods and pieces of equipment that might be useful in your particular studies.

The aspirator. The simple piece of equipment shown in Figure 4-16 works like a miniature vacuum cleaner to capture tiny insects. By sucking on the flexible tubing while holding the end of the intake tube beside a small insect, you can draw the insect into the bottle. In this way specimens can be removed from a net or captured directly from a natural site such as the bark of a tree or a blade of grass. It is recommended that a few layers of adhesive tape be wrapped around the top and bottom of the aspirator. This helps to prevent breakage and, also, lessens the chance of injuries if breakage does occur. Aspirators made entirely of clear plastic are commercially available.

Finger tabs. For some people, handling insects by hand is a frightening experience. It may also damage the insects. A very simple set of handling tabs can be made in minutes to avoid these problems. Cut and bend some fairly strong copper wire as shown in Figure 4-17. Cover each side of the loops with cellophane tape. Then tape the other ends to your thumb and forefinger.

Although originally designed for studies of bees, anyone unskilled in the quick capture and steady hand required for these insects should not use this method with bees. The finger tabs can also be used to sort and otherwise handle any dead or living insects where actual touching is undesirable.

Killing bottle. The permanent removal of a few insects from a particular community seldom has any profound effect on it. In most instances, only a small percentage of the total population of any species can be found and removed in any one outing. As a result, some of the insects you capture can be killed, stored, and returned to the laboratory for identification and further study. Close examination under a microscope is often required to detect the intricate structural adaptations of these creatures which, in turn, reveal the reasons why they are so successful in colonizing the terrestrial niches in which they are found. Do not kill any insects which appear to be rare. For example, if you capture an unusual butterfly, examine it carefully and then release it.

Killing bottles must be treated with respect. Cyanide bottles should not be used since they are much too dangerous. Carbon tetrachloride or, better still, ethyl acetate are recommended killing agents. But even they can be harmful if inhaled.

Pour 1 – 2 cm of plaster of Paris over the bottom of a stout bottle for which a tight-fitting lid is available. Heat the bottle, contents, and lid in an oven to drive off any moisture. Cool the bottle to room temperature. Pour in just enough

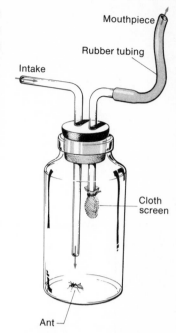

Fig. 4-16
An aspirator for capturing small insects.

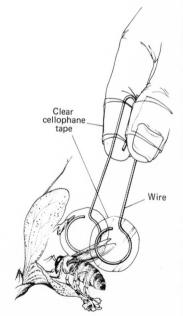

Fig. 4-17
A method for capturing and handling insects.

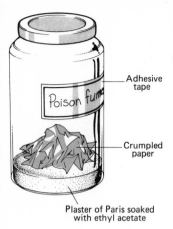

Adhesive
tape

Crumpled
paper

Plaster of Paris soaked
with ethyl acetate

Fig. 4-18
A killing bottle.

killing liquid to moisten all of the plaster of Paris. (Too much moisture is unsatisfactory.) Avoid the fumes by working always in a well-ventilated area or out-of-doors. A small piece of crumpled paper inserted in the bottle gives the insects a surface to grip, discouraging them from flying and injuring their body parts. (See Fig. 4-18.)

Insects placed in the bottle should die within 5 minutes. Transfer dead insects to an ordinary bottle so that freshly caught insects cannot damage them.

Wrap a couple of layers of adhesive tape around the bottle to prevent injury if the bottle breaks. Leave a "window" so you can see when the insects have died. Mark every killing bottle with the words POISON and FUMES in obvious red letters on the outside. Do not let young children use the bottle or play with it.

Discussion

An important question should be asked when viewing an insect or any other arthropod found on a field study. How is this particular organism adapted to the environment in which it was found? There must be something about the structure, behavior, color, taste, smell (or perhaps all of these factors combined) which enables the organism to live successfully. It is your job to figure out how the organisms you find have adapted to ensure survival. Unless you bring back a few live specimens, it may be difficult to state anything about behavior unless you have kept good field notes. Certainly the structure of the specimens can be examined if some have been preserved. Look closely for modifications which aid in eating, climbing, sensing, protection, egg-laying, mating, escaping, and so on.

4.11   ESTIMATING INSECT POPULATIONS

It would be an impossible task to count all of the individuals of a particular species in a large area. Yet, for many ecological studies, this number must be known. If the habitat is fairly uniform and if you can operate a sweep net in the area, you can use the *mark-recapture method* to estimate population size. This method works best for species that are not active flyers. Ladybird beetles, grasshoppers, and crickets are examples.

For simplicity, the following description assumes that you are going to study only the grasshopper population. You should be able to modify the procedure to suit any other insect population or to permit simultaneous studies of several insect species.

Materials

a) sweep nets

b) marking pens (bright color)

c) tally counters (optional)

Procedure

a) Select the study site, preferably one that is fairly uniform throughout. A meadow or a playing field would be suitable. If possible, select a site which has clearly defined boundaries like a road, a hedge, or a river.

b) Mark the boundaries of the study site and determine its total area. An area less than 4000 m² (about 1 acre) should be chosen.

c) Write a careful description of the study site—topography, dominant vegetation, and weather conditions (including air temperature, relative humidity, and the presence or absence of moisture on the vegetation).

d) Sweep about one-fifth of the area with sweep nets. Try to collect at least 200 grasshoppers. Distribute your lines of sweep as evenly as possible throughout the area.

e) Make a small colored mark on the back of each grasshopper. (You may have to anesthetize them with a light dose of ethyl acetate.)

f) After the coloring has dried, count the grasshoppers. Then release them throughout the study area. Do not count any damaged individuals.

g) After several hours, re-enter the area and conduct a second sweep. Collect at least as many grasshoppers as you did the first time. Count the total number of grasshoppers and the number that have your marks on them. *Note:* If the weather is warm and dry, you should allow at least 3 hours between sweeps. In that time the grasshoppers will redistribute themselves evenly through the area. If the weather is cool and wet, you should allow at least a day for dispersal.

Calculations

A simple ratio can be used to estimate the total population from the three measurements that you made:

$$\frac{P_1}{M_1} = \frac{P_2}{M_2}$$

where P_1 = total population
M_1 = total number of marked individuals
P_2 = total number collected in second sweep
M_2 = number of marked individuals in second sweep

Suppose 250 grasshoppers were marked and released, and 280 were captured in the second sweep, 35 of them bearing your mark. Then,

$$P_1 = \frac{P_2}{M_2} \times M_1 = \frac{280}{35} \times 250 = 2{,}000$$

Thus the study site contains about 2,000 grasshoppers.

Discussion

a) Why are well-defined boundaries an aid in this study?

b) What assumptions are made in this method?

c) How could you increase the accuracy of the method?

d) Plan and carry out a study in which one group of students studies the grasshopper population in one environment (for example, short grass) and another group does the same thing in another environment (for example, long grass). Describe and account for observed differences. Be sure that you have adequate controls in the experiment—similar catches, same time of day, similar weather conditions, and so on.

e) If possible, conduct a quadrat study of the grasshoppers in an area. Compare the results to those of the mark-recapture method. Enter the site early in the day and distribute 15 – 20 quadrats, each 0.1 m² in area, throughout it. Mark their locations. Return a few hours later. Approach each quadrat carefully, making sure that your movements and shadow do not warn the insects of your approach. Carefully disturb all of the vegetation in each quadrat. Count the number of grasshoppers that leave. Consult Section 4.4 for a procedure that can be used to calculate the density of the grasshopper population. Knowing the density and the total area of the site, you can easily calculate the total population of grasshoppers.

f) The basic principles of the mark-recapture method have been used to study animal populations of many types. Only some of the procedural steps differ. How would you modify the method to study a bird population, a fish population, and the population of a mammal like the caribou?

4.12 BIRDS: POPULATION AND BEHAVIOR STUDIES

Birds are excellent subjects for ecological studies for many reasons: they are common in most areas at all times of year; most species are active during the daylight hours; any area usually contains several different species; birds display fascinating behavior patterns such as unique perching positions and flight movements; interspecific (among animals of different species) and intraspecific (among animals of the same species) interactions are common, particularly during the breeding season; interesting adaptations to the environment are easily observed and interpreted. All that is required for this study is considerable patience, a pair of binoculars, and a bird identification guide.

This exercise briefly outlines an approach that you can use in an ecological study of birds. You should read all you can about birds before the outing. The knowledge gained will help you to interpret your observations. For example, if you read about bird territories, you would discover that a bird sings mainly to mark its territorial boundaries and that it continues to sing only so long as it has a territory. Further, a bird will attack an intruder of the same species unless the intruder asserts its dominance over part of the territory by more active singing than the original occupant. A bird, being chased on its own territory, commonly will not go beyond the boundaries of its territory. You can see how this knowledge will help you to identify territorial boundaries and to explain the distribution of birds that you spot on the outing. Read, then, about territorial behavior. Read also about nesting behavior, flight and perching habits, special adaptations for feeding, other adaptations to the environment, courting behavior, care of the young, interspecific competition, intraspecific competition, and migration. You obviously cannot do this for all species that you are likely to encounter. However, your local nature club can tell you which species dominate the selected study site. Limit your advance reading to those species. Each student in your class could research one or two species.

Materials

a) binoculars
b) field guide to birds
c) aerial photograph of the area
d) markers
e) compasses

Procedure

a) A day or two in advance of the field trip a group of three or four students should visit the area with the teacher. Select a locality where birds are common. Mark the boundaries of an area that can be effectively studied by the class in the allotted time period. (One student can usually study 4,000 – 5,000 m²—about 1 acre—per hour.) Draw a field map of the area. Show prominent landmarks, the main vegetation types, bodies of water, and other pertinent environmental information. Place markers in the field and on the map so that others can identify the locations of birds using a grid system like the one shown in Figure 4-19. Space the markers 50 m apart. An aerial photograph will assist you in drawing the map.

b) On the day of the study, assign a line to each pair of students. Use one axis only. If possible, one member of each pair should be good at bird identification.

Fig. 4-19
Grid system for a bird behavior study.

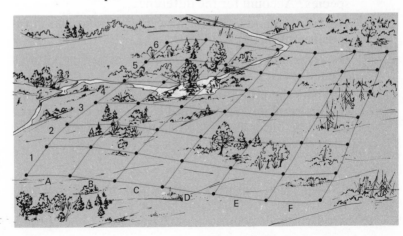

c)   Walk very slowly along the assigned line. When a bird
is observed, stop walking and make no unnecessary
movements. Slowly raise your binoculars and identify
the species. If it flies away before you have identified
it, do not follow it. This will disturb the results of other
groups. Record the following on your map or in your
notebook: the species; its habitat; its location in the
habitat (for example, upper limb of a hawthorn tree);
its sex; the direction in which it flew; its manner of flying (soaring, undulating, erratic, etc.); its food, method
of feeding, and beak type; its songs and calls and the
location of the bird while communicating; evidence of
interspecific interaction; evidence of intraspecific
interaction; its stress behavior (how it reacted to your
presence); and any other special behavior.

If you make up a set of symbols, many of these observations can be noted on your map. Some standard
symbols are x for a singing male, • for a non-singing
bird, y for a young bird, and → for the direction of flight.

Walk each line only once on any given day.

Discussion

a)   For each major vegetation type (coniferous trees,
deciduous trees, shrubs, grass, marsh, etc.) list in order
of abundance the species of birds that were observed.
Account for the results.

b)   Mark on your map what appears to be the territory
occupied by each bird.

c)   What differences in behavior and appearance did you
notice between males and females of the same
species? Account for the differences.

d)   Describe and account for any interspecific and intraspecific interactions.

e)   Describe and account for the main behavior patterns
of each species.

f)   Estimate the bird population of the area. How reliable
is your estimate? Why? Would you expect this population to be different at another time of day or in some
other season? Why?

Notes

a)   Although you will get results at any time of day, you
will get better results early in the morning when bird
activity is at its peak.

b) To get a better idea of the bird population in the area, the study should be repeated several times during the year.

c) During nesting, the mating season, and migration, birds usually show strange but interesting behavior. Pay particular attention to this aspect if the occasion warrants. For example, if you perform the study during the spring nesting period, students could be stationed in secluded sites to observe with binoculars the nesting behavior of certain species. Which sex builds the nest, incubates the eggs, and feeds the young? During the spring and fall migration, birds which are not normal residents will stop in your area. Observe them carefully and try to determine why they do not remain for long in your area.

d) A great deal can be learned about bird behavior and adaptation by observing the birds that come to feeders near your home or school. Establish feeding stations, each containing a different type of food—seeds, suet, minced meat, berries. Set them up about 5 − 10 m from a window where you can sit quietly and observe the birds without disturbing them. Set up a schedule and watch the feeders for specific times throughout each day for several days. Observe such things as the food preferences of each species, and special adaptations such as beak structure, foot shape, and color. Account for your observations. What niche does each species occupy? Describe and explain any unique behavior such as apparent domination of the feeder at a certain time of day by one species.

4.13 ANIMAL BEHAVIOR

During what part of the day is a particular animal active? When does it feed? What does it eat? When and where does it sleep? Does it have a courtship ritual? How does it react to animals of the same species (intraspecific interaction)? How does it react to animals of a different species (interspecific interaction)? How large is its territory? How aggressively will it defend its territory? What habitat does it prefer? Why?

These are just some of the questions that one can ask regarding animal behavior. In the search for answers to such questions you will ask and answer many more questions on the behavioral aspects of ecology.

Squirrels and chipmunks are generally abundant within walking distance of most schools. Also, they are not as afraid of humans as are many other animals. Thus this study focuses on these animals. However, if you can visit the country, a similar approach can be used to study the behavior of animals like groundhogs and porcupines.

Materials

a) binoculars

b) field guide to mammals

c) tape measure

Procedure

a) Prepare a data table into which you can insert observations that will help you to answer the questions in the first paragraph of this section.

b) Prepare a map of the area to be studied.

c) Assign each pair of students a path to follow through the area. The path could, but need not, be on a grid system as described in Section 4.12.

d) Walk your assigned path slowly and quietly. Stop from time to time and remain motionless and quiet. Look and listen for squirrels and chipmunks. Even relatively tame squirrels and chipmunks tend to stop all activity when humans are active in the area. As a result, you may not detect them. However, they soon resume activity if you do not frighten them with your movements and noise.

e) When a squirrel or chipmunk is spotted, use your binoculars to observe it from a distance. Note the species and mark its location on your map. Study its behavior until you have completed most of the columns in your data table. Pay particular attention to territorial behavior. What animals are allowed to come into the territory? How does the occupant react to intruders of the same and different species?

f) When you have a good idea of how far the territory extends, move into the area and determine its size using the tape measure. What shape is it? Mark its boundaries on your map.

g) Look for drinking and feeding spots in the territory.

h) Try to locate the animal's nest. Check the ground for droppings, food remnants, runways, footprints, and other evidence that will help you to confirm the territorial boundaries.

i)   Proceed to the next sighting and repeat the study.

Discussion

a)   Use the class results to estimate the population of the area.

b)   What is the habitat preference of each species? Why? What niche does each species occupy?

c)   Describe and account for evidence of territorial behavior. Does any one species appear to be dominant? Compare the sizes of the territories of the different animals. Are the territories of fixed size? How do interspecific and intraspecific interactions differ? Why?

d)   Why do animals establish territories? Do men behave like other animals in this respect? Why?

e)   Name an animal that you think does not set up a territory. Explain why it does not do so.

Notes

a)   Instead of following paths, each pair of students can be assigned to a specific quadrat on a grid system. The pair should remain in the quadrat, quiet and motionless, making notes on squirrel and chipmunk behavior for about 2 hours.

b)   More reliable data can be obtained by repeating the study at other times of day and in other seasons.

c)   Careful observation of squirrels and chipmunks at feeders near your home or school will yield a great deal of information on animal behavior. For example, you might try setting up a small feeding station well within the territorial boundaries of one squirrel. Then observe what happens when animals of the same and different species enter the territory.

4.14   ANIMAL SIGNS AND TRACK CASTING

Direct evidence of the presence of wildlife in natural habitats is sometimes hard to come by. Wild animals do not usually enjoy man's presence. Thus they take flight or hide at the mere sight, smell, or sound of human beings. Often, all that remains are the "signs" that animals were present at some previous time. It requires a real Sherlock Holmes type to find the "signs" and then to determine the identity of the animal that was there. Here are clues that you might look for:

a) evidence that the vegetation has been used as food—twigs browsed by deer, shrubs nibbled by rabbits, and husks of acorns discarded by squirrels;

b) the presence of scats (fecal material) which give, through their size, distribution, and composition, an indication of the size of the animals, the time spent in the area, the number of animals, and the nature of their feeding habits (herbivorous or carnivorous);

c) tracks, which are as good as fingerprints in determining the identity of the animal.

Browsing or feeding studies can be carried out by examining the vegetation to determine which species are being used as food and to what extent. This information is useful in managing an area for the production of larger populations of given species.

Fecal material (especially that of herbivores) can be collected in plastic bags and either dried in the laboratory or preserved in a 10% formaldehyde solution. This material can be broken apart and examined under a dissecting microscope to obtain evidence as to the type of foods being eaten.

Tracks made in mud, sand, or snow can be followed to trace some of the animal's activities. For example, they may indicate feeding or bedding sites. Obvious trails are usually better indicators than a single set of tracks. Interspecific and intraspecific interactions can be investigated by observing the relationships between the trails of different animals using the same area. Territorial boundaries can often be estimated using tracks. Of course, you must be able to identify the tracks. Carry with you a copy of *A Field Guide to Animal Tracks* by O. Murie, Houghton Mifflin, 1954. Alternatively, you can sketch or photograph the tracks and identify them later. Or, you can make a permanent record of track impressions in moist clay or mud.

Materials

a) plaster of Paris

b) mixing container

c) water container

d)   stirring stick

e)   cardboard strips 2 cm wide and 30−40 cm long (optional)

Procedure

a)   After locating a suitable track (not necessarily the first one seen), clear away any leaves, grass, or particles that have fallen into the impression.

b)   Make a circular wall around the print in one of two ways (Fig. 4-20). Build a mud barrier by placing the mixing container over the print and packing mud around the base (A) or make a collar from the cardboard strips (B).

c)   Place an appropriate amount of water (enough to nearly fill the impression and surrounding pool) in the mixing cup. Gently sprinkle in an equivalent amount of plaster of Paris.

d)   Stir the mixture. Add more plaster or water to get a thickness similar to that of pancake batter.

e)   The mixture should *flow* into the crevices of the print as you fill the pool.

f)   Let the cast harden for 20 minutes or more. Then loosen it from the ground. Before removing any earth, wrap it in newspaper and store it to be returned to the laboratory.

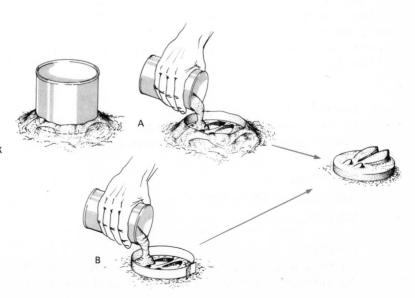

Fig. 4-20
Two ways of making a track cast.

g) Let the cast dry completely. Then use a brush to remove any clinging soil particles.

h) You are left with a model of the tip of the animal's paw or hoof. It is, of course, a *negative* cast of the original print. It is a simple matter to get a *positive* track cast. (Hint: Use petroleum jelly, soft soap, or melted paraffin to insure separation of the positive cast from the negative cast.)

Discussion

Only general guidelines have been given here for the use of animal signs in the study of animal behavior. If you wish to do a detailed study of an area, model your procedure on that of Section 4.13. Determine the boundaries of the study site, allot specific paths or quadrats to each pair of students, and search the site thoroughly for the clues described here. Back in the classroom, try to use your clues to answer questions like those asked in Section 4.13.

4.15 SUCCESSION IN A ROTTEN LOG

After a tree dies, it passes through a number of well-defined stages before it decays completely and becomes part of the soil. Each stage has a microcommunity consisting of characteristic organisms. When the organisms of one stage use up their food supply or otherwise make the microhabitat unsuitable for themselves, they are succeeded by other organisms. Thus a succession of communities occurs in a rotten log in much the same way that a succession of communities occurs on a sand dune or in a vacant lot.

Materials

a) thermometers (air and soil), light meters, hygrometers, and other instruments for measuring environmental conditions

b) pocket magnifiers

c) collecting and killing bottles

d) hatchets (optional)

Procedure

a) Within a woodlot locate trees of the same species in the following stages of succession: a dead tree that is still standing; a tree that has recently fallen; a log with a rotten core but firm exterior; a totally rotten log.

b) Make careful measurements of the environmental factors near each site. If you have the instruments, measure the air and soil temperature, the relative humidity, and the light intensity. If you lack instruments, make qualitative observations of these factors. Note also the condition of the soil—moist or dry, impacted or loose, its color, evidence of organic matter, and its state of decomposition.

c) Identify the plant species that appear close enough to influence the microcommunities at each site.

d) Check the standing tree for evidence of the past activity of vertebrates. Look for woodpecker holes, bird nests, and squirrel nests. Estimate when the activity took place. Note the species and location of any fungi present. Examine the bark remaining on the tree. Note its moisture content. Remove some of the bark and look for invertebrates under the bark and in the wood. Identify as many of these as you can and note their relative abundance. If necessary, collect one of each species and take it back to the laboratory for identification and closer examination. Make accurate notes regarding the habitat of each species.

e) Examine the newly fallen log. Compare the ease with which bark can be removed from it and the standing tree. Note the moisture content and hardness of the wood. Compare these to the standing tree. Check for fungi, mosses, lichens, and herbaceous plants. Study the invertebrates as in d).

f) Approach the partially rotten log slowly. Look around and under it for vertebrates like snakes and salamanders. Look for signs of animal life such as tunnels, runways, nesting sites, and food caches. Use a hatchet, if necessary, to remove part of the hard outer shell. Break this apart and make observations on the invertebrate population as in d). Search through the rotting core for invertebrates, snakes, and salamanders. Note the color, moisture content, and odor of the rotting core. Describe its state of decomposition. Check for fungi, mosses, lichens, and herbaceous plants.

g) Examine the totally rotten log as you did the core in f). Compare the color, moisture content, odor, stage of decomposition, plants, and animals of the two stages.

Discussion

a) Describe the microsuccession that occurs in a rotten log from the time the tree dies to the time it becomes part of the soil.

b) Which organisms were most abundant at each stage? Why?

c) Which stage had the greatest diversity of life? Why?

d) Account for the succession that occurs by relating the changing biotic factors to the changing abiotic factors.

e) Make up as many food chains as you can for each of the four stages.

f) What organisms are responsible for the odor of a rotting log? What niche do they occupy?

g) What do you think is the most important niche in a fallen log microcommunity? Why?

Note: These logs are the homes of many organisms that are essential components of the forest ecosystem. Therefore, leave things much as you found them. Do not chop an entire log apart when a small cut will do. If you turn a log over, return it to its original position to protect the homes of salamanders and other animals that have established residence under it.

4.16 PRIMARY SUCCESSION ON A ROCKY SURFACE

The first plants to colonize barren rock are generally crustose and foliose lichens (Fig. 4-21). *Crustose* lichens send rhizoids several millimeters into the rock, thereby attaching themselves firmly to the surface. They usually appear as fine-textured patches that are difficult to remove by hand. The leaf-like *foliose* lichens are not so firmly attached. In fact, large pieces can be easily pulled off the rocks. To obtain nutrients these lichens secrete acids that attack the rocky surface. The weakened rock crumbles, forming parent soil material in which other species of plants can become established. Pioneer mosses usually invade the area at this stage. They grow in clumps which make a major contribution to soil development by trapping wind-blown earth and organic matter. Further soil buildup occurs as mosses and lichens die and decay.

Fig. 4-21
Pioneer lichens.

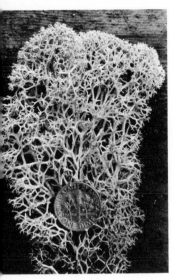

Fig. 4-22
Cladonia, or reindeer moss, one of the most common fruticose lichens.

Fruticose lichens like reindeer moss (Fig. 4-22) and larger mosses now appear. These branching plants trap still more wind-blown material. Also their great bulk quickly builds up the organic portion of the soil. Ferns often appear at this stage. Seed-bearing plants, usually hardy annual weeds, now begin to grow in the area. Biennials and perennials, the latter commonly grasses, follow. By now the soil is up to a foot deep on the rock. Shrubs like the sumac can grow in this soil. The usual succession of tree communities follows.

Only those of you who live near large expanses of rock are likely to find an area showing all of these stages. Many of you will have to restrict your studies to the microhabitat of a single large rock. Regardless of the extent of the rock succession, investigate it as closely as you can. Pay particular attention to the manner in which biotic and abiotic factors interact to produce the succession of communities.

A. STUDY OF A SINGLE ROCK

Materials

a) field guides to lichens, mosses, flowering plants, trees
b) soil trowels
c) soil test kit (pH and common minerals)
d) pocket magnifiers
e) collecting bags and jars
f) tape measures and other materials for vegetation studies
g) scalpels and forceps
h) soil thermometers
i) compasses

Procedure

a) Note the overall pattern of vegetation on the rock. Draw a map of the surface of the rock showing the location and shape of each major patch of vegetation. Show a north-south axis on your map.

b) Identify the common vegetation types. Record these on your vegetation map. The use of symbols will help. For example, use CL for crustose lichen, FoL for foliose lichen, and FrL for fruticose lichen. Do any particular species prefer the sunny side of the rock? The shady side? Small specimens could be collected and returned to the laboratory for later identification and further study. Use scalpels and forceps so that you remove only very small samples. You should not disrupt in a few minutes something that took nature hundreds of years to develop. Make notes on the strength of the "rooting systems" of each species as you attempt to remove samples.

c)   Look for evidence of intraspecific competition. What role does this appear to play in succession?

d)   Look for evidence of interspecific competition.

e)   Study the soil around and beneath each major vegetation type. Note its depth, texture, temperature, pH, mineral content, moisture content, and organic content. The last two factors may be studied qualitatively in the field or small samples of soil may be returned to the laboratory for quantitative determination.

f)   Identify the major invertebrates associated with the community. If they appear to prefer a certain microhabitat, note this in your records. Determine the niches that they occupy in the community by observing their behavior closely and by examining them with pocket magnifiers.

B. STUDY OF A LARGE EXPANSE OF ROCK

If you can find a study site where successional stages from bare rock to forest are visible, you have sufficient study material to occupy your entire class for a full day. Consult Section 5.4 for a master plan that you can use. You will, of course, have to make some modifications in the procedure to adapt this master plan to a study of succession on a rocky surface.

If you plan a qualitative study of the vegetation, lay out one or more lines running from the bare rock to the forest. Then set up quadrats of suitable size (see Section 4.4) along each line, so that one quadrat is in each major vegetation zone. Perform the usual tests of abiotic factors in each quadrat and look for animal life and evidence of its presence. If you plan a quantitative study, the line intercept method (Section 4.5) is probably your best choice. Here, too, perform tests of abiotic factors and search for animals at intervals along each line.

Discussion

a)   Interpret your findings in the light of the ecosystem concept. How did the interaction of biotic and abiotic factors cause the succession of communities on the rock or rocky surface that you studied?

b)   What community do you think is the most important stage in the development of soil on bare rock? Why?

c)   What roles, if any, do the animals present play in succession?

4.17   INTRASPECIFIC COMPETITION IN PLANTS

Intraspecific competition is the rivalry among members of the *same* species for light, minerals, and water. If plants having identical requirements are growing close together, competition is inevitable. If the requirements are plentiful, the results of competition will not be too obvious. However, as the availability of light, minerals, and water decreases due to crowding, the results clearly show up. What do you think will be the results of crowding on the growth of plants?

Materials

a)   4 flats (planting boxes)

b)   potting soil

c)   seeds of one species, preferably a broad-leafed plant such as tomato, bean, or sunflower

d)   ruler and pencil

e)   drying oven (optional)

f)   balance (optional)

g)   string and tacks (optional)

Procedure

a)   Place soil to a depth of at least 5 cm in the 4 flats. Smooth and gently pack the surface.

b)   Using a ruler and the point of a pencil, gently lay out a grid system in one flat, crisscrossing the surface of the soil with lines 10 cm apart. If the lines do not show up well, use the string and tacks to mark the grid system (Fig. 4-23).

c)   Place the grid lines 5 cm apart in the second flat, 3 cm apart in the third, and 1 cm apart in the fourth.

d)   Make small holes of the same depth at the centers of all of the squares marked out by the grid systems. Consult the planting directions on the seed package for the proper depth.

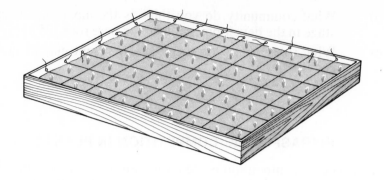

Fig. 4-23
Grid system for plant competition studies.

e) Select the largest seeds of one species that are approximately the same size. Place one seed in each of the holes and cover it with soil.

f) Water the flats and place them in a warm bright location. All flats must have the same conditions of temperature, light, and moisture.

g) (Advisable) Germinate a few extra plants in another flat so that you will have seedlings to plant in those positions where seeds fail to germinate.

h) Whenever the first flat requires watering, use the same amount of water to water the other three flats.

i) Allow the plants to grow until the results of competition are obvious. Then make the measurements and observations necessary to complete Table 10. Consult Section 3.14 for techniques.

TABLE 10

	Flat 1	Flat 2	Flat 3	Flat 4
Percent of plants surviving				
Average height of plants				
Average width of leaves at widest location				
Average length of roots				
Total weight of plant tissue				
Average weight of plant tissue				

Discussion

a) Summarize the effects that crowding appears to have on plants. Account for these effects.

b) What advice do you have for gardeners as a result of this investigation?

c) Which do you think is more important to a farmer, the average weight or the total weight of a crop? Why?

d) For this investigation you selected the *largest* seeds. What would have happened if you had selected the smallest seeds? What would have happened if you had alternated large and small seeds in the holes? As an extra project you could set up further flats to test these predictions.

e) Over a long period of time, intraspecific competition generally results in a strengthening of the species. Why?

4.18 INTERSPECIFIC COMPETITION IN PLANTS

Interspecific competition is the interaction between two or more species living within the same habitat and competing for some or all of the same abiotic factors.

Materials

as in Section 4.17 except that the seeds must be of at least two varieties. Wheat and rye seeds are advised.

Procedure

a) Perform steps a) and b) of the *Procedure* in Section 4.17, making the grid lines 2 cm apart in all 4 flats.

b) Make small holes of the same depth at the centers of all of the squares marked off by the grid system. A depth of 0.5 cm is suitable for wheat and rye. Consult the planting directions on the seed packages for other species.

c) In the first flat, plant one wheat seed in each hole.

d) In the second and third flats, alternate the planting of wheat and rye seeds in the holes as shown in Figure 4-24.

x	o	x	o	x	o	x	o	x	o
o	x	o	x	o	x	o	x	o	x
x	o	x	o	x	o	x	o	x	o
o	x	o	x	o	x	o	x	o	x
x	o	x	o	x	o	x	o	x	o
o	x	o	x	o	x	o	x	o	x

Fig. 4-24
Positioning of wheat (x) and rye (o) seeds.

e) In the fourth flat, plant one rye seed in each hole. In all cases, select large seeds of about the same size.

f) Perform steps f) to i) of the *Procedure* in Section 4.17. Your data table will, of course, require double columns under "Flat 2" and "Flat 3."

Discussion

a) Summarize the effects that wheat and rye plants appear to have on one another. Account for these effects.

b) Was the faster growing species in the pure stands also the faster growing species in the mixed stands?

c) Suppose that a farmer wishes to have a 1:1 mixture of wheat and rye in his granary. Would it be wise for him to plant a 1:1 mixture of wheat and rye to attain this result? Why?

4.19 INTERSPECIFIC COMPETITION IN PLANTS: CHEMICAL WARFARE

Plants compete for minerals, water, and sunlight. One way to win the competition is to grow fast and establish widespread root systems which can tap more of the soil's minerals and water. Some plants have difficulty establishing root systems in soil robbed of these items. Likewise, fast-growing plants may capture most of the sunlight, thus preventing slower-growing competitors from getting enough sunlight. Thus slow-growing plants are eliminated.

Recently, a remarkable twist to the business of plant competition has been revealed. Apparently some plants can secrete chemicals into the soil to inhibit the germination and growth of competitors. If this type of interaction between plants is as widespread as some biologists think it is, the structure of plant communities may be much more difficult to understand than was once believed.

The black walnut is one plant capable of chemically altering the soil around itself to make it difficult for other plants to grow there. The following investigation uses the walnut to demonstrate interspecific competition with chemicals.

Materials

a) 2 flats (planting boxes)

b) potting soil

c) walnut hulls (preferred) or walnuts

d) sunflower seeds

e) centimeter ruler and pencil

f) string and tacks

Procedure

a) Grind up the hulls of 10 or more walnuts. Make a powder of them, if possible. If hulls are not available, use walnuts instead.

b) Place soil to a depth of at least 5 cm in the flats. Sprinkle the powdered walnut over the soil in one flat. Mix it thoroughly with the soil. Smooth and gently pack the surface of the soil in both flats.

c) Lay out a grid system in each flat as described in step b) of the *Procedure* in Section 4.17. Place the grid lines 8 cm apart.

d) Make small holes 1 cm deep at the centers of all of the squares marked off by the grid systems.

e) Plant 3 seeds of about the same size in each hole.

f) Water the flats and place them in a warm bright location. Both flats must be exposed to the same conditions of light and temperature, and should always be watered with the same amount of water.

g) After the sunflowers have sprouted, select the best seedling at each site. Kill the others by clipping off the growing tip.

h) Continue the investigation until the results of competition are obvious. Then make the measurements and observations necessary to complete a data table comparable to Table 10 in Section 4.17.

Discussion

a) Summarize the effects that the walnut powder had on sunflowers.

b) Some aspects of this investigation are obviously not equivalent to natural conditions. How do you think the process works in nature? (Note: The roots of walnut plants give off the same chemical as the hulls.)

c) A plant called pussytoes *(Antennaria)* can compete well on dry exposed hillsides, even though it is a very small plant. It can do so because it uses chemical warfare. If you can find a few of these plants, grind them up and place them in a liter of boiling water. Allow the mixture to sit for at least 15 minutes, but no longer than 1 day. Use this mixture in place of the walnut powder to see how pussytoes affect sunflowers.

If you wish to study a third example, leafy spurge *(Euphorbia esula)* can be used in the manner described for pussytoes.

4.20 INTRASPECIFIC COMPETITION IN ANIMALS

Competition for the same resource by organisms of the same species is called *intraspecific competition*. This investigation studies the effect on population growth of limited food and space while physical factors like light, relative humidity, and temperature are constant and optimal.

Materials

as in Section 3.12, with only one climate control chamber (and related materials) required.

Procedure

a) Using the techniques described in Section 3.12, establish a temperature of $28-30°C$ and a relative humidity of $30-70\%$ in the chamber. Keep these factors and the light conditions constant throughout the investigation.

b) Place 2 male and 2 female flour beetles *(Tribolium confusum)* in the jar along with 50 grams of flour. Place the jar in the chamber. Do not disturb it except during counting periods.

c) Determine the population structure after 2 weeks as described in Section 3.12, *Procedure* step e). Add all of the life stages to a fresh 50-gram sample of flour in the jar. Return the culture to the chamber.

d) Repeat step c) at 2-week intervals for several months.

e) As the density of flour beetles increases, pay close attention to changes in behavior, population growth, and number of individuals at each stage of development. Graphs of time versus number of eggs, larvae, pupae, and adults will help you summarize and interpret your results.

Discussion

a) Account for the results of this investigation.

b) Does the death rate of any particular stage appear to determine the rate of population growth? Explain.

c) What changes would you expect if, after two months, you began using 100 grams of flour instead of the suggested 50 grams? Why?

d) Is increased food production a solution to widespread starvation in the human population? Why?

4.21 INTERSPECIFIC COMPETITION IN ANIMALS

This investigation studies the competition between two species of flour beetles, *Tribolium confusum* and *Tribolium castaneum*. The microclimate is often an important factor in determining whether a particular species can maintain itself when in competition with another species in a particular microhabitat. Thus, in this investigation, you study competition between the two species of flour beetles at a variety of different temperatures and relative humidities.

Materials

a) flour beetles of 2 species, *Tribolium confusum* and *Tribolium castaneum*

b) as in Section 3.12, with 6 climate control chambers (and related materials) required

Procedure

a) Using the techniques described in Section 3.12, establish 6 climate control chambers with conditions as close as possible to the specifications in Table 11. (You may have to insert a small heating element into the chamber to reach the 34°C temperature.)

TABLE 11

Chamber	Temperature	Relative humidity
1	24°C	30%
2	24°C	70%
3	29°C	30%
4	29°C	70%
5	34°C	30%
6	34°C	70%

b) Make sure you can distinguish between the two species of flour beetles, *Tribolium confusum* and *Tribolium castaneum*.

c) Place 2 male and 2 female flour beetles of each species in each jar along with 50 grams of flour. Place one jar in each climate control chamber. Do not disturb the jars except during counting.

d) After 2 weeks determine the number of adult beetles of each species in each jar. (See Section 3.12 for techniques.) In each case add all of the life stages of both species to a fresh 50-gram sample of flour in the jar. Return the jar to the correct chamber.

e) Repeat step d) at 2-week intervals for several months.

f) Plot graphs of time versus number of beetles of each species for each microclimate.

Discussion

a) How does this investigation illustrate interspecific competition?

b)   Describe the role of microclimate in competition between *Tribolium confusum* and *Tribolium castaneum*.

c)   Describe an example of interspecific competition that
occurs between a domestic animal and a wild animal.

4.22   BEHAVIOR STUDIES WITH CRICKETS

If a species is to insure its own chances of survival, its individual members must respond in the proper manner toward one
another. Mating must take place. Hopefully the healthiest
individuals will be the ones to mate and reproduce more of
their own kind. Survival of the fittest leads to the reproduction
of the fittest because the good qualities of an organism can be
passed on in heredity.

Crickets are useful for demonstrating some of the
types of behavior that insure reproduction of the fittest in
animal species. Basically, all that is required for this investigation is a small population of common field crickets (such as
Acheta pennsylvanica or *Acheta domesticus*) and a simple
terrarium to hold them.

Materials

a)   glass terrarium and glass lid

b)   sand to cover the bottom 2 cm deep

c)   5 or 6 male crickets (from the genus *Acheta*)

d)   1 or 2 female crickets (of the same species)

e)   a food supply of cracked corn, oatmeal, or chicken
mash

f)   4 match boxes

g)   bottle and lid for each cricket

h)   quick-drying paint

i)   (optional) cotton batting or pieces of apple or pear

Procedure

a)   Set up the terrarium and place a match box in each
corner. Number each match box.

b)   Place small drops of paint at slightly different positions
on the thorax of each male cricket to identify them.
Give each a number and record its distinguishing
mark.

c)   After isolating the crickets in separate bottles for at
least a day, introduce 5 or 6 males into the terrarium.

d)   During the first 15 minutes keep notes on the manner in which the crickets get accustomed to their new environment. Try to observe and record information pertinent to each of the following questions: What happens when males meet? What areas of the terrarium are investigated most? What use is made of the match boxes, and by which males? Do any males appear to be more aggressive than others? To what extent is singing important in the population, and for what purpose? Do any males appear to be dominant over the others and how?

e)   Leave the crickets for a number of days before carrying out further experiments.

f)   After a few days re-examine the terrarium for about 15 minutes. Note whether any individuals have established homes and territories. How does the amount of activity compare to the first 15 minutes in the terrarium? Explain any differences.

g)   On the next day force confrontations between specific males by placing a large-mouthed bottle upside down over the home of one cricket. Then introduce a strange cricket into the bottle. Note the results.

h)   Describe the results of such confrontations in terms of any aggression evident.

i)   Try to determine the dominant crickets as a result of these confrontations.

j)   Leave the crickets for a number of days.

k)   Introduce a female cricket (unmarked) into the colony. Try to observe any differences in confrontations; if matings occur and with which males; the importance of singing, if any; variation in the nature of singing between males to females and males to males.

Discussion

a)   A number of important questions have already been asked in the *Procedure*. Be sure that you have answered them.

b)   Do crickets show forms of behavior which insure that the strongest (and presumably fittest) males show dominance over weaker males; establish themselves as the owners of the best territories (having shelter, etc.); end up mating with the females of the population? Summarize evidence supporting your answer.

Major Field Studies

5

5.1 ECOLOGICAL STUDIES IN A WOODLOT OR FOREST

Objective

The main objective of this study is to investigate the relationships between the abiotic and biotic factors of a forest ecosystem.

Place

The ideal region is a large woodlot or forest that has been relatively undisturbed by man or domestic animals for several years. Parks, conservation areas, and forests under government control are examples. A mixed woodlot usually contains the greatest diversity of life, but a pure coniferous or deciduous stand also offers many interesting studies. Further diversity is often added when the woodlot is located on the side of a hill that runs from a wet lowland area to a dry upland area. In all cases, the most meaningful results are obtained if the studies are performed when the canopy is fully developed.

In the absence of an ideal site, you can perform most of the suggested studies in such places as a wooded area of a city park or a farm woodlot that is open to cows. In the former case, be sure to include in your study a search for evidence of the impact of man on the region. In the latter, try to determine the effect of the cows on the woodlot.

Pre-field Preparation

(a) Examine topographical maps and aerial photographs of the region. From the aerial photograph, determine the area of the woodlot. (If you know the scale of the photograph, you can determine the area by laying out a system of grid lines of known spacing over the photograph.) What surrounds the woodlot? Where are the nearest sources of water? Is the topography flat, rolling, or hilly? Locate one or more open glades in the woodlot. Try to identify tree associations like groves of cedar trees and large expanses of deciduous trees.

(b) Prepare a preliminary field map of the region. Mark on it the various things you discovered in (a). Select what you feel would be good locations for the base camp and study sites. Insert on your map any prominent landmarks that might help you find the study sites.

(c) Investigate the past history of the area. Trace its ownership as far back as you can. For what purposes did each owner use the area? Has the area experienced, within recent times, a forest fire? When was the last time that logging, commercial or therapeutic, was conducted in the woodlot?

Materials

a) labels and marking pens
b) notebooks and pencils
c) topographical maps and aerial photographs
d) identification guide books
e) collecting jars for soil samples and insects
f) preservative for insects (80% denatured ethanol)
g) beating sheets and sweep nets
h) pocket magnifiers
i) insect aspirators
j) trowel or small shovel
k) soil sampler
l) soil thermometers
m) soil test kit (pH and main minerals)

n)   sling psychrometers

o)   light meter (foot-candles)

p)   increment borer

q)   tape measures, meter sticks, compasses, and other equipment required for a quantitative vegetation study (see Unit 4)

r)   wind velocity gauges

s)   boards, 10 cm × 10 cm

t)   thermometers (air)

u)   clinometers and equipment for profile and/or contour studies (see Unit 3)

v)   binoculars

Procedure

a)   Walk slowly through the woodlot in small groups. Visit the areas that you marked on your preliminary field map as possible study sites. Observe the overall nature of the woodlot. What trees appear to be dominant? How old do you think the largest trees are? What plants appear to be dominant in the shrub and ground strata? At what successional stage does the woodlot seem to be?

b)   Watch closely for birds, mammals, and other larger animals. Use binoculars to help you to identify the species. Note also the location of each species. What stratum was it in? Was it in dense cover or in a clearing? Was it at the edge of the woodlot or in the interior?

c)   Return to the base camp and discuss your findings with the other groups. Update the field map.

d)   Determine the boundaries of the region to be investigated. Mark these clearly by tying colored ribbon to shrubs and trees along the boundaries. Determine the total area of the study region.

e)   Decide whether your vegetation analysis is to be qualitative or quantitative. If it is to be qualitative, lay out 100-m² systematic quadrats as described in Section 4.4. Identify the tree species in each quadrat and describe the abundance of each species using *abundant (a)*, *frequent (f)*, *occasional (o)*, and *rare (r)*. Using nested quadrats, repeat this for the shrub and ground strata.

f) If the vegetation analysis is to be quantitative, select the appropriate method from Unit 4 and proceed as instructed. If your interest is only in the trees of the area, you can do your analysis most quickly with the random pairs method. If an environmental gradient is clearly evident (as often occurs if the woodlot is on the side of a hill), the line intercept and belt transect methods yield useful information. The quadrat method, though often more time-consuming, is the best choice if this is your first outing to a woodlot.

g) Study the animal life (or evidence of it) at each study site. Look particularly for insects and other arthropods. Use the insect aspirator to collect visible specimens from vegetation. Use beating sheets to collect arthropods that drop from shrubs as you shake them. Use sweep nets to sample the arthropods of the herb layer. Be sure to note the type of vegetation on which each animal was found. Examine each animal closely with a pocket magnifier, noting special adaptations such as the structure of the mouthparts. These observations will help you to determine the niche occupied by the animal. Look under fallen logs, bark, and other debris for animals. Return such objects to their original positions after your examination. (Why?) If you plan to study the soil fauna, consult *A Guide to the Study of Soil Ecology* by W. A. Andrews et al., Prentice-Hall, 1973, for techniques. Look for evidence of woodpeckers and other birds. Examine hollow trees and other possible homes of mammals.

h) Investigate the following abiotic factors at each site: Light intensity (Section 3.17), relative humidity (Section 3.11), wind velocity (Section 3.10), soil and air temperatures, and soil conditions (Section 3.23). All groups must measure soil temperatures at the same depth and air temperatures at the same height.

i) If you can return to the site in 2 or 3 weeks, place a 10 cm × 10 cm board at each study site. After the elapsed time, turn the boards over. Note the name, number, and unique features of each species of animal on the boards. Consult *A Guide to the Study of Soil Ecology.*

j) Investigate the past history of the forest. Use the increment borer to sample representative trees of different species. Keep the cores for the follow-up session by wrapping them in paper. The number of rings and their spacing will give you interesting information on the history of the stand. Examine stumps. Determine the ages of the trees when cut and estimate when the cutting occurred.

k)   If certain areas appear to be heavily used by humans for recreation, try to determine the impact that humans are having on the woodlot. For example, you could compare the percolation rate of water into the soil in impacted areas and loose areas. You could also examine the various strata for evidence of damage.

l)   If slope appears to be a significant abiotic factor in the woodlot, determine it as outlined in Section 3.3. Profile and contour studies may also be performed if time permits. (See Sections 3.5 and 3.6.)

Notes

a)   If you wish to shorten the field trip, study only one quadrat in each of a few selected areas: a wet area, a dry area, the bottom of a hill, the top of a hill, a clearing, a predominately coniferous stand, a predominately deciduous stand. Such a study will not, of course, tell you as much about the area as the more extensive study.

b)   The study outlined here requires the talents of 30—40 well-prepared persons working for a full day. Some time-consuming activities like a quantitative vegetation analysis and soil testing at every site may have to be restricted if you lack time and preparation.

Follow-up

a)   Summarize in tabular form the abiotic measurements made at each study site.

b)   Summarize the biotic data for each study site.

c)   Interpret your summaries using the ecosystem concept. For example, how does the vegetation modify the abiotic factors? How do the abiotic factors affect the vegetation? What plant-animal relationships did you discover?

d)   Construct as many food chains as you can for the woodlot. If possible, put these together in a food web.

e)   Has the woodlot been managed? If so, would you judge this management as a positive or negative factor? Why? How would you like to see the area managed? Why?

5.2 ECOLOGICAL STUDIES IN MEADOWS AND WEEDY FIELDS

Objective

The main objective of this study is to investigate the relationships between the abiotic and biotic factors of a meadow or weedy field ecosystem.

Place

An ideal location for this study is an "old-field" community adjacent to a meadow that supports domesticated grazing animals like cows. The "old-field" community should have been undisturbed for at least 4 or 5 years. Such situations are common in rural areas. Farmers frequently put up a fence to keep cattle out of a particular region, thereby creating the ideal study site. Of course, permission must be obtained before you enter private land to perform this study.

Other suitable sites are parks and conservation areas where an undisturbed grassy area is adjacent to a mown area. (The mower has replaced the cow as an ecological factor.) If you can include within the boundaries of your study area a region of permanently wet soil, a greater diversity of plants and animals will be noted.

Many schools have playing fields that are acceptable sites for this study.

Pre-field Preparation

(a) Investigate the past history of the area. How long has the "old-field" community been undisturbed? How long has the meadow community been grazed or mown? What is the climax vegetation of the region? If the area was once a forest, when were the trees removed? Why were they removed?

(b) Study the topography of the site using topographical maps. Is it flat, rolling, or hilly? What effects might the topography have on the plant and animal life?

(c) Prepare a preliminary field map of the region using aerial photographs and topographical maps. (Be sure to check the dates of the photographs and maps!) Select suitable locations for the base camp and study sites.

Materials

as in Section 5.1, with the deletion of p)

Procedure

a) Update your preliminary field map. Show the locations of prominent landmarks like rock piles, solitary trees, fence rows, and bodies of water.

b) Before you disturb the site too much, scan it thoroughly with binoculars. Note the species, relative abundance, and habitats of birds and mammals.

c) Mark the boundaries of the study site with 4-foot poles bearing colored ribbon. If possible, include equal portions of undisturbed and grazed land. A permanently wet area is also desirable. The total area should not exceed 10,000 m² (2 or 3 acres).

d) Lay out a system of 1 m² quadrats over the area as outlined in Section 4.4.

e) Assign one-half of the class to the undisturbed area and the other half to the grazed area.

f) Approach each quadrat carefully, making sure that your movement and shadow do not warn inhabitants of your approach. Slowly disturb the vegetation and note the species and relative numbers of insects that leave the quadrat. Search through the surface debris for other animals. Use the sweep net to collect specimens for closer examination. Note special adaptations such as the structure of the mouthparts. Note also the type of vegetation on which the insects (or other arthropods) resided. If you wish to study the soil fauna, consult *A Guide to the Study of Soil Ecology* by W. A. Andrews et al., Prentice-Hall, 1973. Look for evidence of larger animal life—moles, voles, mice, and so on.

g) Perform a vegetation analysis. If you select the qualitative method, identify the 10 or so most common plant species in each quadrat and classify each species as *abundant (a), frequent (f), occasional (o),* or *rare (r).* If you select the quantitative method, proceed as outlined in Section 4.4. Keep the results for the undisturbed and grazed sections separate from one another to facilitate comparisons in the follow-up.

h) Investigate the appropriate abiotic factors at each site. Since light intensity, relative humidity, and wind velocity will vary little over the area, perform these studies only if time permits. Concentrate on soil conditions (Section 3.23). Try to determine the soil preferences of unique plant associations. Studies of percolation rates should indicate one way in which grazing animals affect an area.

i) If you can return to the site in 2 or 3 weeks, place a 10 cm × 10 cm board at each site. After the elapsed time, turn the boards over and note the name, number, and unique features of each species of animal on the boards. Consult *A Guide to the Study of Soil Ecology.*

j) To reduce the time required for this study, perform some of the time-consuming exercises like soil testing and insect investigations in just 2 or 3 quadrats in each of the grazed and undisturbed areas.

Follow-up

a) Compare the abiotic measurements made in the grazed area with those made in the undisturbed area. Account for any differences.

b) Compare the animal life—soil fauna, arthropods, birds, and mammals—of the two regions. Account for any differences.

c) Summarize in words the effects of grazing on the area. Would these effects disappear if grazing were stopped?

d) List any evidence that you saw of secondary succession. Describe the long-term changes that would occur in the area if grazing were stopped.

5.3 THE MEADOW-WOODLOT ECOTONE

Objective

The main objective of this study is to investigate the effects of the changing abiotic factors between a meadow and a woodlot on the biotic component of the region.

Place

Any ecotone region is exciting to study because of the great diversity of life that it contains. However, the most interesting region is one that consists of an undisturbed meadow adjacent to an undisturbed woodlot. Recent inhabitation of either the meadow or woodlot by domestic grazing animals like cows generally reduces the diversity of life. Nonetheless, meaningful studies can be conducted in grazed areas, particularly if you include as a part of your study an investigation of the effects of grazing on the area.

Ecotone studies can also be conducted in most city parks and in greenbelt areas that have both open and wooded areas. Many such regions probably exist close to your school.

Pre-field Preparation

(a) Consult topographical maps and aerial photographs to gain an overview of the nature of the area. How extensive is the woodlot? How large is the meadow? How long is the ecotone? Is the terrain hilly, rolling, or flat? Is there water nearby? Do the prevailing winds blow from the woodlot to the meadow or from the meadow to the woodlot? What differences will this make?

(b) Determine, if possible, the history of the area. What has man been doing to the area over the past few years?

(c) Using the topographical maps and aerial photographs, sketch a preliminary field map of the area. Then select what you feel are the best locations for the base camp and study sites.

(d) Five abiotic factors will probably vary from the meadow into the woodlot—soil conditions, moisture (soil and air), temperature (soil and air), wind velocity, and light intensity. Predict how these factors might change along a line running from the meadow into the woodlot. Then predict the accompanying biotic changes.

Materials

a) labels and marking pens
b) notebooks and pencils
c) topographical maps and aerial photographs
d) identification guide books
e) collecting jars for soil samples and insects
f) preservative for insects (80% denatured ethanol)
g) insect nets (sweep, aerial, and beating)
h) insect aspirators
i) trowel or small shovel
j) soil sampler
k) soil thermometers
l) soil test kit (pH and main minerals)
m) soil sieves

n) sling psychrometers

o) light meter (foot-candles)

p) increment borer

q) strong cord (or rope) and markers

r) tape measures and meter sticks

s) wind velocity and wind direction gauges

t) rain gauges

u) compasses

v) boards, 10 cm × 10 cm

w) thermometers (air)

x) clinometers and equipment for profile and/or contour studies (see Sections 3.5 and 3.7)

Procedure

a) Prepare a large field map of the area using the technique described in Section 3.9.

b) Walk slowly through the area, checking for changes in abiotic and biotic factors. Watch for birds, mammals, reptiles, and amphibians. Many of these animals will leave the immediate area because of your subsequent activities. Record species, habitat, and numbers, where possible. Binoculars are an asset. Are the strata in the woodlot clearly defined? Which strata do the various animals seem to prefer? Why?

c) Lay out a base line in the meadow, roughly parallel to the edge of the woodlot (Fig. 5-1). The line should be clearly within the meadow, not in the ecotone.

Fig. 5-1
The meadow-woodlot eco-
tone.

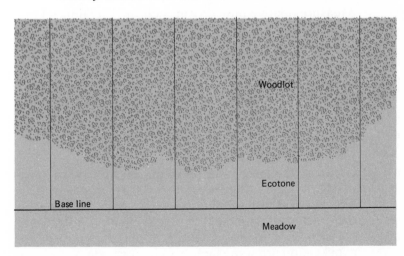

d) At suitable intervals along the base line, place markers to designate the starting points for the crews. Consult Section 4.4 for ideas regarding the spacing of the lines.

e) Beginning at each marker, lay out a line perpendicular to the base line and running well into the woodlot. The length of the line may vary from 20 to 100 or more meters, depending on how abruptly the vegetation changes in the ecotone. If the change is abrupt, a short line will do. If the change is gradual, a longer line should be used.

f) If the area appears to have sufficient slope that this may be an important factor, determine the slope as outlined in Section 3.3. Profile and contour studies may also be performed at this time. (See Sections 3.5 and 3.7.)

g) Select study sites along each line. You should have at least two in the meadow, two in the ecotone, and two in the woodlot. Lay out a quadrat at each site. (Consult Section 4.4. for spacing and size.)

h) Carefully examine the vegetation in each quadrat. Note its density, the species present, and unique features—leaf area, shape, and size; flower type, arrangement, and size; other adaptations to the environment. Alternatively, you may wish to perform a quantitative study of the vegetation using the line intercept method (Section 4.5) or the belt transect method (Section 4.6). Leave markers at each site since you will be returning to perform further studies.

i) Measure the light intensity at each site (Section 3.17).

j) Measure relative humidity at each site (Section 3.11).

k) Measure the soil and air temperatures at each site. Be sure to make all soil measurements at the same depth and all air measurements at the same height.

l) Perform the appropriate soil tests at each site (Section 3.23). To complete this step, samples must be collected and taken back to the laboratory.

m) Determine the wind velocity and direction at each site (Section 3.10).

n) Compare the insect species of the meadow with those of the woodlot. (See Section 4.11 for capture techniques.) Watch particularly for special adaptations to their selected habitats. Protective coloration, flight patterns, structure of mouthparts, and thickness of the exoskeleton are some factors of importance.

o)   If you can return to the site in a few weeks, rain gauges could be placed at selected sites (Section 3.13). Possible vandalism should be considered before this step is taken.

p)   Place one of the 10 cm × 10 cm boards at each site. Return in 2 weeks, turn the boards over, and note the name, number, and unique features of each species of animal on the boards. Consult *A Guide to the Study of Soil Ecology* by W. A. Andrews et al., Prentice-Hall, 1973.

Notes

a)   Whether you can perform the study as outlined depends on the size of your group, the time period allotted, and the equipment available. As outlined, this is an all-day outing for a group of 30–40 persons who have rehearsed the techniques involved and have carefully planned the day's activities. You may find it necessary to delete some time-consuming activities like the quantitative vegetation analysis and the contour study. Soil testing may have to be restricted to one line only.

b)   Some of the activities can only be performed at certain times of year. For example, the insect studies will be most effective in the early fall.

Follow-up

a)   Complete your large map of the area. Show the location of prominent landmarks and bodies of water.

b)   Describe and account for any changes in abiotic factors along a line from the meadow into the woodlot.

c)   Describe and account for any changes in biotic factors (plant and animal) along a line from the meadow into the woodlot.

d)   List evidence to support the statement that the ecotone generally has a greater diversity of life than either of the communities that form it.

e)   Construct as many food chains as you can for the area. If possible, put these together into a food web.

f)   Describe man's impact, if any, on the area. Would you judge this impact as negative or positive? Why?

g)   Suggest a management plan that you would like to see implemented in the area. Account for your suggestions. Are they ecologically sound?

5.4 SUCCESSION ON SAND DUNES

Objective

The main objective of this study is to find out how the abiotic and biotic factors of a dune region interact to form the unique distribution of communities found in such a region.

Place

Sand dune successions commonly occur on the leeward shores of large bodies of water, particularly where large expanses of sand are exposed to the prevailing winds. As you walk inland at the ideal site, you should be able to see or feel changes in abiotic factors—light intensity, soil conditions, relative humidity, wind velocity, and temperature. On this same walk you should be able to spot a succession of reasonably well defined plant communities.

If an outing to a true dune area is impossible, visit any large sandy beach. Many of the successional stages will probably be present there.

Pre-field Preparation

(a) Read Section 1.5. Answer the first two questions of *For Thought and Research.*

(b) Find out all you can about the history of the area. If it is a government park, when and why was the land acquired by the government? What is the estimated age of the oldest forest in the area? When did the last major blowout occur? What caused it?

(c) Use aerial photographs and topographical maps to prepare a preliminary field map of the area. Select what you feel is the best location for the study. If possible, a small group should visit the area in advance of the main outing to pinpoint the exact location. What unique set of circumstances led to the formation of the dunes?

(d) Carefully rehearse any study techniques that you will be using. A hot sand dune is no place to learn how to operate a sling psychrometer or how to lay out a belt transect!

(e) Thoughtless behavior on sand dunes often leads to serious problems. Simply pulling up some sand grass in the wrong place could trigger a blowout. To ensure that your group acts responsibly, prepare a list of rules of conduct to be followed by all on this study.

Materials

a) as in Section 5.3, with the deletion of items t) and v)

b) maximum-minimum thermometers

c) pocket magnifiers (for examining soil)

Procedure

a) Make corrections on and add further details to your preliminary field map. You may wish to prepare a more accurate map using the method in Section 3.9.

b) Begin at the water margin and walk slowly inland toward the wooded area. Look carefully at the soil and vegetation. Watch for birds, reptiles, and other large animals. Make a note of all abiotic and biotic changes that you encounter.

c) Return to the water margin by a different route, making similar observations.

d) Begin your detailed investigation of the area by marking the boundaries of the study area.

e) If you plan to do quantitative vegetation studies, lay out the lines for a line-intercept study (Section 4.5) or the belts for a belt-transect study (Section 4.6).

f) If your vegetation study is to be qualitative, you should still lay out lines as described in Section 4.5. Follow these lines as you perform your investigations of abiotic and biotic conditions at a number of sites. Suggested sites are the wet sand margin, the middle beach, the windward slope of dune 1, the top of dune 1, the leeward slope of dune 1, the hollow between dunes 1 and 2, the top of dune 2, the cottonwood region, the pine region, the oak region, and, finally, the maple-beech region. (Some of these regions may be absent in your area.)

g) Investigate the following abiotic factors at each of the sites listed in f): light intensity (Section 3.17), relative humidity (Section 3.11), wind velocity (Section 3.10), soil and air temperature, and soil conditions (Section 3.23). Leave a maximum-minimum thermometer on the ground at each site for the duration of the study. Examine the soil at each site with a pocket magnifier. Summarize your findings in a table like Table 12.

h) If you are performing a qualitative vegetation study, investigate the plants at each of the sites listed in f).

TABLE 12   ABIOTIC FACTORS

Study site	Light intensity	Relative humidity	Soil temperature	Air temperature	Maximum-minimum temperature	Wind velocity	Soil texture and horizons
Wet sand margin							
Middle beach							
Windward slope, dune 1							
Top, dune 1							
Leeward slope, dune 1							
Hollow between dunes 1 & 2							
Top, dune 2							
Cottonwood							
Pine							
Oak							
Maple-beech							

Describe the abundance of each species using the following terminology: *abundant (a), frequent (f), occasional (o), rare (r).* Note the structure of the leaves and stems of the dominant species at each site. Do not disturb the soil to examine the roots. However, if some roots are exposed, note their structure. In wooded areas note carefully the composition of each stratum of vegetation.

i)   If your vegetation study is to be quantitative, omit step h) and proceed with a line intercept study (Section 4.5) or a belt transect study (Section 4.6).

j)   Note the animal life (or evidence of it) at the various sites. Look particularly for insects and other arthropods. If you capture any of these, examine them closely for special adaptations to their habitats. For example, if you capture an insect on the middle beach area, check it for protective coloration and adaptation to the xerophytic conditions of this harsh environment.

k)   Look for evidence of man's impact on the environment—the effects of paths, picnic sites, roadways, and motorized recreational vehicles.

l)   Examine a blowout area. What kinds of trees once stood there? What was their average age when the blowout occurred? (Use the increment borer.)

m)   Determine the average age of the trees in each successional stage. Get permission from the authorities before you use the increment borer on live trees.

Follow-up

a)   Gather together for each site the measurements of abiotic factors and the results of vegetation and animal studies.

b)   Summarize in words any gradients in abiotic and biotic factors that are obvious from your studies.

c)   Interpret this summary using the ecosystem concept.

d)   If conditions warrant, suggest a management plan that you would like to see implemented in the area. Account for your suggestions.

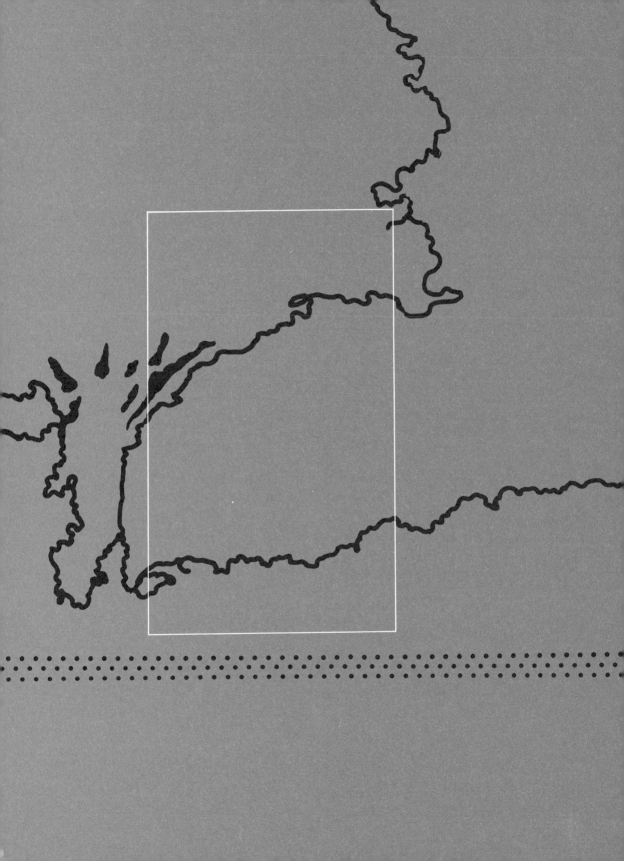

Research Topics

6

This unit contains a number of topics that are of great importance to all of us. Examine the topics closely and select one that interests you. Research it thoroughly, by yourself, or with several other students.

A list of things that you might do has been included with each topic. This list will help you to get started on your project. It is *not* complete. Many other ideas will come to mind as you research the topic. Some references have been included. You should also consult encyclopedias and other books in your school and community libraries. Many government agencies, industries, conservation groups, and nature clubs supply free information on some of these topics. You need only ask for it. Letters, telephone calls, and visitations are effective ways of obtaining information.

At the end of your study you should prepare a written report so that others in your class can benefit from your work. Your teacher will give you instructions regarding the nature of the report.

6.1 ENDANGERED SPECIES

Why do animals become extinct? Since about 1600 A.D., 27 mammal and 65 bird species have disappeared. Even today, after all of the lessons we should have learned about the extinction of animal species, 300 kinds of birds and mammals are in great danger of extinction.

What common patterns and processes reduce huge numbers of animals to the extinction level? Sometimes extinction occurs naturally. Changes in climate can destroy niches and habitats that a species occupied. For example, the ice ages destroyed much vegetation and, along with it, those animal species which could not tolerate the harsh conditions. Also, competition for food and space often becomes so intense that one species drives out another. Further, natural selection has played a critical role in the disappearance of many wildlife species. Generally those animals with low reproductive rates and high energy requirements are the first to go. Why is this so?

Too often man brings a species to the endangered or extinction level. He has often destroyed a population of wild animals by exploiting it for food, clothing, or sport. The overkill which occurred in man's quest for buffalo hides, beaver and otter pelts, and whale oil represents thoughtless exploitation of what were considered inexhaustible resources. Pests of domestic crops and predators of livestock were often ruthlessly wiped out as man tried to bring civilization to a hostile environment.

The webs of ecology are intricate. Man has often failed to realize that cutting forests, draining swamps, and spraying fields with pesticides destroy habitats and food cycles of creatures he seldom sees. Waterfowl and woodpeckers have found themselves homeless. Other birds have found the DDT content of earthworms deadly to digest. Although man cannot be blamed for all cases of species extinction, the majority of cases have resulted largely from his action.

One need not be a conservationist or ecologist to recognize the tragedy of the extinction of an animal species. A museum full of animal skeletons and skins cannot replace the unique structural and behavioral patterns that each living species represents. Ecologically we know that each species is a building block in the pyramid of life in an ecosystem. Remove too many blocks and the foundation loses its stability. When a species disappears, food chains and webs are broken. But, more importantly, we lose a part of ourselves. In spite of all our scientific advances, we still belong to nature.

For Thought and Research

The following are some aspects to investigate:
1   Why did dinosaurs become extinct?
2   Why did the American mastodon become extinct?

3 Why is the California condor in danger of extinction? Can steps be taken to ensure its survival?
4 The sea otter and oil pollution.
5 How was the trumpeter swan saved from extinction?
6 The role of hunting in species extinction.
7 The role of habitat destruction in species extinction.
8 The problem of the ivory-billed woodpecker.
9 Buffalo Bill and the bison hunters.
10 Pesticides and their effects on reproduction of ospreys, peregrine falcons, golden eagles, and other birds of prey.
11 The role of zoos and forest reserves in the protection of endangered species.
12 Wolves: pests or ecologically essential animals?
13 Whales in danger of extinction.
14 Common patterns and processes that lead to extinction of species.
15 Techniques for ensuring the survival of endangered species.

Recommended Readings

1 *Biological Conservation* by D. W. Ehrenfeld, Holt, Rinehart & Winston, 1970. This book explores in a most interesting fashion causes, effects, and solutions of the problems of species elimination.
2 *Vanishing Wild Animals of the World* by R. Fitter, Midland Bank, London, 1968. This well-illustrated book describes endangered animals and conservation methods at a beginner's level.
3 *Wildlife in Danger* by J. Fisher, N. Simon, J. Vincent, Viking, 1969. This book deals with many species, including plants, fish, and reptiles.
4 *Fall of the Sparrow* by J. Williams, Oxford University Press, 1951.
5 *The Land and Wildlife of North America* by P. Farb, Time, Inc., 1964.
6 *Extinct and Vanishing Animals* by V. Ziswiler, Springer-Verlag, 1967. This excellent book on endangered species throughout the world discusses the nature of extinction.

6.2 TERRITORIAL BEHAVIOR

Why do birds sing? Scientists believe that some singing is a bird's way of saying "This territory is mine." His song claims a certain area of space for his mate and himself, in which they can feed, nest, and raise their young. What we consider harmonious sounds may be a warning to male intruders and a cordial welcome to females seeking a prominent land owner.

The singing of birds is just one important aspect of a phenomenon called territorial behavior. Nearly all species of birds, mammals, and some insects parcel out the environment into tiny lots so that each active member of the species has a territorial space. The *territory* is defined as that area of space which an animal guards as its exclusive possession and which it will defend against all members of its species. *Territorial behavior* is the set of ritual behavior patterns which each species activates when it sets up or defends the area it considers home. Bird song and other territorial displays are most evident during periods of feeding and breeding. This set of gestures is a peaceful means (rather than a fight to the death) of communicating to members of one species the way in which the environmental resources will be shared.

This process of animal behavior has evolved from the beginnings of life and, strangely enough, it offers animal populations a number of advantages. At nesting time each mating pair can hatch and raise their young in a peaceful neighborhood with few intraspecific quarrels. Territories are usually large enough to contain sufficient food for adults and young alike. Indirectly, then, territories prevent over-exploitation of food resources and also control the population size in a given area. Animals without territories are often excluded from the habitat and are generally prevented from breeding.

Sizes of territories vary from species to species. But researchers have found a close link between food supplies and territorial space. Some warblers occupy territories one-tenth of an acre in size during insect outbreaks. Yet in times of food shortage and drought this area increases in size. A golden eagle often controls a territory as large as 40 square miles. Colonial sea birds crowd into nesting areas which are only a few feet square, just out of reach of their neighbors' sharp bills.

In recent years there has been a keen interest in the concept of animal territories. Some scientists have suggested territories are an innate method of population control, a factor just as important as food in population dynamics. Robert Ardrey has examined the territorial behavior in many species, especially man. The problem of each person having enough breathing room or territorial space is an important consideration in a crowded environment. Have a close look at the world of territories and, as you learn about this exciting set of relationships within a species, consider how some of these concepts might apply to the human population.

For Thought and Research

The following are some aspects to investigate:
1   The territorial behavior of a particular bird species. Include response to intruders, nesting behavior, and courtship ritual. You may wish to do some of this research by direct observation. (See Section 4.12.)
2   The territorial behavior of a particular mammal species such as the wolf, squirrel, beaver, or deer. (See Section 4.13.)

3 The territorial behavior of a particular insect species such as the cricket. (See Section 4.22.)

4 Do domestic animals like cows, horses, cats, and dogs display territorial behavior?

5 The relationship between territorial size and the chances of a species becoming endangered or extinct. Include some examples and your thoughts on possible solutions.

6 The ecological reasons for the closely packed territories of colonial nesting birds such as gulls and terns. Investigate also the location and size of such colonies and the behavior of the birds within the colonies.

7 The behavior of birds that do not establish territories, for example, the cowbird or cuckoo. How do they raise their young without the protection offered by territorial boundaries?

8 The effects of crowding on animals. What happens when animals like mice are forced to live closer than territorial boundaries would have placed them?

9 Territorial behavior in early and modern man.

10 Ghetto problems—a need for territorial space?

Recommended Readings

1 *An Introduction to Ornithology* by G. J. Wallace, Macmillan, 1955. This authoritative book deals with most aspects of bird life in a readable manner.

2 *The Birds* by R. T. Peterson and the Editors of *Life*, Life Nature Library, Time, Inc., 1963. This well-illustrated book presents in an interesting fashion a brief but broad description of bird life.

3 *Ecology and Field Biology* by R. L. Smith, Harper & Row, 1966. Contains accurate information on territorial behavior.

4 *The Territorial Imperative* by R. Ardrey, Atheneum, 1966. Discusses territorial behavior in many species, including man.

5 *Territory in Bird Life* by H. E. Howard, Atheneum, 1964. A small book which discusses the securing and defense of territory and the links of song, migration, and reproduction with territorial behavior.

6.3   MIGRATION

For centuries the migration of animals has intrigued men. Most of us associate migration with birds because they are the most noticeable seasonal travelers. Often we overlook the long migratory journeys of insects such as the Monarch butterfly and of mammals such as bats, mule deer, and caribou (Fig. 6-1). This two-way journey of terrestrial and aquatic creatures has long been an unsolved puzzle to scientists. However, recent research has provided us with a few clues which may unravel some of its mysteries.

Modern banding techniques and reported sightings have provided us with enough information to map out most of

Fig. 6-1
Migration of caribou across the Canadian barrens. (Courtesy of Ontario Ministry of Natural Resources.)

the well-traveled paths of almost all North American migrants. The journey from a breeding area to a winter home is not always from north to south. Birds like the evening grosbeak travel from east to west. Mountain dwellers like some elk, mule deer, and song birds simply migrate to the warmth of a lower altitude during the winter months. The well-used migration routes which huge flocks prefer to travel twice each year are called flyways. There are four in North America: the Atlantic, Mississippi, Central, and Pacific. Each funnels birds to and from the Gulf of Mexico. Not all birds migrate. Many species winter in the north while other species journey only a few hundred miles.

The Arctic tern, golden plover, and bobolink are three long-distance flyers that journey more than 10,000 miles across two continents to reach their destination. Waterfowl may travel at migration speeds as fast as 60 miles per hour. Geese crossing mountain ranges have been sighted at heights of 20,000 feet. Storms and unusually cold weather are natural forces which have always prevented some birds from reaching their destination. Now the combination of foggy nights and tall man-made obstacles have caused thousands of disoriented birds to crash to their deaths.

Considerable research has enabled us to predict which species will migrate where. But what causes the start of migration is still not fully explained. Just what makes animals migrate like clockwork at approximately the same time each year? Some believe that in northern areas the dwindling food supply prompts bird species and caribou to seek out new feeding grounds farther south. Also, environmental factors like temperature, humidity, and photoperiod are probably seasonal stimuli which prepare animals physically and psychologically for migration. A movement of cold polar air from the north in the autumn or a warm moist air front from the Caribbean in the spring is often the spark which initiates the migratory journey.

Scientists are still guessing about that special sense of birds which allows them to navigate across unknown terrain to places they have never seen. Many theories have been suggested but all are only partial explanations. In some cases older birds remember shorelines and landmarks and the younger birds follow their lead. Experiments by a German scientist, Gustav Kramer, showed how birds could use the position of the sun to help orient themselves. Birds are believed to use the position of the stars in nocturnal flights.

As you investigate migration, you will realize that answers to many of the critical questions are still unknown. Your research, however, should give you a better understanding of this fascinating process of nature.

For Thought and Research

The following are some aspects to investigate:
1   Methods of determining migration routes of animals—banding and radio techniques.
2   The migration behavior of a particular bird species. How, where, when, and why does it migrate?
3   The migration behavior of a particular mammal. How, where, when, and why does it migrate?
4   Migration of Monarch butterflies.
5   Which birds migrate the farthest, fastest, highest, and longest?
6   Birds using the flyway closest to you.
7   Navigation by homing pigeons.
8   Man's interference with migration of a bird or other animal, and his attempts to assist migration.

Recommended Readings

1   *The Birds* by R. T. Peterson and the Editors of *Life*, Life Nature Library, Time, Inc., 1963. A picturesque and exciting book which presents many of the important issues of bird study.
2   *Ecology and Field Biology* by R. L. Smith, Harper & Row, 1966. A short but good discussion of migration of insects, reptiles, mammals, birds, and fish.
3   *Paths Across the Earth* by L. Milne and M. Milne, Harper & Row, 1958. An excellent, easily read description of the major aspects of migration.

4 *An Introduction to Ornithology* by G. J. Wallace, Macmillan, 1963. A complete text for the study of birds. Read Chapter 11 for bird migration.
5 *Ornithology: An Introduction* by A. L. Rand, New American Library, 1969. An inexpensive pocket book on birds, with selective chapters on migration and orientation. Excellent references are given for each chapter in the book.
6 *Bird Migration* by D. R. Griffin, Natural History Press, 1964. Contains excellent chapters on homing experiments, observations of birds by radar and airplane, and different theories on celestial navigation. Suggested for advanced or very interested students.

6.4 FOREST AND WOODLOT MANAGEMENT

Throughout much of North America, urban and farming regions were created by the cutting of forests. Usually, however, patches of trees were left standing. The result is a scattering of small woodlots. Recently government officials have realized the economic and ecological importance of these woodlots. As a result our governments now encourage and support the management of such woodlots. Management generally means removing crooked, crowded, and diseased trees. It also means removing tree species that have little commercial value. Unfortunately, management of this type also removes the habitats of many animals. Since management practices have been weighted toward the economic side, with little consideration for the ecological side, forest management has received much criticism in recent years. Ecologists and conservationists see mechanized cutting as a threat to irreplaceable wilderness environments and wildlife reservoirs. Yet we cannot ignore the fact that the forest industry of Canada and the United States plays a major role in the economy of both nations. As Canada's largest industry it consumes over 13% of the nation's electrical power.

Your main task in this research topic is to find out if forests and woodlots can be managed in such a way that both economic and ecological values are realized.

For Thought and Research

The following are some aspects to investigate:
1 Economic values of woodlot areas.
2 Ecological values of woodlot areas.
3 Effects of domestic animals like cows on woodlots.
4 Insects and diseases that attack various tree species.
5 The most commercially valuable trees. How are their wood products used?
6 The impact of mechanized cutting.

7 Can mature trees be harvested without damaging younger trees?
8 Do wilderness areas (regions where no cutting is allowed) serve useful purposes?
9 Managing a maple sugar bush—past and present.
10 Methods of reforestation.
11 Advantages of reforestation.

Recommended Readings

1 *The Forest* by P. Farb and the Editors of *Life,* Time, Inc., 1961. An exciting and colorful examination of the forest environment, its history, life, and future development.
2 *The Life of the Forest* by J. McCormick, McGraw-Hill, 1966. A colorful and enjoyable description of the forest community.
3 Ask your federal and state or provincial Forestry Departments for booklets on farm woodlots, managing land for wildlife, forest conservation, insects and diseases that attack trees, maple syrup production, and reforestation.

6.5 FOREST FIRES

Since the beginning of time fire has exerted a powerful influence on the evolution of nature and the history of mankind. After climate and soil, forest fires rank next in importance among the factors that control the vegetation and wildlife of a forest. After years of study of past records and research in new forestry techniques, scientists now understand this destructive force much better.

For years Smoky the Bear has warned us of the terrible destruction of timber and life which human carelessness in the wilderness brings. About 80% of forest fires are caused by thoughtless smokers and campers. But fires are not all bad. Controlled burning of small areas has been used to clear land for agriculture and to rejuvenate aging woodlands.

Early settlers along the St. Lawrence Valley and in the eastern seaboard states viewed the massive virgin hardwood forests as obstacles which impeded farmland development and progress. Because the supply of timber was so abundant, trees were regarded as an infinite resource. As a result, forest fires were deliberately set to clear the land for farming. Too often the fires burned out of control, destroying millions of acres of forest.

Even with modern equipment and well-trained fire fighting personnel, we usually cannot control the awesome fury of a large forest fire. When burning conditions are right, fire moves with a lightning speed that sometimes mocks the

Fig. 6-2
A forest fire. (U.S.D.A. Photo by Bluford W. Muir.)

swiftness of the spotters who detect the initial blaze and the smoke jumpers who parachute to stop the fire before it gets out of control. In the majority of cases, however, early detection and speedy reaction stop small fires before they have an opportunity to become uncontrollable monsters.

Preventive fire control and forest management have reduced the chance of large fires. Closely packed stands have been thinned, fire breaks and roads constructed, and controlled burning allowed at safe periods of the year. Yet improper cutting and lumbering which produces slash still promote fires. And, artificially grown pure stands of conifers in managed forests create extremely hazardous fire conditions. Education, legislation, and more research are greatly needed as a comprehensive approach to solving the problem of forest fires.

For the majority of people who have never experienced the fearsome magnitude of a huge fire, it is hard to imagine what it is like (Fig. 6-2). Thick clouds of smoke block out the midday sun. Breathing is almost impossible. Huge green trees burst into flames like dry match sticks. The very air seems to be on fire as sparks and flames leap upward and outward far in advance of the main blaze. Once the cyclone of fire has finally burned itself out, only the charred skeletons of once magnificent trees remain. Animal life is non-existent on the blackened landscape. A whole priceless ecosystem, often centuries old, has been completely consumed in a few frightening hours.

The value of our woodlands at a time when this natural resource is beginning to dwindle has made people realize the importance of research in this area. The scope of such research is almost limitless.

For Thought and Research

The following are some aspects to investigate:
1 Behavior of small and large forest fires.
2 Ecological consequences of forest fires.
3 Modern fire fighting techniques.
4 Prevention of forest fires.
5 Uses of controlled fires in land management; prescribed burning.
6 A large forest fire of the past.
7 Weather and forest fires.
8 Derivation of the "fire danger index."
9 Fire-resistant tree species.
10 Fire-successional tree species, in particular, jack pine and lodgepole pine. Why are they first in their ranges to become established after a fire? What ecological role do they play?

11 The return of forest life after a fire—succession.
12 Forest management: a cause of or a cure for forest fires?

Recommended Readings

1 *Elements of Forest Fire Control* by the Food and Agriculture Organization of the United Nations, Forestry Division. Available in Canada from McGraw-Hill Ryerson Ltd.; in the United States from Columbia University Press, International Documents Service.
2 *Forest Conservation*, Department of Northern Affairs and National Resources, Forestry Branch, Queen's Printer, Ottawa, 1959. An excellent introduction to all aspects of the forest.
3 *Forest Fire Control and Use* by K. P. Davis, McGraw-Hill, 1959. This text describes thoroughly the effects and behavior of fire, the control of forest fires, and the use of fire in land management.
4 *Principles of Forest Fire Management* by R. C. Clar, California Office of State Printing, 1966. A thorough examination of fire behavior, control, and forest management, presented in simple terms.
5 *Burning an Empire* by S. Hollbrook, Macmillan, 1943. An excellent account of fires which have made history because of the great damage inflicted on man and nature.
6 *Analysis of Forest Fire Behavior* (A Programmed Text), Forest Protection Branch, Ontario Ministry of Natural Resources, Queen's Park, Toronto, Ont. An excellent programmed learning booklet on the major aspects of forest fires.
7 "The Natural Role of Fire in Northern Conifer Forests" by M. L. Heinselman, *Naturalist*, Vol. 21, No. 4, Natural History Society of Minnesota, 1970. This article presents a strong case for prescribed burning as a means of maintaining natural forest ecosystems.

6.6 ADAPTATIONS OF ANIMALS TO TEMPERATURE

It is not unusual for temperatures in the Arctic to drop from a summer high of 35°C (95°F) to a winter low of −50°C (−60°F)—a change of 85°C (155°F). In the so-called temperate regions of North America the seasonal temperature change often exceeds 60°C (110°F). Even in the deserts of the American southwest the seasonal temperature change can be over 55°C (100°F).

What adaptations have evolved that make it possible for animals to survive such temperature extremes? How do they behave during unusually hot and cold periods?

For Thought and Research

The following are some aspects to investigate:

1 Adaptations displayed by invertebrates such as protozoans, crustaceans, insects, molluscs, and various types of worms. (For example, cyst formation, egg production, pupation, and diapause.)

2 Adaptations displayed by poikilothermic vertebrates such as fish, snakes, turtles, frogs, and toads. How do they react to unusually high and low temperatures during a day? How have they adapted to seasonal temperature fluctuations? Do they hibernate? If so, where and how?

3 Adaptations displayed by homoiothermic vertebrates—birds and mammals. (For example, migration, storage of fat, higher food intake and more activity, hibernation, semi-hibernation, and estivation.) Animals of particular interest are shrews, mice, and other rodents that remain active all winter; hummingbirds, which enter a strange dormancy at night to conserve energy; polar bears, seals, whales, and other mammals of the frigid Arctic waters.

Recommended Readings

1 *Animal Physiology* by K. Schmidt-Nielsen, Prentice-Hall, 1970. Contains sections on the adaptation of animals to temperature.

2 *Ecology and Field Biology* by R. L. Smith, Harper & Row, 1966. Contains an interesting and informative section on responses of animals to environmental factors and their adaptations to them.

3 *Biosphere: A Study of Life* by N. M. Jessop, Prentice-Hall, 1970. Discusses briefly at a relatively advanced level many of the adaptations of animals to temperature.

4 *Vertebrate Adaptations*, readings from *Scientific American*, W. H. Freeman, 1952—68. This collection of articles covers in depth most vertebrate adaptations to temperature.

5 Most biology texts contain chapters on animal adaptation.

6.7   SPECIES POLLUTION

An animal population, in its natural environment, is usually kept in balance by predators, parasites, diseases, climatic extremes, and competition for food and space. Plant populations are regulated by many of the same factors. But when plants and animals are transported to new locations where some of the population-limiting factors are absent, rapid growth of the population often occurs. This commonly results in extensive economic losses and the elimination of competing native species. The term *species pollution* is used to describe such an event.

For Thought and Research

The following are some aspects to investigate:

1 For at least one of the following, research the origin of the species pollution problem, its development, its ecological consequences, and the procedures used to combat it:
   a) the rabbit explosion in Australia;
   b) the starling and house sparrow explosion in North America;
   c) the water hyacinth problem in Florida;
   d) the carp in North America;
   e) the sea lamprey in the Great Lakes;
   f) any exotic species of your choice that exhibits species pollution.

2 Repeat question 1 for an exotic species that has proven to be beneficial, for example, the ladybird beetle.

3 Methods of eliminating species pollution.

4 Can the importation of exotic animals be justified when the danger of species pollution exists? (See if you can find examples of an endangered species being helped by moving some of its individuals to a new location where population controls are not so prevalent.)

5 Why should man be particularly cautious when transporting rodents from their natural habitats? Could the common rodent pets—gerbils and hamsters— cause a species pollution problem if a number of them were released in your part of North America? In any part of North America?

Recommended Readings

1 *Biological Conservation* by D. W. Ehrenfeld, Holt, Rinehart & Winston, 1970. This interesting and readable book lists and discusses the more important exotic species that have contributed to species pollution in North America.

2 *Before Nature Dies* by J. Dorst, Collins, 1965. Discusses worldwide examples of species pollution—in particular, the problems in New Zealand and Australia.

3 *The Ecology of Invasions by Animals and Plants* by C. S. Elton, Methuen, 1958. A more advanced source of information.

4 Look up particular animals in encyclopedias and animal books.

Case Studies

7

These case studies are derived from actual information collected by scientific means. They are included here to give you a chance to find out if you can apply the knowledge that you have gained from this book.

7.1   PEST CONTROL

An insect pest has attacked about 20% of the trees in a pure stand of white pine. In an effort to reduce his economic loss, the owner has his forest crop sprayed each spring with a relatively new pesticide. The species which he is trying to eliminate is normally preyed upon by other insects, a parasite, and song birds from nearby woods. To the south of his property is a bird sanctuary for rare species of waterfowl and the carnivorous osprey. He has been assured that natural barriers and the wind direction will keep the pesticide out of the wildlife area. The three areas shown on the diagram (Fig. 7-1) were carefully studied over a five-year period by researchers from a nearby university. Insect populations were estimated, fish and bird populations studied, soil samples collected, and pesticide concentrations measured in an effort to determine the overall environmental influence of this new pesticide. The results are recorded in Table 13.

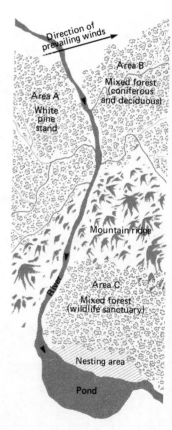

Fig. 7-1
A problem in pest control.

TABLE 13

Year	Area	Insect population	Species of insect predators	% of pests with parasites	% fish mortality (adults)	Pesticide concentration in fish (ppm)	Carnivorous birds		No. of soil species
							% nesting success	Insecticide in eggs (ppm)	
1965	A	200,000	4	50	10	50			42
	B	50,000	7	30	10	50			60
	C	50,000	8	30	8	30	80	70	74
1966	A	4,000	2	10	10	150			30
	B	2,000	3	20	10	120			55
	C	40,000	8	30	8	100	25	170	70
1967	A	200	0	4	50	250			24
	B	1,000	1	10	40	200			50
	C	40,000	8	25	10	150	10	240	68
1968	A	800,000	0	2	80	400			20
	B	80,000	1	5	70	350			46
	C	50,000	7	25	50	250	4	300	60
1969	A	1,400,000	0	0	90	500			7
	B	100,000	0	3	90	450			25
	C	50,000	7	30	70	300	2	400	56

Questions

1   Plot a graph which shows the changes with time of the population of the insect pests in each area. Explain the graphs. Why did the population increase in 1968 when, in 1967, it appeared that the pest had been almost eliminated in Area A? What caused the difference in population dynamics between Areas B and C? What indication is there that Area C has not been directly affected by aerial spraying of the pesticide?

2   Discuss the effect on natural pest controls that the pesticide had in each area. How will this eventually influence the size of the pest population?

3   Why is the concentration of pesticide so high in fish and bird species? Suggest a food chain which would link the pine stand vegetation to the poor nesting success of the birds.

4   What methods could be used to remedy this "eco-mess"? What concentrations of pesticide in the fish and in the birdlife represent the point where a significant change in mortality occurs? What other methods could have been used to control the pest?

5   Use the data to evaluate the effect of the pesticide on species diversity and, hence, on environmental stability. (See Section 1.2.)

7.2 INTRODUCTION OF AN EXOTIC INSECT SPECIES

A species of insect has been accidentally introduced from Asia into the North American forest. The success of this organism depends on its ability to find a suitable habitat, that is, one with the proper abiotic conditions for all of its life stages. The larval stage is very sensitive to changes in temperature, humidity, and light conditions. Exposure to situations outside the tolerance limits of this species results in a high mortality rate. Data showing the influence of the three physical variables on the larva are presented in Table 14. The data for each variable were obtained while the other two variables were kept constant at optimum conditions.

TABLE 14

Temperature (°C)	% mortality	Relative humidity (%)	% mortality	Light intensity (f.c.)	% mortality
15	100	100	80	200	0
16	80	90	10	400	0
17	30	80	0	600	10
18	10	70	0	800	15
19	0	60	0	1,000	20
20	0	50	50	1,200	20
21	0	40	70	1,400	90
22	0	30	90	1,600	95
23	20	20	100	1,800	100
24	80	10	100	2,000	100
25	100	0	100	—	—

Questions

1 Plot graphs that show the effect of temperature and humidity on the mortality rates of the introduced species. Use the format illustrated in Figure 7-2.

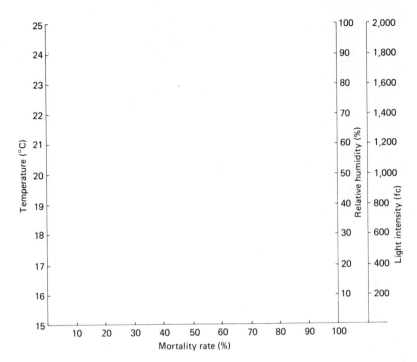

Fig. 7-2
Effect of temperature and
humidity on mortality rate.

2   Mark on the graph the area which represents suitable conditions for the insect larvae to survive the combined effect of these two environmental factors.
3   How much does the suitable area for the temperature factor decrease when the humidity factor is added?
4   Add to your graphs another to illustrate the effect of light on the mortality of the larvae. Compare the suitable area for insect survival to the area in question 2.
5   Mark the most desirable area when all three factors—temperature, light, and relative humidity—are considered. State the temperature, relative humidity, and light ranges which are optimal for the larvae.
6   One spring morning while the larvae were feeding in the open, the temperature dropped to 18°C and a strong wind lowered the relative humidity to 40%. The light intensity was 400 foot-candles. Which factor had the greatest influence on insect mortality?
7   What other factors determine whether terrestrial organisms can find a niche in the environment?
8   Suggest a habitat which might suit this insect. How could it react to intolerable temperatures, relative humidities, and light intensities?

7.3   THE WHOOPING CRANE: WEATHER AND NESTING SUCCESS

The whooping crane has long been in danger of becoming an extinct species. Its population has been carefully studied by the Canadian Wildlife Service since its breeding grounds in

Wood Buffalo National Park were discovered in 1954. The whooping crane migrates north from the Aransas Refuge in Texas. It builds its nest in marshy areas of Wood Buffalo National Park and feeds in numerous nearby shallow potholes. The weather in the summer breeding areas has a substantial effect on the nesting and feeding habits of these birds. Heavy rainfall may flood nests and cause a high mortality in young birds. Temperature extremes or heavy snowfall early in the season may also disturb the nesting success. Data are presented which show the bird population of the northerly migrating whooping cranes over the past 15 years. Nest sites

TABLE 15

Year	Migrating adults	No. of nests	Eggs laid	Hatched eggs	Rainfall (inches)	Snowfall (inches)
1955	21	6	6	4	3.5	1.4
1956	20	3	2	0	5.9	0.2
1957	20	4	4	3	4.6	0.8
1958	22	5	5	4	2.4	1.1
1959	23	4	6	2	2.5	5.6
1960	23	8	8	4	3.2	1.8
1961	30	6	6	5	2.9	0.03
1962	32	0	0	0	7.6	3.0
1963	28	4	6	2	5.9	0.5
1964	26	10	10	7	3.2	0.8
1965	32	10	10	6	2.9	1.0
1966	36	2	2	0	5.4	2.9
1967	30	4	4	3	3.5	0.4
1968	32	3	4	3	2.8	0.7
1969	33	3	3	1	5.8	2.4
1970	32	5	5	4	2.1	0.6

were carefully examined without disturbing the birds and the number of hatching eggs counted. Measurements of snowfall and rainfall during the summer period were recorded. Not all of the birds which migrated north from the winter area in Texas were in the same breeding area. The results of the study are summarized in Table 15.

Questions

1   Plot a graph to show how the crane population has changed over the past 15 years.
2   When was the population highest? When did it reach its lowest level?
3   During which years did the population increase the most? What year was adult mortality the greatest?
4   Which six years were the poorest breeding years for the cranes? When were the most eggs laid and hatched successfully?
5   Rainfall and snowfall were high some summers. During which four summers was rainfall greatest? Was snowfall ever high the same year as the rainfall? How was the hatching success those years?
6   What percent of the eggs hatched when rainfall and snowfall were lowest?
7   Plot a graph which relates hatching success to rainfall. Why would a daily or weekly account of rainfall be more helpful?
8   What other factors besides weather might influence the population growth of the whooping cranes? What lowered its population to the endangered level in the first place?
9   Suppose 1964 and 1965 had been poor years due to high precipitation. Would this have greatly altered the population?
10   What factors prevent a rapid increase in the number of cranes? Suggest natural or man-made factors which could rapidly snuff out this species.

7.4   DEER: PREDATION OR STARVATION?

In 1960 the deer population of an island forest reserve about 200 square miles in size was about 2,000 animals. Although the island had excellent vegetation for feeding, the food supply obviously had limits. Thus the forest management personnel feared that overgrazing might lead to mass starvation. Since the area was too remote for hunters, the wildlife service decided to bring in natural predators to control the deer population. It was hoped that, eventually, natural predation would eliminate the weakest deer, thereby preventing the herd from becoming too large while, at the same time, increasing the quality of the herd. In 1961, 10 wolves were flown into the island. The results of this natural predator program are presented in Table 16.

TABLE 16 — *1:100 apparently holds the pop. constant with no starvation*

Year	Wolf population	Deer population	Deer offspring	Predation	Starvation	Population change
1961	10 *1/200*	2,000	*40%* 800	*20%* 400	*5%* 100	+300 *+15%*
1962	12 *1/191*	2,300	*40%* 920	*21%* 480	*10.4%* 240	+200 *+11.5%*
1963	16 *1/156*	2,500	*40%* 1,000	*25.5%* 640	*20%* 500	−140 *−5.6%*
1964	22 *1/107*	2,360	*38%* 944	*37%* 880	*7.6%* 180	−116 *−4.9%*
1965	28 *1/80*	2,244	*44%* 996	*50%* 1,120	*1.16%* 26	−150 *−6.7%*
1966	24 *1/87*	2,094	*40%* 836	*46%* 960	*9.6%* 2	−126 *−6%*
1967	21 *1/94*	1,968	*40%* 788	*43%* 840	*0%* 0	−52 *−2.6%*
1968	18 *1/106*	1,916	*40%* 766	*38%* 720	*0%* 0	+46 *+2.4%*
1969	19 *1/103*	1,952	*40%* 780	*39%* 760	*0%* 0	+20 *+1.02%*
1970	19 *1/104*	1.972	*40%* 790	*38.5%* 760	*0%* 0	+30 *+1.52%*

Questions

1   Plot the fluctuations in the deer and wolf populations on a graph for the nine-year study period.

2   Would it have been better for the ecosystem if more wolves had been introduced in 1961? Why?

3   Explain why the wolf population declined after 1965.

4   In which year was deer starvation greatest? From your data and knowledge of ecology, explain why so many deer died.

5   Predict what might have happened if hunters had been allowed to kill half of the wolf population in 1964 (for the bounty).

6   Is wolf predation a limiting or a controlling factor on this reserve? What other factors control or limit a deer population?

7   How does the size of the deer population influence the number of wolves on the island? If no hunting is allowed, what natural mechanisms will control the wolf population?

8   If the deer population is to remain steady at 2,000 and the number of deer offspring is 1,000 in 1971, how many deer would 25 wolves have to eat in a year?

9   From the data which describe the herd in 1970 (Table 17), plot a survivorship curve. Which stages in the life of the deer have the highest mortality? Suggest environmental factors which might make this so.

236   Case Studies

TABLE 17   AGE STRUCTURE OF HERD IN 1970

Age	No. of deer
0 – 1	860
1 – 2	345
2 – 3	262
3 – 4	168
4 – 5	105
5 – 6	88
6 – 7	68
7 – 8	56
8 – 9	42
9 – 10	6
Total	2,000

10 Use the data from 1970 (Table 17) to draw an age pyramid for the deer population. What percentage of the population are fawns? Suppose the percentage of fawns was 65%. What would that indicate about the growth of the herd? Would the population be increasing?

11 How could knowledge of survivorship curves and age pyramids aid in the management of the herd population?

7.5   ANALYSIS OF A TERRESTRIAL SUCCESSION

An ecology class studied succession from a meadow through a shrub area to a mixed woodlot. Along a line transect they measured temperature, relative humidity, light intensity, evaporation rate, and wind velocity at representative sites in each vegetational area. The results are in Table 18. The covers of the dominant plant species were calculated. Soil analysis included measurement of soil acidity, estimates of soil litter, and calculations of the number of earthworms per square meter. Spider species were counted and collected in each area and observations of different bird species were recorded. The purpose of the field trip was to observe differences in three stages of the terrestrial succession and to investigate how the interactions of physical factors, plant species, and animals in each habitat created three different environments.

TABLE 18

		Meadow	Woodlot margin	Mixed woodlot
Tempera-ture	maximum	30°C	27°C	24°C
	minimum	10°C	12°C	15°C
Relative humidity		70%	75%	90%
Evaporation rate		50 ml/day	42 ml/day	15 ml/day
Wind velocity		10 mph	5 mph	0 mph
Light (percent of open field)		100%	30%	4%
Soil litter		250 gm/m²	370 gm/m²	700 gm/m²
Soil pH		6.9	6.8	6.0 (coniferous) 6.6 (deciduous)
Earthworms		100/m²	130/m²	25/m² (coniferous) 220/m² (deciduous)
Spiders		8 web builders 10 non–web builders	18 web builders 26 non–web builders	62 web builders 110 non–web builders
Bird species		14	28	32
Plant species and cover		grass: 76–100% clover: 51–75% goldenrod: 6–25% dandelion: 6–25%	grass: 76–100% blackberry: 26–51% hawthorn: 26–51% goldenrod: 6–25% oak seedling: 6–25% cherry: 6–25%	grass: 26–50% oak: 26–50% white pine: 26–50% fern: 6–25% maple: 51–75%

Questions

1 Examine the data for the physical variables in each stage of the succession. Which environment has the greatest range of temperature, of light, and of evaporation rate? Why? Compare the tolerance of animal species living in the meadow and in the forest.

2 Account for the changes in wind speed and relative humidity along the line.

3 Which environment seems most suitable for earthworm populations? Which factor do you feel has the greatest influence in determining where the earthworms live: light, evaporation rate, or temperature? Justify your decision. Explain from the data provided on soil acidity why you might believe earthworms are sensitive to pH changes. Which type of soil can an earthworm not tolerate, acidic or basic? Why is the coniferous area acidic?

4 Where would you expect to find the thickest soil litter? In general, what effect will a thick litter layer have on soil moisture, soil temperature, and the number of soil animals?

5 In which stage of the succession would you expect to find the shade-tolerant mosses and ferns? What three physical variables provided in your data would encourage their presence in one particular area?

6 Why would you expect to find a greater diversity of birds in the forest? Name three bird species which you would find only in a meadow and three that you would find only in a woodlot. Give reasons for your selections in each case.

7 How does the vegetation type and diversity seem to influence the distribution of spider species? Is there any relationship between the number of niches in a habitat and the diversity of species found in that habitat? Explain your answer using the information on plant species in each area and the diversity of birds and insects.

8 What other data do you feel this class could have collected to help clarify the relationships between physical factors, plants, and animals in a terrestrial succession?

INDEX

Numbers in **boldface** represent pages with illustrations.

A

Abiotic factors, **3**, 6, 13–29, 41–42, 184–186, 198, 201–207, 209–211, 213
  adaptation to, 14–21, 26–27, 48, 52–54, 59, 62, 65, 69, 71, 77, 85, 109, 143, 145, 170, 174, 177, 201, 208, 226–227
  of coniferous.forest, 62–**63**
  in the desert, 80–81
  field and laboratory studies, 90–138
  in grasslands, 75
  interspecific competition for, 189
  and microenvironments, 28–29
  of temperate deciduous forest, 70
  in tundra, 50–52, **51**
  and vegetation analysis, 146, 158, 159
Acorns, 42, 72
Adaptation, 48, 109, 143, 145, 170, 174, 177, 201, 208
  in coniferous forest, 65, 69
  in the desert, 85
  in grasslands, 77
  to moisture, 15, 17–20
  to sunlight, 26–27
  in temperate deciduous forest, 71
  to temperature, 14–15, 226–227
  in tundra, 52–54, 59, 62
  to wind, 21
Aeration, 116
Aerial net, 167
Aerial photo analysis, **92**–93
Alfalfa, 19
Algae, 18
Alpine tundra, *see* Tundra
American beech trees, **70**
Ammonia, **39**, 40
Amphibians, 14, 59, 60, 73
Animals: adaptation to temperature, 226–227
  behavior studies, 177–179
  interspecific competition, 177, 179, 180, 193–195
  intraspecific competition, 177, 179, 180, 192–193

light intensity and, **126**–128, **127**
light photoperiod and, 124–126
light quality and, 128–**129**
migration, 220–223
response to temperature, 131–133, **132**
signs of, 179–182
track casting, 179–182, **181**
Annuals, in desert, 81
Antarctica, 51–52
Ants, 42, 59, 60, 73, 80, 166
Aphids, 73
Appalachian Mountains, 65, 71
Apple trees, 71
Aransas Refuge (Texas), 234
Arctic Circle, 50–51
Arctic fox, 55, 58, 60
Arctic hare, 55, **57**
Arctic tern, 221
Arctic tundra, *see* Tundra
Ardrey, Robert, 219
Arrowhead (plant), 18
Arthropods, 14, 27, **126**, 131
  collecting, 169–**171**, **170**
Ash trees, 20, 43
Aspirator, **170**, 201
Asters, 45
Atmospheric humidity, 16–17, 20, 81
  temperature and, 16
  See also Relative humidity
Autotrophic (self-feeding) organisms, 5
Autotrophic succession, 45

B

Bacteria, 5, 13, 27, 37, **39**, 40, 45
  in coniferous forest, 63–65
  in grasslands, 77
  in temperate deciduous forest, 74
Badgers, 61, 79
Badlands grizzly bear, 76
Balsam fir, 45, **64**, 65, 67–68
Bark beetles, 68
Barren ground caribou, 58, 60
Basswood trees, 43, 45
Bats, 68, 74, 85, 220
Bearing-intersection mapping method, 104–106, **105**
Bears, 4, 9, 48, 57, 60–61, 67–68
Beating net, **167**
Beating sheets, 201
Beavers, 72, 217
Beech trees, 10, 43, 44, 70, 71
Bees, 24, 59, 60, 73
Beetle larvae, 72, 74

Beetles, 42, 45, 57, 60, 68, 171
Belt-transect vegetation analysis, 159–**161**, **160**, 201, 208, 212
Berries, 74
Biogeochemical cycles, *see* Nutrient cycles
Biological clock, 125
Biomass, 34–**35**, 43
Biomes, North America, 48–85
  abiotic factors, 50–52, **51**, 62–**63**, 70, 75, 80–81
  altitude and, 49–50
  biotic factors, 52–62, 64–85
  coniferous forest, 62–69
  desert, 80–85
  distribution, 48–50
  grasslands, 74–80
  latitude and, 49–50
  temperate deciduous forest, 69–74
  tundra, 50–62
Biotic factors, **3**, 4–6, 8–12, **9**, 28, 41–42, 48, 198, 203, 205, 207, 209–211
  of coniferous forest, 64–69
  in the desert, 81–85
  field and laboratory studies, 140–196
  in grasslands, 75–80
  of temperate deciduous forest, 70–74
  in tundra, 52–62
  vegetation analysis, 146–166 200–201, 204, 207, 211, 212
Birch trees, 52, 65, 72
Birds, 2, 4, **9**, 12, 14, 15, 27, 32, 42, 43, 46, **60**, 230
  in coniferous forest, 67–69
  in the desert, 82, 83–84, 85
  in grasslands, 79, 80
  migration, 24, 26, 58, 62, 68, 220–223, **221**
  population and behavior studies, 174–177, **175**, 218–220
  succession study, 237
  in temperate deciduous forest, 72–74
  territorial behavior, 218–220
  in tundra, 55, 58–61
  vegetation analysis and, 166
Bison, 57, **75**–76, 80, 217
Black flies, 59
Black Hills, 77
Black oak trees, 42-43
Black spruce trees, 65
Black willow trees, **70**
Blowouts, **21**, 210, 213
Blueberries, 52